PELICAN BOOKS
A581

THE GREEKS OVERSEAS
JOHN BOARDMAN

John Boardman, Fellow of Merton College, Oxford, and Reader in Classical Archaeology in the University of Oxford, was born in 1927. He was educated at Chigwell School and Magdalene College, Cambridge, then went to Athens as Student and later Assistant Director (1952–5) of the British School at Athens. From 1955 to 1959 he was Assistant Keeper of the Ashmolean Museum. He was elected Fellow of the Society of Antiquaries in 1957, received the Cromer Greek Prize in 1959, and has been a Corresponding Member of the German Archaeological Institute since 1961. He has travelled widely in Greek lands and excavated in Smyrna, Knossos, Chios, and Libya. His previous publications include *The Cretan Collection in Oxford*, *Island Gems*, *The Date of the Knossos Tablets*, and various articles on the archaeology of archaic Greece. He has served as editor of the *Journal of Hellenic Studies* since 1958. John Boardman is married, with two children.

JOHN BOARDMAN

THE GREEKS OVERSEAS

*

*With seven maps, twenty-four plates,
and seventy-five text figures*

PENGUIN BOOKS

Penguin Books Ltd, Harmondsworth, Middlesex, England
Penguin Books Inc., 3300 Clipper Mill Road, Baltimore 11, Md, U.S.A.
Penguin Books Pty Ltd, Ringwood, Victoria, Australia

—

First published 1964

—

—

Made and printed in Great Britain
by Hazell Watson & Viney Ltd
Aylesbury, Bucks
Set in Linotype Granjon

CONTENTS

CONTENTS

LIST OF PLATES

LIST OF TEXT FIGURES

LIST OF MAPS

EDITORIAL FOREWORD

MOST of us are familiar with the glorious achievements of the
Greek classical period, and can easily conjure up a vision of the
Akropolis, the Parthenon, and the masterpieces of Greek art in
stone, in metal, and in pottery, as well as the Greek literary
genius. But we are less familiar with the Greek legacies abroad
and archaeologists are striving to learn more about the way in
which the Greeks approached barbarians and civilized peoples
overseas. Much encouragement has been given to these studies by
cruises throughout the Mediterranean, which have stimulated an
ever-widening interest in this subject.

We may now proceed to trace the stages by which the Greeks
left their imprint east and west, beginning with the first steps
that had already been taken by Greek-speaking Myceneans at the
end of the Bronze Age. The most rewarding period for examina-
tion has been that which lies between the beginning of the eighth
century and the aftermath of the Persian invasions of the fifth
century B.C. Shortly before 700 B.C. there was a powerful orientalizing influence on Greek art which can be discerned through imports on Greek sites, but after 700 B.C. this eastern style was
gradually transmuted and hellenized, as the Greeks brilliantly
transformed eastern inspiration and made it their own. And how
fascinating it is to discover the imprint of the Greek genius in
the most distant parts of the civilized world, for example at
Pasargadae in Achaemenian Iran, where recent discoveries have
renewed our understanding of the capital founded by Cyrus the
Great: we find that his tomb carries on it a Greek architectural
innovation. Soon, Persian sculptured draperies were to follow a
Greek mode, and the Persian city of Susa was importing Greek
vases.

At a period at which Greek pottery may be found in Babylon
or Nubia, Greek bronzes on the Seine, and Urartian bronzes in
Olympia we find ourselves confronted by a flux of cosmopolitan

trade delicately poised between the counter-pressures of politics and economics. We have yet to discover to what extent, if at all, the Greeks were aware of the importance of maintaining a balance of payments, although of necessity when they established rich trading stations at Naucratis in Egypt they had to bring wine, oil, and silver in exchange for corn.

Mr Boardman tells us with sensitive understanding about relations between Greeks and Phrygians, Lydians and Persians, and finally confronts us with Italy, Sicily, and the West. He himself is about to explore more Greeks overseas at the site of Tocra in Cyrenaica where early sixth-century Greek pottery has recently been found. To anyone travelling in the Mediterranean, on the Black Sea, or along the coast of Spain this book should be an indispensable companion, for Greek evidence is a part of the historical scene which still excites our enthusiasm and requires our personal exploration.

M. E. L. MALLOWAN

January 1964

ACKNOWLEDGEMENTS

THE author is indebted to the Ashmolean Museum, the Museum of Fine Arts in Boston, the Hermitage Museum in Leningrad, the British Museum, and the Griffith Institute for photographs. Mrs M. E. M. Cox prepared many of the drawings. Mr W. G. Forrest has kindly read the typescript and suggested several improvements.

J.B.

Summer 1961
Oxford

PREFACE

Rhubarb, rhubarb; *Barbara buzz buzz* – stage conversation which is intended to be unintelligible stresses the *bar-bar-bar* noises of ordinary conversation. Foreigners make similar incomprehensible noises, and it was not only the Greeks in antiquity who characterized those whose speech they could not follow as *bar-bar* talkers – '*barbarians*'. When Greek met Greek the result may often have been violent, but at least they could understand each other's language, and this bond of speech was one which the Greeks always acknowledged and respected. But the Greeks did not use the term 'barbaros' quite as we do 'barbarian'. For them it embraced all non-Greek-speakers, both the 'rude, wild, and uncultured' of our dictionary definition, and the kings and subjects of the great empires of the east.

This book deals with the material evidence for the early relations between Greeks and barbarians. When it was first proposed it was suggested that it should be about the Greek Colonies. This seemed so much part of the history and archaeology of Greece herself that the Editor kindly agreed to let me widen the scope to include an account of all early Greek ventures overseas, whether they were for trade or the establishing of colonies, whether they are attested by the sure evidence of Greek settlers or only by the presence of Greek goods. Even so, this will be more an account of the archaeological *evidence* for the Greeks overseas, since their 'archaeology' proper is at one with that of the Greek homeland. We shall be looking for the material effects of their presence on foreign soil – their relations with and effect upon native populations, and the effect of the natives upon them. In their travels to the east and Egypt it is the latter which is the more important, for contact with the older civilizations of Mesopotamia and the Nile Valley provided the spark which fired the new Greece, and kindled that flame which the discerning may still cherish in modern western civilization. To do as full justice as possible to these matters, it has proved necessary to devote part of the book to a study of the effect of the Near East and Egypt upon the Greeks at home, as well as on the Greeks overseas. Only in this way could the whole story be told. Even so, we deal here with material things only, and the reader must turn elsewhere for an account of the debts of Greek literature, religion, and thought to the east and Egypt.

The testimony of ancient historians will also be used. More than most 'archaeological' histories of ancient cultures, this should be read as a supplement to what is known from other sources, although our evidence may often fill gaps in the record or even correct it.

It must be remembered that this is only part of the story of the Greek renaissance, and can take little account of the Greeks' own genius except in so far as it led them to explore and learn from older civilizations. With so much left unsaid it might even seem that classical Greece could have been nothing without this inspiration, but we have only to look at what the Greeks made of what they had borrowed and how soon they outshone their models. Sappho wrote her poems only 200 years after the Greeks had learnt their alphabet. The Parthenon and its sculpture appear only 150 years after Greece's first steps in monumental architecture and sculpture. And all these things – alphabet, architecture, sculpture – the Greeks had in some degree learnt from the 'barbarians'.

Then there is the other side to the story. With their colonizing and trade in the west and the north, the Greeks made contact with people who were less advanced culturally, and we are able to observe the beginnings of the spread of Greek civilization into Italy and Western Europe.

Learning in the east and south; teaching in the west and north. The story is a balanced one, and the two parts run concurrently. The eighth century B.C. sees the first moves to east and west; the seventh, the first moves to north and south; the sixth, consolidation in the face of powerful opponents and rivals – Persians, Phoenicians, Etruscans. In these three centuries the Greeks passed from isolation and comparative poverty to a position of power and enjoyment of the highest culture. This is the 'archaic' period in the broadest sense of the term. In these years the foundations of classical Greece were laid, and it is these formative years only that we shall be studying. They culminate in 480 B.C. with the Greeks' successful stand against the challenge of Carthage in the west, of Persia in the east, and in this book we shall rarely be led to consider the fortunes of the Greeks overseas after that date.

The interested reader and student will find in the bibliography of each chapter some works which may help explain the background and some of the arguments. To the curious who may be puzzled by remarks about an object or event, I can only apologize and say that, fully documented, this work would have needed three volumes, not one.

My descriptions of sites and particular objects are not often, I fear, based on first-hand experience of them. Where my dating of objects differs from that given in some publications (as it often does), this is deliberate and, I hope, in better accord with the evidence now available. Many of the monuments and objects which have to be considered are of no less documentary value for being considerable works of art. This is, after all, one of the many compensating factors in any archaeological study of ancient Greek affairs.

It is usual to give some explanation or apology for the spellings of place-names and personal names, and to excuse inconsistencies. I have preferred to accept the inconsistencies, and my spellings are those which are most familiar to me and come most readily to my pen. I doubt whether anyone will be seriously misled, and I hope few will be annoyed by the lack of system in this matter.

to 700 B.C.

to 600 B.C.

to 480 B.C.

🔺 Greek settlement   x Greek objects found

THE NATURE OF THE EVIDENCE

ARCHAEOLOGICAL EVIDENCE

T is not too difficult today to recover the archaeological history
of any well-excavated Greek site. Studies in the stylistic development and chronology of pottery, bronzes, and other likely finds
have been carried to a degree not matched in the scholarship
devoted to any other culture of comparable antiquity. A large
part of the evidence is afforded by decorated pottery – the
archaeologist's bread and butter. A vase of fired clay may be
broken readily enough, but its pieces are almost indestructible.
As the fragments were virtually useless, they were left about
ancient sites, or dumped in pits, to be dug up and diagnosed by
archaeologists. Regularly, too, whole pots were put into tombs.
Other objects disappear too readily – iron corrodes, bronze and
precious metals are melted down for re-use, marble feeds the
lime kilns – but potsherds had no value and so have survived.
A Sunday-newspaper columnist has written with wit and sym-
pathy of the 'blue-saucer folk' whose ware litters his and many
other back gardens in England. A small fragment may give
away what the whole shape was – a teapot, saucer, or cup.
A scrap of willow pattern, a '. . . ade in Birm . . .', part of a
monogram from a Coronation mug, may reveal design, provenance, and date. Antiquity has left similar clues in its rubbish
dumps, and on or under floors. And in ancient Greece it was the
potter who provided vessels for purposes now served by bottles,
tins, glasses, cardboard boxes, and even barrels. But even with
our mass of evidence, interpretation is a tricky matter. The
willow-pattern plates still made today prove no close cultural ties
with contemporary China ! But there *is* an explanation for them,
which *could* be worked out by some post-atom-age archaeologist.
In the same way, if a town rubbish dump were to yield in its
lowest (earliest) levels empty packets of Woodbines, and in its

upper levels empty packets of Gauloises, or of chewing-gum, th
deduced changes in habits might lead to a reasonable gues
fragments which will form a great part of our evidence in thi
book may seem miserable substitutes for fine whole vases, but i
need hardly be remarked that such pottery evidence is not les
important because it has failed to survive intact.

The importance which the Greeks attached to the vase
painter's art in the centuries with which we shall be dealing
and the characteristically Greek sensitivity to changes in decora
tive fashions, mean that arguments based on *stylistic* study o
vases can carry much weight. Add to the stylistic sequence
which can be determined for the various Greek wares some in
dications of *absolute* dates, and you have a system which wi
permit the dating of decorated pottery to within a generation, o
sometimes a decade. This is already to some degree true in th
mid eighth century B.C., and the degree of precision increase
through the seventh and sixth centuries. Not only can dates b
assigned, but regional studies have made possible the attributio
of most wares to particular cities, and in many instances we ar
able to distinguish even individual workshops, painters, an
potters.

This is no place for any detailed survey of the background t
the systems of dating which we shall be using throughout thi
book, but something must be said of the most important ware
which will be mentioned and the grounds for dating them.

Furthermore, although the interpretation of finds on a home
land Greek site may be a comparatively easy matter, we hav
to deal largely with Greek finds on foreign shores or in newl
founded Greek settlements overseas. It is necessary therefore t
say something of the principles which should – but rarely do –
govern the interpretation of such finds, for they often form ou
only evidence to support some far-reaching theories.

First, then, the pottery wares and their dating. We begin i
the early Iron Age, the 'Dark Ages' of Greek history after th
collapse and decay of Mycenaean civilization by about 1100 B.C
The finds in Athens cemeteries show that after only a few

generations, perhaps by about 1000 B.C., the new 'Protogeometric' style of vase-painting had been evolved from the debased Mycenaean forms. The decoration is simple, precise, and extremely effective, often of neat concentric circles or semicircles, and the patterns are never allowed to crowd the surface of the vase. The style is most distinctive, and although finds elsewhere in Greece show that many other towns, most of them less prosperous than Athens, evolved their own 'Protogeometric' idioms, these were always dependent – artistically – on Athens. Examples of this, and some of the later styles we shall be mentioning, appear in Fig. 1. In the ninth century, the feeling for proportion and restraint in the matter of decoration weakens, and a growing repertoire of Geometric patterns spreads like a rash over the surface of the finer vases. After 800 B.C., figure decoration – animal, then human – is admitted, with formal geometrical stylization for natural forms. Athens still leads, but other cities have their own distinctive Geometric styles, in varying degrees still dependent on Athens: especially Corinth, Argos, Boeotia, Crete, and the Eastern Greeks.

The influence of the Near East is seen first in Greek pottery in the second half of the eighth century. We shall have more to say of the nature and source of this influence in Chapter 3. In Corinth a new, refined style, which has become known as 'Protocorinthian', is evolved, and 'orientalizing' figures and decoration are used as well as a new incising technique known as 'black-figure', which may have been inspired by eastern incised metalwork. Now, too, we have some indications of absolute dating. Ancient historians give dates for Greek colonies in Sicily, and the earliest Greek pottery found in each of those sufficiently well explored can be plausibly attributed to the first generation of the colonists. Even in detail the sequence of dates given by historians, and the stylistic sequence of the earliest pottery found in the various sites (Syracuse, Megara Hyblaea, and later Gela), agree remarkably well. Some confirmation too is provided by the find of an Egyptian scarab, naming a king, with Greek vases. Corinth now sets the pace, and the sequence of fine Protocorinthian vases can be followed down to beyond the middle of the seventh century. Athens, meanwhile, went her

1. Types of early Greek vases: (a) Protogeometric; (b) Geometric; (c) Protocorinthian; (d) – about 700 B.C.; (e) – about 650 B.C.; (f) Corinthian, about 600 B.C.

own way with the older silhouette and outline techniques of drawing, although orientalizing patterns were admitted, and by now human figure decoration and mythological scenes had become more common. The East Greeks and Cretans too were slow to follow Corinth's lead, and they developed their own highly individual styles. Fortunately the Corinthian vases were popular, and it is possible to determine reasonable chronologies for these other wares from contexts – as in graves – in which imported Corinthian vases are found beside local products. The foundation of another Sicilian colony, Selinus, gives another 'peg' date for the stylistic sequence. We rely very much on the dating of Corinth's vases in these years, but it is easy to fall into the error of saying that 'the earliest imported vases found at X are Corinthian', when all that can fairly be said is 'the earliest *datable* vases . . . are Corinthian'.

In the last third of the seventh century the Corinthian black-figure or full 'Corinthian' series begins. The style of drawing coarsens as the output increases. Around the turn of the century the foundation of Marseilles and the destruction of Smyrna may give us other 'pegs' for dating, but by now the Athenian potteries are again commanding attention. They have accepted the Corinthian black-figure technique, and apply it with a sense for narrative and the monumental which had always escaped the Corinthians. While the Corinthian painters coarsened their work, or attempted to ape the Athenian, the vases of Athens were winning ground, and by the middle of the sixth century were able to drive the Corinthian out of the markets and out of production. The contexts of Athenian, Corinthian, and other Greek vases in tombs of these years confirm the clear stylistic sequences and allow a chronological system which has been worked out for one to be applied to the others. In the 560s can be set the earliest vases which were made in Athens to celebrate the re-inaugurated Panathenaic Games; around 545 and 525 comparisons with sculptured reliefs on independently dated buildings at Ephesus and Delphi (the Siphnian Treasury) give further 'pegs'; and, again in 525, the Persian dismantling of a Greek-manned frontier fort in Egypt (Daphnae) gives another terminus.

By about 530, the Athenian painter had developed a new vase-painting technique – the red-figured – in which the figures are reserved in the clay ground of the vase, the background filled in, and the details painted, where before, in black-figure, they had been incised in the black silhouette (Fig. 2). The new style appears beside the old into the fifth century, when it becomes paramount, and now the Athenian red-figure vases virtually command all markets. Dating points become more frequent – the Persian sack of Athens in 480; funeral monuments with vases in them at Marathon (490), Thespiae (424), and Athens (the grave of the Spartans: 403); the dumping of the contents of graves from Delos on Rheneia during the purification of the island in 425; and, a less sure criterion, the appearance on vases of complimentary remarks about handsome youths. The last

2. Athenian vase painting: (a) black-figure and (b) red-figure drawing.

depends on the identification of the youth in his later career, military or political, an estimate of his age then, and a general estimate of the span of years in which a Greek youth might be called beautiful (*kalos*). Women were seldom thus celebrated, and at any rate we could hardly expect to find any independent historical evidence for their ages.

Allowing, then, some degree of confidence in assigning vases to one Greek city rather than another and in dating them within fairly narrow limits, we have still to determine their possible historical significance when they appear on foreign sites. It is easy to attach undue significance to stray finds of Greek vases or other objects. The archaeologist may overestimate the importance of the evidence or be unrealistic in his explanations for its appearance. The historian may not be able to judge well enough of the circumstances and archaeological background to the finds. In the study of Greek history in the eighth, seventh, and sixth centuries B.C. there is still much need for intelligent liaison between the two professional disciplines, one which works primarily from recorded evidence, the other which works from the first-hand evidence of objects.

For our immediate problem it may help to discuss the various reasons why Greek painted pottery may have travelled overseas in antiquity.

1. The first and most obvious occasion would be for the supply or use of Greeks overseas who had not their own kilns or could not be satisfied with local non-Greek products. Emigrating families would take with them their best dinner service, and probably domestic utensils, and in their new homes they would be likely to create a demand for replacements of the same type of pottery from home. Until local kilns were built – probably to produce imitations of the wares most familiar to them – the pottery used by, say, Corinthian families in Sicily was likely to be much the same as that they were used to at home. The identification of our emigrant Greeks will then depend on what we know of tastes at home. When we deal with well-known pottery producing centres like Corinth, the matter may seem easy – too easy; for other Greeks may have been used to Corinthian vases and have had no distinctive local wares of their own. I think of Aegina, where there was no production of decorated pottery and where Corinthian vases were in general use. Ancient historians tell us much of Aegina's overseas trade, but if Aeginetans settled or carried pottery overseas they could not be recognized archaeologically or, from the pottery, distinguished from Corinthians. Again, many colonial Greek sites have been better explored than their mother cities in Greece – than Chalcis and Megara, for example.

What is important for us is the probability that minor vases which would never have travelled as containers or *objets d'art* may be taken as proof of the residence or at least regular visits of Greeks. In quantity they should imply some kind of settle-

ment, but the presence of even a few such vases may be a
indication of regular trade in other commodities which the
accompanied casually, or perhaps of temporary quarters fo
Greek traders or their agents.

2. Vases which travelled by way of trade may have had con
mercial value (a) from what they contained, or (b) for their ow
sakes as *objets d'art*.

(a) Oil and wine were generally exported in large, plai

a   b

3. (a) Chian wine jar; (b) Athenian oil or wine jar.

vases, but it is not until the sixth century that we are able
readily to distinguish the containers of the various producing
centres, like the Chian wine jars, and the Athenian oil o
wine jars of Fig. 3. Then, it becomes possible to make usefu
observations about the distribution of these commodities
Stout, plain vases may of course be re-used, perhaps even re
exported. Thus, a sixth-century Chian wine jar was re-sealed
in Egypt with cartouches of King Amasis (Fig. 38, p. 147)
Perfume, or perfumed oil, may have been carried in bulk, bu
was certainly also carried in elegant small flasks – *aryballo*
or *alabastra*. To help sell their contents, these regularly carriec

elaborate decoration or were moulded into unusual or striking shapes. A very large proportion of the finest paintings by Corinthian artists in the 'Protocorinthian' period is to be found on these flasks (as Fig. 1d, e, p. 28). Corinth, it seems, was a major exporter of perfume in the flask. At least, it is difficult to see why she should have specialized for so long making these flasks if she did not also fill them. Crete may have shared in the trade in the later eighth and early seventh centuries, and after the late seventh century Rhodes came to rival Corinth. There was probably a lot of opportunist trading by Greek and non-Greek skippers, but where a considerable quantity of, say, Chian wine jars or Rhodian perfume flasks have been found, it seems not unreasonable to think that the carriers were Chians and Rhodians. But it is, of course, not necessary. The Aeginetans were exclusively carriers, not producers, and any captain would probably have been happy enough to carry a load of fine Corinthian perfume flasks.

(b) The elaborate decoration of the small perfume flasks would certainly have encouraged a taste for finely decorated pottery, and it may well be that already in the mid-seventh century other Corinthian vases were being carried for their own sakes, as *objets d'art*, or at least best plate, particularly to the west. Later, the Corinthians exploited the uncritical welcome given to their painted wares by increasing production and coarsening finish. Athens was already beginning to challenge in both the eastern and western markets, in the first quarter of the sixth century, with her fine black-figure vases which must certainly have been carried for their intrinsic value. In the second quarter of the century the Corinthians rallied with a line in mixing bowls (craters) decorated with mythological scenes, and often also deliberately copying the surface appearance of the Athenian vases. These found some favour in Etruria, but their success was short-lived. In the same years some Athenian potteries were making vases (we call them 'Tyrrhenian') for the Etruscan market, and these, together with the finer products, won the day. The 'Tyrrhenian' vases are cheap, gaudy things, often carrying mock inscriptions to impress the Etruscans who could probably not read Greek at any rate. Even after their success, the Athenians had to face the competition of new shops set up in Italy itself, many of them staffed by emigrant or refugee Ionian artists. One Athenian potter, Nikosthenes, went so far as to copy a purely Etruscan vase shape (Fig. 58, p. 212) and decorate it in the current Athenian style in place of the plain grey ware (*bucchero*) in which the shape was familiar in Etruria. From this time on Athenians were the only Greeks to make money from the export of painted pottery. From the prices which merchants scratched on some of the vases, the profit could not have been great and certainly could never have formed an important part of the state revenue, even through taxes. Other works of art – in bronze or ivory – would have commanded higher prices, and we can see some evidence of Corinthian and Spartan success in the export of bronze vases in the sixth century, but finds in these materials are naturally far more rare than those of pottery. Much the same problems about carriers apply here as they do with the commodity containers (see (a) above). It was certainly not Athenian traders only who carried the fine red-figure vases which have been found from Spain to Persia, from South Russia to the Sudan. Indeed many of the merchants' marks scratched on the vases suggest East Greek hands.

3. Casual finds of Greek vases may mean many things. I have already mentioned the possible significance of the plainer small vases which had no commercial value. Otherwise stray pieces could wander far from any colony or trading post, and probably not in the hands of Greeks or necessarily because there was a specific demand for them. Such would be travellers' or native traders' curios, and can tell us nothing of importance. An example of different material may be the little Spartan bronze warrior which was picked up in the South Arabian desert, but even this has been cited to support the theory that there was a Greek post on the Red Sea in the sixth century B.C.

Objects other than clay pottery will concern us little in the search for Greeks overseas, but there will be occasion to mention many other works whenever we have to deal with the reciprocal effects of overseas contacts and trade upon the Greeks at home.

Coinage and weight-standards, although of considerable historical importance, will also not often be mentioned. Coins could circulate too far, too long, and too freely, but where the evidence is plentiful some useful conclusions can be drawn. Thus, it has been argued that the number of North Greek coins in Egypt shows whence the East Greeks trading there acquired the bullion to pay for their corn, and in part explains East Greek interest and colonizing in the silver-producing areas to the north of Greece (Thrace). It is not until the end of the sixth century that enough coins were in circulation to contribute much to the archaeological record, and the significance of the different weight standards used in various parts of the Greek world and outside it is still not easily judged. We shall have something to say about the eastern inspiration for the use of coinage in Greece in Chapter 3.

LITERARY EVIDENCE

There are no contemporary Greek historical records of the centuries which most concern us, although some asides by early poets are relevant to our theme: notably the remarks by Alcaeus about his brother, a mercenary in the pay of the Babylonians. Sappho's remarks about *her* brother, a wine exporter to Egypt who had become infatuated with a lady of easy virtue there, are unfortunately not all repeated verbatim by the later writers who mention the affair. Snatches of Callinus and Mimnermus sing of Ionian struggles against the Cimmerians and Lydians in Asia Minor.

In the later part of the sixth century B.C. Hecataeus of Miletus wrote his *Periodos* – a *Journey round the World*. 'This is the story told by Hecataeus of Miletus. I write here what I consider to be true, for the tales of the Greeks are manifold and, in my judgement, ridiculous.' Unfortunately we have his work only in fragments quoted by later writers. They show that he had an acute interest in geography and assembled the available information about the ends of the earth from the reports of Ionian captains, and perhaps in part from his own travels. He liked legend too, and may not have satisfied modern standards

in his tempering of fantasy to fact, but there can be no doubt
that he would have had much of importance to tell us of early
travels by the Greeks. Even in his day a Carian traveller, called
Scylax, had been sent by the Persian King Darius to explore
India as far as the Indus (?) and to circumnavigate Arabia;
while, yet earlier, Phoenicians had sailed round Africa for an
Egyptian king.

Some information of value can be gleaned from early non-
Greek sources. Assyrian historical inscriptions, dealing with the
res gestae of the Kings, have occasion to mention the 'Yaman'
and 'Yavan' which the Assyrian met in Cilicia, Cyprus, and
Palestine. The 'Yavan' are 'Ionians', the 'Yaman' Cypriots, but
we are at times at a loss to know exactly who is meant. The
major campaigns which led to the overthrow of the empires of
Assyria, Babylon, and Lydia are also recorded in inscriptions.
There are no direct references to Greeks here, but at Babylon
and Susa there is epigraphical evidence for the presence of
'Ionians', some certainly craftsmen.

Our first detailed account of early Greek history from a Greek
pen is in the *Histories* of Herodotus, the very Father of History.
He was born in East Greece, at Halicarnassus, at a time when
his countrymen were being pressed into the Persian service
against the cities of mainland Greece. He was writing about the
middle of the fifth century. The aim of his work was simple:
'To preserve the memory of the past by putting on record the
astounding achievements both of our own and of the Asiatic
peoples; and, more particularly, to show how the two races
came into conflict.' Fortunately, then, for our purpose, he was
led to discuss at length the dealings of the Greeks with the
countries of the east. He digresses readily, to tell of the earlier
fortunes of the peoples who play the major parts in his story.
The Persians, of course, receive his full attention, and the story
of the first Greek intercourse with the east leads him to an
account of Lydia. The growth of the Persian Empire and expeditions of its Kings give us long accounts of Egypt, Babylonia,
Libya, and Scythia; and it seems there was also a long section on
Assyria, which is missing in our texts. Much of his information
he picked up on his own travels from the Black Sea to Syria and

Egypt. He asked questions and recorded the answers, generally registering how much he believed to be true. 'My business is to record what people say, but I am by no means bound to believe it.' His descriptions of the offerings of foreign kings to Greek sanctuaries may sometimes tax the archaeologist, but they can generally be explained in terms of excavated finds.

Of later historians Thucydides helps us very little. The fourth-century historians, notably Ephorus, may have commanded more

4. The world as known to Herodotus.

'documentary' evidence in the form of king lists, priest lists, foundation stories, or local chronicles, but by their day a great part of this evidence may have been artificial, the invention of local savants, and at any rate the historians' works are lost to us except in so far as they were used or quoted by later writers. Herodotus remains our single literary source of any real importance. We may be grateful that so much of his work survives, grateful too for his curiosity and interest in the affairs of countries outside Greece. Plutarch, a tireless biographer with a singularly poor appreciation of character who would have serialized well in an ancient Sunday paper, criticized him for being over-fond of the barbarian – '*philobarbaros*'. We are perhaps better able to appreciate such quality in a man and a historian.

Bibliography

Richter's *Handbook of Greek Art*, 1960, and *Archaic Greek Art*, 1949, are excellent surveys with good bibliographies which introduce general and specialist works. For Greek vases there are Payne, *Necrocorinthia*, 1931, and Cook's *Greek Painted Pottery*, 1960. Rumpf's *Archäologie*, I and II, 1953 and 1956, are good introductions to Classical archaeology, and are to appear in an English translation.

Of the texts, there are translations of Homer, Herodotus, and Thucydides in the Penguin Classics. For general books on early historians see Myres, *Herodotus, the Father of History*, 1953, and Forsdyke, *Greece before Homer*, 1956.

For the historical background to the period covered in this book, Burn's *The Lyric Age of Greece*, 1960, is a detailed work which takes some note of archaeological evidence, and Andrewes's *The Greek Tyrants*, 1956, treats of one important aspect of Greek political development in these years. The literary evidence is summarized in Hammond's *History of Greece*, 1959, and at greater length in the *Cambridge Ancient History*, where the archaeological evidence cited is by now somewhat out of date.

CHAPTER 2

THE BACKGROUND

In the days of her flourishing Bronze Age civilization, of the Minoan palaces and Mycenaean citadels, Greece had been in close contact with those other early civilizations which bordered the Eastern Mediterranean. It is not my purpose here to tell of this age, but much the same ground was to be covered again by the Greeks, and it is as well to bear in mind that the seventh century B.C. was not the first 'orientalizing' period in Greece, and that the Greek language must have been heard in Egypt more than 500 years before the East Greeks built their new trading town on the Nile Delta. So a few words on these early contacts will not be wasted.

Many of the earliest stimuli to the growth of the Minoan civilization of Crete can be traced to both Egypt and the Near East. The connexions remained strong, and when the Mycenaean Greeks succeeded to the to-them-foreign supremacy of Crete the contacts were maintained. This we can tell from the finds of Mycenaean pottery in Egypt and the apparent influence of Minoan–Mycenaean art forms on the Egypt of Akhenaten and his successors – the Amarna period. Some would have it too that relations might have been closer even earlier, and that Mycenaeans fought for Egypt against the Hyksos invaders.

With the east too there were close ties. The original population of Crete – perhaps even that of Greece – may have come from Asia Minor (Anatolia), although the parallels to be drawn between the cults and architecture of Asia Minor and Crete in the second millennium B.C. are not wholly convincing. The coasts of Syria and Palestine gave access to the riches and technical skills of Mesopotamia. Nor was the only contact a matter of trade in necessities or luxuries because the Minoans, and then the Mycenaeans, seem to have planted trading posts or colonies at various points on the coasts of Asia Minor and Syria.

These overseas ventures by Mycenaean Greeks are another

39

story of which I shall tell part in the introductions to later chapters. Here I want to set the scene, introduce the protagonists, and carry their story down from the collapse of Bronze Age Greece to about the eighth century B.C. when the Greeks again set out in earnest to buy, learn, fight, or settle on foreign soil.

The course of the twelfth century B.C. saw the destruction and abandonment of almost all the important Mycenaean citadels and towns. The archaeological record is clear. The literary record tells of an invasion, or succession of invasions, of other Greek-speakers – the Dorians – from the north, and when we are again able to distinguish the Greek races, by their dialect or customs, we find that the Dorians are in possession of much of southern Greece (the Peloponnese) and the southern islands, including Crete and Rhodes. The story of the overthrow of the Mycenaean palaces may not, of course, have been such a simple matter. Other, non-Greek tribes may have passed through Greece, and the arrival of the Dorians need not have been the most destructive of these visitations, although it had the most lasting effect.

Across the Aegean the story is much the same. The Hittites in Asia Minor succumbed to northern invaders. The countries of the Near East were torn into small states and kingdoms by tribes moving down from the north, joined, it may be, by Mycenaean Greeks from the west – the Akaiwasha (Achaeans) and Daniuna (Danaans) of the Egyptian records.

The islands were restless, disturbed among themselves; they poured out their people all together. No land stood before them. ... The countries which came from their isles in the midst of the sea, they advanced upon Egypt, their hearts relying on their arms.

Egypt withstood the invasions with difficulty, but the upheaval left her too exhausted, and happy enough to let well alone those new cultures of Greece and the Near East who knew iron but had, it seems, no heart for their predecessors' arts and achievements.

The succeeding 'Dark Ages' in Greek history present a real challenge to the archaeologist, and perhaps a too ready field for the ingenuity of scholars attempting – with some justification, it is true – to rescue the history of the illiterate centuries from the myths and poems remembered and recorded by later generations.

To the archaeologist the picture is deceptively simple. On most homeland Greek sites there seems to have been the sort of cultural break which betokens either complete abandonment or considerable depopulation. To this there are two notable exceptions, where folk lived still in a sort of Mycenaean twilight. These are Athens and Crete. The literary record tells us that Athens did not fall to the Dorians or any northern invaders, and the archaeological evidence from the city suggests that this was certainly true, although she may have been hard-pressed and her people confined to within the stout walls of her Acropolis. The finds in her cemeteries, and from nearby Salamis, show that Mycenaean forms and decoration were still remembered, though often much debased. In Crete the Mycenaean tradition, heavily tinged by the native Minoan, survived in two different ways. First, in the refugee settlements – like Karphi, on a nearly inaccessible hill-top where the people sought to avoid the disasters of the preceding generations by removing themselves from contact with possible enemies. Secondly, in the open city of Knossos, which seemed still able to maintain some cultural contact with mainland Greece. Knossos was Dorian by this time, yet it is the cultural influence of non-Dorian Athens which is most strongly felt.

In Athens, before the end of the eleventh century, the first new Iron Age culture of Greece was born. We know it as the 'Protogeometric' because the patterns on its pottery foreshadow the 'Geometric' styles of the ninth and eighth centuries, and it is from its pottery that its character can best be judged. From the finds made with the pottery in tombs, we can see that iron was coming to be used more and more both for ornaments – the big dress-pins – and for weapons. Cremation too was adopted in Athens, although many other parts of Greece were slow to make the change from ordinary inhumation of the dead. It was as though Athens was sloughing off the worn-out idioms of Greece's Bronze Age, and replacing them by the new discipline and precision which were to remain hallmarks of Greece's later achievements in the arts. In the tenth and ninth centuries the archaeological evidence for the awakening and growing populations of other once-rich Greek centres shows that in their arts and crafts they were in varying degrees dependent on Athens' lead. This was true even of Crete, although Knossos and other cities of the lowlands were still highly conscious of their past, and the mountian refuges were at last being abandoned. This Protogeometric spirit is wholly and simply Greek, not Dorian or Ionian or Aeolian. The cultural '*koine*' cuts across the otherwise clearly defined boundaries of speech or politics. And to the historian a common way of life may be of greater significance than a common dialect.

These centuries saw not only the regeneration of prosperity in Greece, but also the beginnings of renewed interest in lands overseas and of migrations to new homes. I write of these events here rather than in later chapters because, for the greater part, they involve a return to towns and islands in the east which had already once been visited by Mycenaean Greeks. In some respects these Eastern Greek states may never have lost their Hellenic character after the débâcle of the end of the Bronze Age. The interruption in their archaeological record may be interpreted in much the same terms as it is for the many homeland Greek sites which seem dead in the eleventh and tenth centuries. And although the Dark Age migrations may have had to displace non-Greek peoples, the political aspect of what we call 'East Greece' cannot from now on be divorced from that of the rest of Greece, and many of the East Greek states are to play leading roles in the later enterprises overseas which are our main interest.

The tradition, which is perhaps only in part the fabrication of patriot-historians, assigned Athens a position of considerable importance as the departure or marshalling point for the migration of the Ionians to their ultimate homes on the eastern shores of the Aegean. Athens' survival of the disaster which attended other Mycenaean cities, and her record through the Dark Ages, show that there is likely to be more than a grain of truth in this. The tradition also speaks of yet earlier migrations by the Aeolians, who settled the islands and cities on the northern half

44

of the coastline of Asia Minor while the Ionians were busy in the south. Ancient historians tried to rationalize these two migrations into two separate and organized movements, while it seems far more likely that the dispossessed or homeless peoples of Greece were crossing the Aegean on many different occasions from the eleventh to the ninth centuries, following the routes explored by their predecessors, or still remembered from the days of Mycenaean trade and settlement.

The later importance of many of the cities, and the fact that the migrations led directly to more immediate contact with 'the barbarian' and set a pattern for later colonial development, justify a brief survey of the archaeology of these early East Greek sites. The equating of this archaeological record with the quasi-historical indications in ancient authors is again a matter of some difficulty which need not be dwelt upon. In general the literary evidence gives higher dates for the migrations than the archaeological evidence so far available, and it is still not possible to say whether this is due more to the incomplete nature of the latter than to the semi-mythical or contrived background of the former.

The questions we should ask about each of the new towns in the east are the following:

1. What sort of site has it; and why was it chosen?
2. Had it been occupied by Greeks (i.e. Mycenaeans) before?
3. Was Greek occupation continuous through the Dark Ages?
4. If not, are there signs of non-Greek occupation?
5. When and whence did the new settlers come?

Of the native Anatolian peoples with whom the Greeks might have had dealings, or whom they may even have had to displace, we know best the Phrygians. They were the heirs to the empire of the Hittites on the plateaux of north-central Anatolia, but, like the Hittites, only intermittently interested in the fortunes of the western seaboard. We shall have more to say of their relations with the Greeks in Chapter 3. The people who occupied the coastal areas of Asia Minor in the Early Iron Age are still little known archaeologically. Their plain pottery is related to the grey Phrygian wares, but there is no quantity of painted pottery until the seventh century, when we see other influences at work. The literary record, on the other hand, offers a plethora of names of peoples whom the Greeks met. Some may refer rather to the state of affairs which the Mycenaean Greeks had found in Asia Minor, but others, like the Carians, survive as recognizable units into later periods. Archaeologically they are not so easy to recognize in the years which interest us, but 'Submycenaean' people in East Greece may have been Carians, and it was perhaps they who were responsible for the survival of some Mycenaean motifs in East Greek art. Where we meet archaeological evidence for a native population we will try to explain it, but otherwise our concern is with the character of the new Greek towns and what has been found in them. The character of the material evidence from them is such that we unfortunately cannot yet make useful deductions about the exact provenance of the new settlers.

We begin in the south, with those places where there is either some possibility of continuous Greek occupation or at least only a short break in the Dark Ages.

The island of RHODES, with Cos, Calymnus, and no doubt others of the Dodecanese (still little explored), was a flourishing Late Mycenaean centre with several important settlements. These were all abandoned at the end of the Bronze Age, but Cos, and to a lesser degree Rhodes, have yielded evidence of reoccupation by Greeks using Protogeometric pottery, possibly from the Argolid and perhaps before the end of the tenth century, so the break was not a long one. There is no sign of any other inhabitants in the interim. From this time on there is a steady and rapid increase in population and multiplication of settlements. The history of the cities of Rhodes is tied so closely to that of the Greek mainland that despite the island's geographical position, its reoccupation in the tenth century can barely be considered an adventure on foreign soil.

On the mainland opposite we still have much to learn of the earliest Greek cities HALICARNASSUS and CNIDUS, and their archaeological relationship with non-Greek peoples. Cnidus lay near the tip of the long peninsula at the extreme south-west point of Asia Minor; Halicarnassus was in a similar position on the next peninsula to the north. A considerable Carian element in the population of Halicarnassus in classical times is shown by personal names, and the town must always have been much involved with its Anatolian neighbours. At ASARLIK (Greek Termera), a hill town near the tip of the Halicarnassus peninsula, a small cemetery has yielded early Protogeometric pottery (now in the British Museum) of Attic type, and has suggested to some that there may have been a shortlived Greek community here which came over from Athens early in the Iron Age. Nothing else has been excavated there, but there are surface indications of sixth-century Greek material, and occupation may after all have been continuous. At all events it would be rash to talk about early Greek settlement soon overwhelmed by the natives on the evidence of one excavated cemetery only. It may be remarked too that one theory would explain the cemetery at Asarlik, and most of the Mycenaean finds in this quarter of Asia Minor, as evidence of Carians living within the Mycenaean cultural ambit and not of Greeks themselves.

MILETUS may tell a somewhat different story from Rhodes, for all that it lies actually on the mainland. Cretans had settled there in the Middle Bronze Age, and Mycenaeans had followed them in the Late Bronze Age. The story of the Greeks taking Carian wives from the native population they found there might belong to the transition between Minoan and Mycenaean settlements, but at the time of Homer's Trojan War Miletus was, it appears, Carian and not Greek. The German excavators allege continuity of Greek occupation, through the Submycenaean and Protogeometric periods, to Classical and Roman times, and what they have published seems to bear this out. The main site lay, at all periods, on the peninsula which projected north into the bay (now silted up) at the mouth of the River Maeander. It commanded good farm land, but the inland route along the Maeander valley may not have been of great importance at first. Details of the early town are obscured by Hellenistic and Roman building, but recent excavations may teach us more. There may too have been other communities near by. On Kalabaktepe, a hill barely half a mile away, there was a settlement from the eighth century on, with its own circuit wall and temple. This was perhaps at first a place of refuge in the years when Cimmerians and Lydians were threatening the city. All the pottery found at Miletus is Minoan, Mycenaean, or Greek, so any Carian occupation did not interrupt the at least superficially Greek character of the site. Miletus will play an important part in our story of the Greeks overseas, and it is a pity that excavations there have so far denied us any very clear idea of the specifically Milesian products – especially pottery.

Of the other sites near by, both MYUS and PRIENE may have occupied peninsula sites in the same bay, but the earliest settlement at the first has been barely explored, and that of the second has yet to be found. MAGNESIA lay inland, on the Maeander, commanding a route to the north and Ephesus; it did not become Greek until the seventh century, but an ancient tradition implies some Bronze Age Greek or Cretan settlement there. Farther south Mycenaean pottery has been found at MYLASA.

At the other side of the Mycale headland, Protogeometric pottery has been found at PYGELA, and Mycenaean and Protogeometric at Tsangli, near the later site of the headquarters of the Ionian League (PANIONION). The town of MELIE here was destroyed by the Ionians. An eighth-century cemetery has been found, but there is later occupation too and the date of the destruction is still not wholly clear. This whole area, according to ancient writers, had to be wrested from the Carians.

EPHESUS lay at the mouth of the River Cayster. It commanded good farmland and was readily accessible from the north and inland. The earliest Greek settlement has yet to be found, but the sixth-century Temple of Artemis (the 'Diana of the Ephesians') probably occupied the site of its earliest sanctuary and Mycenaean pottery has been found near by. Protogeometric pottery has been reported some way to the south.

North of Ephesus lies the great Erythraean peninsula, bounded to the north by the Gulf of Smyrna. On its south flank are the cities of TEOS and LEBEDOS, neither of them excavated. The former figures in Bronze Age myth-history. A little inland is COLOPHON, which has been described as strikingly like the sites of the major Mycenaean cities of Old Greece, on a steep

cropolis commanding a rich plain. Excavations have been un-
ucky in that the finds were lost, but it seems there was a
Mycenaean walled town here. Geometric pottery is reported, but
we cannot say whether occupation could have been continuous.
The full literary record suggests that Cretans preceded the
Mycenaean Greeks and that the later Greeks came straight from
Pylos and established themselves by force of arms.

ERYTHRAE lies on a bay at the extremity of the peninsula to
which it gives its name. The earliest town may lie on a small
peninsula site some way from the later Classical town. It has
not been excavated. Later tradition implies a Bronze Age Greek
settlement here. On the northern arm of the peninsula, within
what was later the territory of Erythrae, is a small peninsula
site (Mordoğan) with Protogeometric and later pottery, and we
should perhaps assume that the larger sites on the peninsula
were occupied just as early. On the north coast of the main
peninsula, looking on to the Gulf of Smyrna, stood
CLAZOMENAE. Parts of the archaic cemetery have been excavated, but not the town, which stood at the end of a low spur
near the shore, and was later removed to an offshore island
when the Persians threatened. The literary record of the Greek
foundation seems to refer to the Iron Age settlement, but some
quantity of Mycenaean pottery has been found, and since there
is no mention of evidence for a native town, this too may have
been twice settled by the Greeks.

SMYRNA, or Old Smyrna – to distinguish it from the Hellenistic and modern city (Izmir) – lay on a small promontory, well
served by harbours on either side of the causeway leading to the
mainland. It has been excavated in recent years by British and
Turkish archaeologists, so that much of its early history is now
clear, although the publication of the finds has barely com-
menced. Here there are clear signs of a flourishing native – or
Anatolian – Bronze Age settlement, and the few Mycenaean
sherds suggest an awareness of the Greeks but not settlement by
them. Some painted Protogeometric vases show that the Greeks
had arrived there, perhaps by about 1000 B.C., but the mass of
plainer grey pottery which accompanied them proves that these
were Greeks who shared the culture of Aeolis, not Ionia, and in

this the archaeological and historical records are at one. By the eighth century, the pottery which we associate rather with the Ionians is predominant, and we read of the city's capture by them. Old Smyrna affords the most complete picture we have so far of an early Greek settlement in Asia Minor, and its colossal walls, laid out in the ninth century and remodelled in the eighth, are witness both to the strength of the city and the very real threat presented by its barbarian neighbours, notably the Lydians. A view of the town as it may have appeared at the end of the seventh century is shown in Fig. 5 (after a drawing by R. V. Nicholls).

Phocaea lay on the north side of the mouth of the Gulf of Smyrna. It is another promontory site with a good sheltered harbour. There has been a false report of Mycenaean pottery

5. A reconstruction of Smyrna in the late seventh century.

rom the site, and recent Turkish excavations have found
nothing earlier than the eighth century.

Of the islands of Ionia, SAMOS has yielded enough Mycenaean
pottery, both from its main town – on a small promontory by a
good harbour – and from the later sanctuary site of the Heraeum,
to suggest Greek settlement in the Bronze Age. There are no
non-Greek 'native' finds of the period which interests us. At the
Heraeum, where the great temple later stood, the Mycenaean
levels are immediately overlaid by heavy Greek Geometric
deposits of the eighth century, although there are reports of
Late Protogeometric, and some Early Geometric (ninth century)
from a tomb, and the excavators thought that the earliest of the
temples there could be of the ninth century. It is possible that
new finds will prove uninterrupted or barely interrupted occupation by Greeks, but there was clearly a significant growth in
prosperity and probably immigration in the Geometric period.

CHIOS tells much the same story. At Emporio, a good harbour site near the south point of the island, recent British
excavations have shown that there was a Late Mycenaean settlement beside and probably on the rocky promontory by the
harbour. This may have been a short-lived refugee settlement of
the twelfth century. In the eighth century there was a new
Greek settlement, not exactly on the site of the Mycenaean,
although the harbourside may have been occupied, and there
was an important sanctuary there, but on a less readily accessible
hill a little inland (Fig. 6). This had an acropolis wall, temple,
and 'palace' ('Megaron hall') within, and the town houses on the
steep hill slope outside the walls. It was abandoned for the
comforts of valley dwelling before the end of the seventh century. Again there is no clear indication of native or 'Carian'
occupation, unless the later Mycenaean or Submycenaean finds
are such. Another important sanctuary and harbour site in the
south of the island, at Phanai, is less well explored but has
yielded Mycenaean and Greek pottery from perhaps the late
ninth century on. The main town of ancient Chios is covered by
the modern city, but here too Mycenaean and Geometric have
been found. At Volissos in the north west, reputed home of the
poet Homer, and on the island Psara there is also Mycenaean and

Archaic town

Megaron hall

Athena sanctuary

Acropolis wall

Cistern

Harbour sanctuary
terrace

0   100   200
yards

6. Plan of Emporio, Chios, in the seventh century.

archaic pottery. As on Samos, there seems to have been a real break in Greek occupation but no recognizable native inter-regnum. The literary record also tells of two periods of settle-ment but admits Carians between them.

We have now looked at the settlements of Dorian Greeks on and off the south-west corner of Asia Minor, and of their Ionian neighbours to the north. Here and there are suggestions of continuous Greek occupation from the Late Bronze Age into historical times – as on Rhodes and at Miletus. The sites chosen, especially in Ionia, are often promontories or peninsulas which afforded protection on the landward side. This in itself implies a fear of hostility, yet each site clearly relied also on its com-mand of good farmland, and only at Smyrna have we seen clear indication of a native settlement being gradually taken over by Greeks. The literary record is full of references to Anatolian peoples met by the Greeks and displaced by them, notably the Carians, but their archaeological presence can only be sought in the Late Mycenaean or Submycenaean culture which they may have absorbed. For it must be remembered that the majority of the sites which have been adequately explored seem to have already been chosen by Mycenaean Greeks for settlement or at least visits.

The main Ionian cities had been organized into a League perhaps by the end of the ninth century. These were Miletus, Myus, Priene, Ephesus, Colophon, Lebedos, Teos, Clazomenae, Phocaea, Samos, Chios, and Erythrae; the last five named may not have been 'founder-members', being, it seems, partly Aeolian settlements at first. Smyrna was never admitted, although it became Ionian after capture by refugees from Colophon. The original function and purpose of the League are not clear, but if there was a military aspect to it there is little reason to think that it was primarily directed against possible barbarian enemies in Anatolia. Ephesus seems to have stood at the head of the League, and there are mentions of her championing Ionians against the native Carians. On the other hand there is evidence for intermarriage between the Ionians and Carians, and Hero-dotus remarks that some of the Greeks set up Lycian kings, or accepted the joint rule of Greek and native royal houses.

The story of Greek settlement in Asia Minor north of Ionia is not so easily told. This is the area of the Aeolians, although it is not possible to define any clear borderline, physical or cultural, between them and the Ionians. The Aeolian sites are fewer and less well explored, but as we have seen already at Smyrna, there are clearer indications of relations with native Anatolian peoples. We are here closer to the heart of the Phrygian kingdom, and the archaeology of the coastal areas is akin to that of western Phrygia, distinguished by the use of monochrome grey pottery, like what is known as *bucchero*, long popular in this part of Anatolia. This was the ware which the Greeks found in use when they first came to Smyrna.

On the island of LESBOS, the great prehistoric site of Thermi yielded Mycenaean pottery in its last phase, and there is some from three other sites in the island. Thermi was violently destroyed, and the story of Achilles' raid on the island at the time of the Trojan War is often cited in this connexion (Homer, *Iliad*, IX : 129f.). Trifling finds of Protogeometric, including an alleged Athenian import, lend a little support for the early date of the new Aeolian settlements suggested by the literary evidence, but otherwise there is hardly anything which need be earlier than the eighth century, from the few archaic sites which have been explored. Characteristic of the earliest finds is the occurrence of fine *bucchero* pottery, unpainted and generally of a silvery grey appearance, in shapes which are not wholly derived from the contemporary Greek repertoire (Fig. 7). The technique and perhaps some shapes may reflect Anatolian fashions, and the great popularity of this ware in Lesbos may be taken as evidence for close relationship with the mainlanders, or with the non-Greek peoples still resident in the island.

We still know very little about the Aeolian cities on the mainland of Asia Minor. From KYME, PITANE, and MYRINA nothing appreciably earlier than about 700 has been published or reported. There is a Mycenaean vase said to be from Pitane, and another, with fragments, from Myrina. Pitane is another peninsula site. The cemetery recently excavated on its isthmus has so far yielded nothing earlier than the early seventh century. Kyme at least must have been an early Aeolian foundation,

sought out for the farmland to which it gave access. The father
of the Greek poet Hesiod had lived there in the eighth century
before moving his family back to Boeotia, and we also hear of
a royal marriage with Phrygia at this time. We shall have
something to say of later Aeolian foundations in Asia Minor in
Chapter 3. As in Ionia, most of the places chosen for the early

7. *Bucchero* from Lesbos and painted vases from
Samothrace.

towns seem likely to have been known to Mycenaean Greeks,
although probably not settled by them.

This is as far as we need pursue the story of the resettlement
of Greeks on the coasts of Asia Minor and the islands. Their
history now is at one with that of the homeland Greeks,
although necessity or convenience at times led them into unholy
alliances with Greece's enemies. By the eighth century, the main
East Greek states are established and rapidly growing. Indeed
they were outgrowing their territories. With that enterprise and
ambition which characterizes people who have established themselves successfully far from home and at the gates of powerful
neighbours, they were ready to join the states of mainland

Greece in those ventures overseas which were to help fashion Greece's new 'Classical' civilization, and at the same time to begin the spread of that new civilization to all corners of the western world.

Bibliography

The settling of the East Greek cities has been studied recently in Roebuck's *Ionian Trade and Colonization*, 1959; the literary evidence is collected in Sakellariou, *La Migration grecque en Ionie*, 1958, and the institutions and Mycenaean elements in Cassola, *La Ionia nel mondo miceneo*, 1957. These give full references and bibliographies. Important new chapters by Desborough and Cook in *Camb. Anc. Hist.* deal with the end of the Mycenaean world and the East Greek settlements.

Recent work on sites in Asia Minor is surveyed by J. M. Cook in *Archaeological Reports for 1959–60*. There are annual reports in *Amer. Journ. Arch.*, and Turkish excavations are described in the periodicals *Anatolia* and *Türk Ark. Dergisi*. The British excavations at Old Smyrna are introduced in *Brit. School Ann.*, LIII–LIV, 1958–9. For Chios see *Arch. Reports* for 1952 to 1955; for Lesbos, articles in *Brit. School Ann.*, XXXI, XXXII, 1930–2, and Lamb, *Thermi*, 1936; Hogarth's *Ephesus*, 1908, for the British excavation of the temple site, and *Journ. Hell. Stud.*, LXXI, 1951; for recent work at Miletus, *Neue deutsch. Ausgrab.*, 1959, and *Istanbul Mitt.* German excavations in Samos are published piecemeal in *Ath. Mitt.*, LV, 1930, on; inter-war Italian excavations on Rhodes are published in *Clara Rhodos* and the Italian School's *Annuario*, and other important works about the island are Kinch, *Vroulia*, 1914; Blinkenberg, *Lindos*, i, 1931; and Johansen, *Exochi*, 1958.

CHAPTER 3

THE EASTERN ADVENTURE

THE Near Eastern peoples with whom the Greeks resumed contact in the eighth century B.C. were heirs to the great civilizations which had flourished in the rich plains of Mesopotamia. Early in the Bronze Age the Aegean world had felt the impact of the

sudden growth of these new cultures, and had come to learn from them their new metallurgical techniques. Indeed the very people of Minoan Crete may have owed their stock to immigrants from the east, despite the independent and brilliant culture which we see they evolved in their island. Relations between the mature Minoan civilization and the east are not easy to make out, but at least in North Syria there is some archaeological evidence for intimate connexions, even in the Middle Bronze Age, before 1550 B.C. At the end of the Late Bronze Age, when Mycenaean Greeks had won ascendancy

57

over the Aegean and succeeded to the Minoan 'empire', ther
are more clear indications of what can almost be called coloniz
ing by Mycenaean Greeks in the Near East, although th
establishments may have been no more than trading post
admitted under treaty with local kingdoms. The most notabl
example is at Ugarit (Ras Shamra), but there was also a fai
quantity of Late Mycenaean pottery imported into Palestine
perhaps from the Mycenaean kingdom of Rhodes rather tha
from the Greek mainland.

The break-up of the Aegean Bronze Age cultures, and th
period – in the myth-historical record – following the Troja
War, saw the migrations of many peoples, from west and north
through the countries of the Near East. Some were carriers o
Mycenaean pottery, themselves surely Mycenaean Greeks, and
to these years may be assigned new Greek settlements in th
east, many of them acquired and no doubt held by force o
arms, although none are long-lived. The archaeological record
shows this most clearly at Tarsus, but the literary record also
tells of other new settlements at this time.

In Cilicia the Theban seer Mopsus was said to have founded
Mopsuhestia and Mallus. A dramatic illustration of this story is
given by the inscription found at Karatepe in 1947, set up in the
eighth century by a ruler who refers to the 'Danunim' – surely a
memory of the Greek Danaans. With other towns, he mentions
Beit Mopsu – the Phoenician form of Mopsuhestia, 'hearth' or
'home' of Mopsus.

The memory of Greek occupation had survived clearly enough
here in Cilicia. As on the Asia Minor coast, it was to the same
areas and cities that the Greeks returned after the Dark Ages,
to found new settlements or open new markets, but here there
was clearly a complete break in the continuity of Greek occupation, despite the survival or memory of names like Mopsus or
the Danaans. During this break, Greek awareness of the countries of the Near East is shown archaeologically by occasional
eastern products which found their way to Greece and sometimes had a limited effect on local crafts. These may briefly be
reviewed, for they suggest a pattern of casual trade with one
part of the Greek world in particular, Crete. But it was not, it

seems, the Cretans who were later to sail east and establish themselves in the eastern markets.

Cyprus provided the intermediary between Crete and the east, and all the 'orientalizing' objects or ideas which Crete accepted during the Dark Ages are either derived directly from Cyprus, or involve the type of object which was as much at home in Cyprus as on the eastern mainland. Even in the depressed period following the end of the Bronze Age, when iron was still barely known and the artist was still working in a Minoan–Mycenaean tradition, there are signs of continued relations between these two islands, which had been among the most

a   b

8. (a) Bronze stand from Knossos, Crete;
(b) Bronze stand from Larnaka, Cyprus.

important centres of the Late Mycenaean world. The evidence lies mainly in the choice of decoration on pottery and in the shapes of some vases (e.g. duck-vases). Iron pikes of a Cypriot type appear with a tenth-century burial at Knossos. In bronze the most important objects which travelled west were openwork vase-stands, largely composed of rods bent into volute patterns. Examples of the simplest form – tripod stands – have been found in Crete (Fig. 8a) in tenth- and ninth-century contexts. The more elaborate form, square in plan with a hoop on top and sometimes wheeled, like that from Larnarka in Cyprus (Fig. 8b), was apparently also known in Crete, to judge from the clay imitation of one found at Karphi. This is a remote mountain village in Crete, sheltered by its position from hostile interference, and so cut off from the cultural progress of other Cretan centres that even when a foreign form is admitted and copied – as with the stand – the decoration on it remains Minoan in its style. This type of stand was later, in the eighth century, copied in Crete in bronze; there are fragmentary examples from the Idaean Cave and Knossos, and another, found at Delphi, may have been made in Crete. The import and limited influence of Cypriot pottery is also admitted in Crete in the eighth century, and we might have expected that the Cretans would be the first Greeks to take the initiative in the east, but it seems that the Cretan Dorian temperament lacked the spirit of enterprise which had characterized the Minoans.

In other parts of Greece the evidence is very slight for even minor and casual imports from the east before the eighth century: a bronze bowl in Athens in a ninth-century tomb is the best example.

It is none too easy to fit in the Phoenicians to this picture of relations in the Aegean in the Early Iron Age – or at least to fit in the reputation which the Phoenicians had acquired as mariners and traders. We shall see that it is only after Greeks establish themselves on the Syrian coast that Greece begins to receive and appreciate eastern products; and there is no clear evidence for Phoenician trading colonies overseas earlier than the Greek ones. For all that, they may have been the carriers of what little did travel into the Greek world from the east before the eighth century. The nature of this trade did not require the establishment of regular trading posts or colonies until Greek example and competition led them to similar undertakings.

With the eighth century, the picture begins to change completely. We may distinguish three main areas in the Near East which were either penetrated by the Greeks, or whose cultures had a profound influence on them. They are:

1. *North Syria*, both in its role as the home of neo-Hittite culture and as the gateway to the Urartian, Assyrian, Babylonian, and Persian Empires, which successively occupied it.

2. *Phoenicia* and *Palestine*, whose cultures and their influence on the Greeks are not always readily distinguishable from those

of North Syria, especially after the Assyrian conquest. Cyprus plays a somewhat equivocal part as intermediary for both North Syria and the countries to its south. It is as an intermediary rather than as an independent centre that it is best considered here. It was peopled largely by Greek-speakers, having been 'colonized' in the Late Bronze Age, and it is still in touch with Crete, as we have seen; but by now its culture has almost nothing in common with Greece, and looks to the east and the adjacent coasts of Cilicia and North Syria.

3. *Anatolia*, and the kingdoms of *Phrygia* and *Lydia*. We have already seen how the Greeks established themselves again on the sea-board of Asia Minor. It will be their relations with these kingdoms of the hinterland which will concern us later in this chapter.

NORTH SYRIA AND THE EMPIRES BEYOND

Al Mina, at the mouth of the Orontes in North Syria,* is the site of what was probably the most important and earliest of the new Greek settlements or trading posts in the Eastern Mediterranean, and it is our best and earliest source of information about the Greeks overseas.

The town was possibly that known to the Greeks as Posideion. Herodotus says that it was founded by Amphilochus, a hero who, like Mopsus, had founded other cities in the east, in Cilicia, just after the Trojan War. This, then, must be yet another Late Mycenaean settlement to which the Greeks later returned. Of its first Greek occupation we know nothing, but Mycenaean pottery has been found near by (at Sabouni), and the new town may not have been in exactly the same place as the old; this is true of several such resettlements.

Al Mina was excavated by Sir Leonard Woolley before the last war. He was exploring in Syria, which he recognized as the key area, for sites which would throw light on the relationship between the countries of the Aegean and Mesopotamia. He was soon rewarded, with the fine Bronze Age site of Atchana, and the no less significant Iron Age port at Al Mina. The site had

* It stands at present within the Turkish border.

been in part washed away by a change in the course of the river. Woolley thought that part of its early history had been washed away as well, but there can be little doubt that we have some at least of the earliest Greek material there. It is not, of course, unlikely that there was an earlier port, perhaps the Mycenaean Posideion, in the neighbourhood, for which Sabouni, the hill town some three miles inland where Mycenaean pottery has been found, served as a mother-city or refuge.

Woolley distinguished ten different levels at Al Mina, numbered from the latest, i, to the earliest, x, but we are concerned with two main periods only, which can be readily picked out from the architectural history of the site and the finds. The first (Levels x–vii) covers the earliest history of the town, down to about 700 B.C. The second (Levels vi–v) carries us to about 600 B.C., when there seems to be a break in the Greek occupation, or at least a serious recession. The excavation was in the town and warehouses, and we unfortunately know nothing of the cemeteries and sanctuaries, Greek or native.

Al Mina: the first period, to 700 B.C.

The configuration of the Delta of the Orontes and the coastline in antiquity is not quite clear, but it seems that the town at Al Mina served through much of its history as a port and depot for sea-going vessels. Its architectural remains of our first period are not particularly impressive. The walls of the buildings were of mudbrick upon a low stone foundation or socle – a type of construction which remained the rule at Al Mina and was common on both Greek and Near Eastern sites at this time. No complete house plans can be made out, but it seems that many of the earliest walls (Levels x–ix) were re-used in buildings of Level viii, and that Level vii was no more than a re-shaping or restoration of existing structures. What is important for us is the fact that Greek pottery is present in some quantity from the earliest levels on.

Before the second main period – the seventh century, Levels vi–v – there seems to be a real break in the history of the site. Not perhaps a long one, but certainly an important one. There is a complete change in the character and origins of the Greek finds, as we shall see, and the new buildings are laid out on quite different lines. Some rooms are more spacious, like store-rooms, and the excavator observed that 'it already becomes possible to recognize – without undue exercise of the imagination – early examples of the type of office and magazine building which was to become the standard for future times'. Level v was a re-modelling of Level vi, and we are not for the moment concerned with the replanning of the town in Level iv and its subsequent history down to its eclipse by the foundation of Seleucia in 301 b.c., although it is in this later period that the form and character of the Greek warehouses are best appre-ciated, because the latest buildings are better preserved.

Who then were the Greeks who established this trading station? What did they buy and sell, and what were their rela-tions with the local population? The finds at Al Mina answer the first question for us; for the others we must appeal both to literary record and to the cumulative evidence of other sites, and we must also for the most part simply guess.

The finds of our first period are largely pottery. The Greek vases fall into a number of clearly defined groups, and by taking first what are stylistically the latest – because they are more readily identified – we can win some idea of the source of the pottery and of the Greeks who carried it. The groups are as follows:

1. The smallest, but most distinctive, is of small straight-sided cups painted with Geometric patterns which are sometimes filled in with a white or cream slip (Fig. 9a). Such vases have other-wise been found only at Eretria and Chalcis in Euboea.

2. There are imitations of the elegant cups (*kotylai*) which were made in Corinth in the later part of the eighth century. Their clay, which is pinkish, and the occasional use of white paint for stripes within, show that they are not true Proto-corinthian (Fig. 9b). Imitations which carry all the features of this group have so far been found only at Eretria in Euboea and in the western colony of the Euboeans, on Ischia (*Pithekoussai*).

3. Cups (*skyphoi*) with simple Geometric patterns in panels (the 'metope' pattern). The class is well known in the islands

of the Cyclades and Euboea, but the general absence of mica in the clay points especially to Euboea, and so does the particularly common pattern of concentric circles on the lip (Fig. 9c).

4. Stylistically the earliest are cups decorated with compass-drawn semicircles (Fig. 9d). Similar vases have been found par-

9. Eighth-century vase-types from Al Mina.

ticularly in the Cyclades and Thessaly, but there are several from Euboea, and they appear occasionally in East Greek (not mainland) sites, in Crete, and in places in the Near East. Their clean fabric again points rather to Euboea, but they may have been made in other island centres also. Their date has been much discussed. The Near Eastern contexts are equivocal, but it seems likely that they were already being made in the ninth century. Their absence in the western Greek colonies suggests that they were going out of use by about the mid eighth century, although there are a very few which appear still in use later.

5. A group of cups (*skyphoi*) of the late eighth century seems likely to have been made by Greeks at Al Mina, not imported. Their clay seems local, details of their decoration and use of colour (bichromy) show the influence of Cypriot-type pottery which was also current in Al Mina at that time, but the shapes and details of technique are wholly Greek. Thus, the striped interior of the cup shown in Fig. 9e is Cypriot, and non-Greek; while the exterior decoration, the use of a multiple brush, and the fine fabric and shape are Greek. Some cups of this type reached Cyprus, where they stand out clearly from the local products, and one or two were found in Phoenician Byblos, on the coast to the south of Al Mina, and at Tarsus.

Of the other pottery which from its level or style belongs here, there are scraps only of vases of a type made in East Greece, especially in Rhodes, and one piece only of true Protocorinthian; nothing Cretan. We shall return to consider the non-Greek pottery in a moment.

It seems likely then that it was the Euboeans who led the Greeks to Al Mina, together perhaps with islanders of the Cyclades, over some of whom Eretria (in Euboea) held some sort of empire. The evidence for this is wholly archaeological. The literary record does not contradict it; indeed it says nothing at all of this truly epoch-making enterprise.

What the Euboeans brought with them to sell we do not know. At this period it could hardly have been pottery, although this no doubt accompanied other goods and was certainly as fine as or finer than anything made in the Near East at this time. It is difficult to see what eighth-century Greece had to offer, except perhaps slaves, but certainly a flow of trade ensued; and this could hardly have been one way, however highly we rate the Greek flair for business, for here they were meeting their equals in this matter. Many Greeks may have travelled east to serve as mercenaries, but they would not have won the commodities which the merchants and rulers at home wanted. From the east came works of art whose profound influence we shall discuss later. Of more immediate importance would have been the supply of metal: iron and copper, which were in particular demand in Greece, where the city states or kingdoms saw the need for increasing their force of arms in step with their increasing prosperity and population, and the growing jealousy of any less fortunate neighbours. It may not be by chance that we hear first of hoplite battles, with armies of bronze-clad warriors, in Euboea, whose merchants had first sought out the new sources of metals for the Greek world. Chalcis in particular held a reputation in antiquity for being the home of various innovations in bronze armour. Her name, the 'brazen town', suggests an earlier association with metal working, but growing demands may have necessitated a search for new sources of material. We cannot say that metals were the main commodities sought by the Euboeans, but they surely played an important part in trade with the east. The initial voyages were probably casual private ventures which opened a new world to Greek eyes, a world which was rich enough and sufficiently disturbed to give promise of quick and profitable business. In effect the new trade route provided something of an escape or outlet to the easterners as well as a source of wealth and inspiration to the Greeks.

When the Euboeans first came to Al Mina, the town probably lay under the suzerainty of Urartu, together with the other cities of the Amq plain by the lower Orontes. The seat of this Urartu kingdom was in what we know as Armenia, but in this, its greatest period, the empire seems to have spread to the shores of the Mediterranean. Urartu was rich in metals and was an important and original metal-working centre, although it is still not always possible with certainty to distinguish Urartian from the Assyrian bronze work, about which there is much more to be learnt. From the start, then, the Greeks visiting Al Mina had access to rich supplies of metal and metal work, and Urartian control of the coast seemed in no way to inhibit free trade overseas and even the establishment of a foreign trading post.

The town at Al Mina was not, of course, wholly Greek. It is

likely that there was already a settlement there of some kind, which only assumed real importance as an emporium when the Greeks began to visit the port and established a small community there. The non-Greek pottery from Al Mina may give us some idea both of the antiquity of the settlement and of the culture of the people who admitted the Greeks. The latter is more easily judged, for the pottery is plain or very simply decorated, and there is nothing like the rapid stylistic and decorative development to be observed that there is in the Greek wares. Also, for all their careful excavation, the chronology of various comparative sites in the east is still the subject of considerable discussion.

A recent study of the non-Greek pottery at Al Mina shows that none of it need be earlier than the mid ninth century. The Greek pottery which was found beside it in the lowest levels can plausibly be dated around 800 or before, so that occupation here before the arrival of the Greeks may have been but slight. Through the eighth century the volume of non-Greek pottery seems to match that of the Greek. All must have been for daily use, since there was no organized trade in Greek pottery at this time, but the majority of the minor objects found are not Greek. The Greek community may therefore have been a minority, although it seems to have been the direct cause of the port's prosperity, if not of its existence. Most of the non-Greek pottery in our first period has a marked Cypriot appearance, but other wares which were current in Phoenicia and North Palestine are well represented. The Cypriots were trading freely with this coast, and part of the population of Al Mina is likely to have been Cypriot, making its own vases there, or near by, in a Cypriot style. The importance of these local Cypriot wares is reflected in the decoration of the vases which, it seems, were made by the Greeks in Al Mina (see our group 5, above).

The Greek pottery found in Cyprus itself – mainly in the coastal towns – is of much the same sources and in much the same proportions as that at Al Mina in these years. An undue number of Geometric vases in Cyprus have been identified as Athenian, but are more probably from the Cyclades or Euboea. There is no question yet of new Greek settlement there. A 'royal tomb' of the mid eighth century near Salamis in Cyprus was furnished with Greek vases, including Athenian, but this indicates only the extravagant or exotic taste of its occupant.

In 743 the Assyrian king, Tiglath-pileser III, broke Urartian power in the west, and by the end of the century Assyrian rule had spread over Syria and Cilicia, to Cyprus in the west, to Palestine in the south. Cyprus logically formed part of any empire embracing North Syria and Cilicia. At Al Mina Woolley declared that his Level VIII bore almost exclusively Cypriot pottery, but there are many Greek sherds from the site labelled Level VIII, and, although the Cypriot element at Al Mina may have been considerable in the eighth century, Level VIII probably begins earlier than 709, the year of the first record of Cypriot submission to Assyria. But it seems unprofitable to attempt to make serious distinction between the pottery labelled from Levels X–VII. It might be suspected that it was the Cypriots who led the Greeks to Al Mina, and the quantity of eighth-century Greek pottery found in the island shows the extent of Greek interest there. They might certainly have travelled via Cyprus. Assyrian domination had no adverse effect on Greek trade. The Greek pottery can be dated by external evidence and clearly continues in quantity at Al Mina to the end of the eighth century, and the same must obviously be true of the Cypriot and other wares found with it.

Before we consider more closely the end of our first period at Al Mina, marked by the abandonment – though brief – of the houses of Level VII, and followed by the new planning of Level VI, we may review what other evidence there is for the Greeks in the Near East in these years. Clearly Al Mina was not the only port which attracted Greeks (see below, on Tell Sukas), but its position must have made it the most important one. Through it some Greek pottery passed to the hinterland and to the south, in the hands either of Greeks or of local traders. Scraps are reported from various sites in the Amq plain behind Al Mina. The distinctive cups with pendent semicircles (our group 4, above) have been found at some five other sites in Syria, and two in Palestine. Other Geometric vases, or fragments of them, have been found in Syria at Hama and Catal Hüyük; in

Assyria at Nineveh (reported, not published); in Palestine at Megiddo, Samaria, and Tell abu Hawam. These are variously identified as Athenian, Cycladic, or Argive, but all – especially the standed bowls (craters) – are well matched by Euboean wares, and in view of the Euboean record at Al Mina it seems unnecessary to look further for the origins of many of them. There is no archaeological evidence for any profound influence on the local arts which might be attributed to these casual contacts with Greek things. Only in pottery had the Greeks anything to teach, and the Near Easterner (outside Cyprus) was not much interested in elaborately decorated vases.

Farther south, at Ashdod, Assyrian records tell of a Yatna or Yamani who was put up as king by rebels. Sargon crushed the revolt in 712, and Yatna fled to Egypt and Nubia, where he was handed over to Sargon by King Shabako. Yatna may have been a Cypriot (Yadanana is Cyprus). Some have thought that a Greek from Cyprus is involved, and invoked the similarity of the eastern name for Greeks – Yavan = Ionians – but the archaeological evidence shows that there was no new Greek (Ionian) settlement in Cyprus at this date. More likely the Assyrians were in the habit of calling Cypriots Ionians, confusing them with, or at least not differentiating them from, the Greek islanders.

To the north, in Cilicia, the evidence is yet stronger, and Geometric sherds have been found in several places, notably Mersin and, even more important, Tarsus, at both of which sites the pendent-semicircle cups appear. Tarsus is another of these sites which had been settled by the Greeks for a short while in the Late Mycenaean period and then returned to in the Geometric period some 400 years later. The Greek pottery from Tarsus, which was excavated by Americans from 1935–9 and 1947–9, has only recently been published and it seems possible that a small Greek settlement had been admitted perhaps as early as that at Al Mina. The types of Greek and other pottery found seem to be much as at Al Mina, with more local Cilician wares. The East Greek element, which appears slight and late in the first period at Al Mina, may have been somewhat stronger at Tarsus.

Cilicia, with Syria, had fallen to the Assyrian king Sargon after his accession in 720. Twenty-four years later the Assyrian governor in Cilicia revolted, the Greeks at Tarsus rose in arms with him, and beside them, perhaps, the Greeks of Injira (if this is Greek Anchiale). Sennacherib, who had come to the Assyrian throne in 705, crushed the revolt and destroyed the city of Tarsus. This we know from Assyrian records, and a destruction level at Tarsus was readily distinguished by the excavators. Later records speak of a sea battle between Assyrians and Ionians, and this may have happened in the course of the campaign. Even if the revolt did not spread as far as Al Mina, it seems likely that the Assyrians would hardly look with favour on Greek or Cypriot undertakings; and as the pottery evidence at Al Mina suggests that the abandonment of the Level VII houses fell at about this date, I am inclined to associate this break in the site's history with the events which led to the destruction of Tarsus in 696.

Al Mina: the second period, to 600 B.C.

The second phase of our story of the Greeks in the east is again best represented archaeologically at Al Mina, in the excavated Levels VI and V. The architectural history of the period has already been discussed. The continuity in the style of the Greek pottery found before and after this break at the start of the seventh century shows that the break was not of long duration. But it was virtually a new town which arose over the ruins of the old, barely acknowledging the lines of the earlier roadways and the limits of individual properties. Levels VI and V at Al Mina bring us through the period of Assyrian domination to its collapse and the spread of the new Babylonian empire to the shores of the Mediterranean.

The Greek pottery seems now to form a more significant proportion of all the pottery found, and is perhaps the major part of it. This would suggest that the Greeks were beginning to command the trade which passed through the port rather than share it with the Cypriots, and Woolley notes that although there is still a certain amount of Cypriot pottery in Level VI, it fails in Level v. The Greek vase fragments will again help us to identify the homes of the Greeks mainly concerned in the eastern trade, for although some fine Greek wares (such as Corinthian) might have been carried by any Greek traders, it is still too early to speak of a serious or deliberate trade in decorated pottery as such. Woolley writes that 'Lesbian *bucchero* was favoured by one or two dealers, and one at least kept . . . Chiote pottery'. These finds, if significant at all, may rather suggest the nationality of the warehouse keepers, for the distribution of decorated Greek pottery in the Near East in the seventh century presents if anything a poorer picture than it does in the eighth.

The main classes of pottery from Al Mina in the seventh century are:

10. Seventh-century vase-types from Al Mina.

1. *Euboean* imitations of Protocorinthian cups – our group 2 above. Sufficient fragments are labelled 'Levels VI–VII' or 'Level VI' to suggest that this ware may still have been arriving.

2. *Corinthian*. Fine Protocorinthian *aryballoi* and cups appear now in some quantity. The earliest may be as early as the first quarter of the seventh century, and the flow continues uninterrupted to near the end of the century.

3. *Athenian*. Scraps of storage jars, called 'SOS amphorae' from the patterns on their necks (as Fig. 3b).

4. *Argive* (?). Some unusual polychrome fragments are similar to fragments from the sanctuary of Hera near Argos, but also to pottery found in the *Euboean* colony of Cumae in Italy.

5. *East Greek*. There are several important types:

(a) 'Bird bowls': shallow cups of fine fabric, decorated with simple Geometric patterns (Fig. 10a). Rhodes must have been an important centre of production, but there were factories elsewhere for this long-popular ware.

(b) 'Bird *oenochoai*' (Fig. 10b): jugs related to the last for their decoration, but they do not long survive the middle of the seventh century on other sites. Again, Rhodes is an important centre, but they were made also in Samos, Chios, and perhaps elsewhere. The Al Mina jugs have round mouths, without the trefoil lip for pouring like many Chian and a few Rhodian.

(c) 'Wild Goat' vases: various shapes decorated with animal friezes – often of goats – in the style which is adopted in East Greece by about the middle of the seventh century. Some of these, particularly the shallow dishes, are clearly Rhodian. Others must be from elsewhere in East Greece – Chios, Samos, or Miletus. There are no examples with the incised 'black-figure' technique which begins to appear on such vases about 600 B.C.

(d) Cups: plain painted cups with reserved stripes at the level of the handles and the lip: the so-called 'Ionian cups', perhaps Rhodian (Fig. 10c).

(e) Polychrome striped vases, mainly fine cups painted black with thin red and white stripes (Fig. 10d); certainly Rhodian.

72

(f) Chian chalices (Fig. 10e) and fragments of other vases with the distinctive Chian white slip.

(g) 'Lesbian' *bucchero* is mentioned by Woolley, but none has been published; and Lesbos may not have been the only place in Aeolis where grey *bucchero* was made in the seventh century.

It is clear from this survey that most of the Greek pottery arriving at Al Mina in the seventh century is coming from parts of Greece other than those which served the Greeks living there in the eighth century. The Euboean interest has virtually disappeared. The years around 700 may have seen the last or most decisive of the struggles between the two main Euboean cities, Eretria and Chalcis (the so-called Lelantine War). Eretria probably won, and it is at Eretria, not (so far) Chalcis, that we find the type of vase still carried to Al Mina; but this may mean nothing. Both cities retire from the arena for many years. The islanders of the Cyclades who came with the Euboeans are also seen no more, although there are scraps of one of the distinctive island wares of the earliest seventh century at Al Mina; perhaps from Naxos.

In their place we find Corinthian and East Greek vases. The evidence of the Corinthian pottery must be treated with caution. It was of the highest quality, worth possessing and carrying for its own sake by any Greek, and need not mean the active participation of Corinthian traders in the east. The vases have been found all over the Greek world – and beyond it – and do not present any very clear pattern of specifically Corinthian trade and interest. The East Greeks, themselves active producers of decorated pottery, were glad enough at times to use this most elegant of all seventh-century Greek wares. But this alone can hardly explain the quantity of Corinthian pottery at Al Mina, especially early in the century; and if not necessarily for Corinthians, we should look for Greeks closely connected with Corinth. I suspect the Aeginetans, who at home nearly always used Corinthian vases, having no local potteries for fine vases. I say 'nearly always', for excavations on Aegina show that Athenian and Argive vases were also imported for use. Athenian, and perhaps Argive too, are the only other recognizable scraps of mainland Greek pottery at Al Mina (3 and 4 above). Finds on Aegina itself indicate an interest in eastern matters throughout the seventh century.

The leading part was now clearly played by East Greeks. They had already been seen in Al Mina in the later eighth century, and it was on these eastern routes that the Samians and Milesians met the Euboeans and became involved in their rivalries. We can certainly identify Rhodian pottery, and Chios, Samos, and perhaps Lesbos are also represented. Miletus clearly should be also, from what we know of her other enterprises in the seventh century, but we still know too little about Milesian pottery. When we know more, it seems likely that the Milesian share will be recognized at the expense of the Rhodian. This is historically the more likely, and it is interesting that the earliest East Greek pottery at Naucratis in Egypt (see Chapter 4) is very like the latest at Al Mina, and at Naucratis there is every reason to look for Milesians. Rhodian pottery may have been used and carried by East Greek states much as Corinthian was by mainland Greeks. The island's role in the expansion of Greek interests in the seventh century has perhaps been exaggerated. It is remarkable how very few of the finest 'Wild Goat' vases have been found in the otherwise prolific cemeteries of Rhodes.

The latest datable pottery from this second main period at Al Mina is of about 600 B.C., and thereafter the evidence for occupation becomes very slight. There are fragments of pottery, East Greek and Athenian, from Al Mina, and especially from Sabouni, the hill town associated with the port, of the middle decades of the century; but it is not until the last quarter of the century that Greek vases appear again in quantity. What is the reason for this break? At the end of the seventh century the Assyrian empire fell to Babylon, and in the early years of the sixth Nebuchadrezzar II extended this empire to the coast of the Mediterranean. If the break in Al Mina's archaeological record is not wholly illusory, it may be connected in some way with this shift of power.

Of the other eastern sites occupied by Greeks, Tarsus revived as quickly after 696 B.C. as did Al Mina, and except for a relative ack of Corinthian pottery, its record through the seventh century seems much as that of the North Syrian town. Slighter evidence of Greek interest, though not settlement, is found elsewhere in Cilicia (Mersin, Sakjegözü, and minor sites), Syria (Çatal Hüyük, Zinjirli), at Babylon, and in Palestine (Tell abu Hawam). The pottery, as at Al Mina, is nearly all East Greek and Corinthian, as are the imports in Cyprus in the seventh century. The foundations from Rhodes of Phaselis and Soloi, on the south coast of Asia Minor, may date to the earlier seventh century, but there is no archaeological evidence for this.

There is a little evidence too for Greek mercenaries in the east in the seventh century. Soldiers dressed like Greek hoplites appear in the siege scene on a silver bowl found in Cyprus (Amathus) but probably of seventh-century Phoenician workmanship. Unfortunately the 'Ionian warriors' which some have detected on a relief from Nineveh are certainly easterners, and the scrap of what might be a Greek helmet shown on a painting from Til Barsip is meagre evidence for any Assyrian representations of Greek soldiers. From the ruins of Carchemish, overthrown by the Babylonians in 605, came one Greek greave and a shield (Plate 6b) with decoration of concentric friezes of animals and a central gorgon's head. This is likely to be Greek work of the mid seventh century or little later, and a similar, rather finer example has been found at Olympia. It is likely, however, that the shield was carried by a Greek serving not the Assyrian or Babylonian king, but the Egyptian king Necho who had occupied Carchemish.

A site near Ashdod and just south of Tel Aviv (Mezad Hashavyahu) is thought by its recent excavators to have included a settlement of Greek mercenaries, paid off by the Egyptian Psammetichos I. It is fortified, and the East Greek pottery there is all of the end of the seventh century. It is suggested that it was abandoned in the face of Necho's invasion in 609; but might not these be Necho's Greeks, ousted by Babylonians (see p. 132).

The sixth century

There is one site on the Phoenician coast, Tell Sukas, where the amount of Greek pottery found may mean another Greek settlement or trading post. The site lies on a low promontory between two good anchorages, about 50 miles south of Al Mina. It was partly excavated before the last war, and digging has recently been resumed there by Danish archaeologists. It was visited by Greeks as early as Al Mina, in the eighth century, but so far the site has yielded little of the seventh century, and its main period of prosperity seems to be after about 600. Most of the pottery is East Greek. There is some Athenian imported pottery of the mid century, but nothing very much later, and there are signs of a destruction about 550. The first excavator of the site, Forrer, thought that its brief life as a prosperous Greek settlement showed that it had been sponsored or at least encouraged by the Babylonians in the teeth of the rival Phoenicians whose capital city Tyre never fell to them, and that the Persians put an end to it. In these respects there is a profound discrepancy between its history and that of Al Mina, which declined on the approach of the Babylonians and only revived under the Persians. It may be that the new overlords found it expedient that the Greeks should continue their trading activities at Tell Sukas rather than Al Mina, but that the Greeks returned to the more favourable port as soon as they were able. Or it might mean that in this period there was more interest in direct trade with Syria and less with the remoter centres served by Al Mina.

There are very few other finds of Greek pottery in the Near East, from Cilicia to Palestine, for some fifty years after the beginning of the sixth century – the Babylonian 'interregnum' between the Assyrians and the Persians.

The Babylonians themselves employed Greek mercenaries. The Lesbian poet Alcaeus sings for his brother Antimenidas 'fighting beside the Babylonians you accomplished a great feat and delivered them from distress, for you slew a warrior who lacked only one span from five royal cubits in height' (i.e. eight feet four inches tall). There is a hint that he served in the Palestine campaign. At Babylon there is inscriptional evidence

or the presence of 'Ionians', but perhaps only from Cilicia, and
ome mid-sixth-century Athenian pottery which reminds us of
he finds at Tell Sukas and scraps at Al Mina (Sabouni).

Babylonian supremacy was shortlived, and a new power from
he east takes the stage. The Persian king Cyrus entered Babylon
n 539 and succeeded to the dominion over Syria, Phoenicia, and
Palestine. He had already subdued the Ionians in East Greece
fter his defeat of Croesus and the Lydians. Under Persian rule,
Greek trade seems to have prospered again in the Near East,
fter its setback under the Babylonians. In Phoenicia and
Palestine there is a little East Greek and Athenian pottery,
mainly of the second half of the century, but in the north the
Greek port of Al Mina was rebuilt and in operation again before
he end of the century. By now it seems to be a wholly Greek
establishment, and its regeneration can only be understood in
he light of positive encouragement of the Greek traders by the
Persians. The new town at Al Mina (Level IV) was laid out in a
quite new plan and style. The buildings or warehouses are
grouped in large rectangular blocks, and some approach the
orm, around a courtyard open on one side, which appears in a
ater stage of the town's history (Fig. 11). Al Mina was to suffer
two more changes in its plan, after fires, but despite these setbacks its prosperity was uninterrupted until its importance was
eclipsed by the new foundation of Seleucia, four miles to the
north, in 301 B.C.

For the identity of the Greeks now dealing with Al Mina we
can no longer rely on the sort of archaeological evidence which
has served us before. Athenian pottery had won all markets
now, and finds of decorated Athenian vases anywhere in the
Greek world or outside it do not imply the active interest there
of Athenians rather than any other Greeks. In view of East
Greek and especially Ionian relations with Persia, and the
analogous record of Naucratis in Egypt, we may reasonably
suppose that the East Greeks still ran most of the trade. From
the end of the sixth century, the Greek decorated pottery at Al
Mina is all Athenian, most of it of poor quality, for an uncritical
market, it would seem. There are still, of course, Cypriot objects,
and some minor trinkets from Phoenicia. Local or native wares

are still in evidence and are profoundly influenced, usually for the better, by the quality of the Greek imports. In general it may be said that the greater part of the fine pottery was Greek but that the minor objects were more typical of the finds in any other Near Eastern port or city with extensive overseas con-

11. Reconstruction of warehouses at Al Mina.

nexions. By now, of course, the Athenian pottery was being imported for its own sake, and it appears with growing frequency on many Near Eastern sites. To confine our attention only to the years after the resumption of trade through Al Mina and before the end of the Persian Wars in 479 B.C., we find

Athenian pottery at some half-dozen sites in North Syria, the remotest being at Carchemish, some at Babylon, and in somewhat greater quantity in Palestine, from Tell abu Hawam in the north (near Haifa) to Tell Jemmeh in the south. It is invariably bad and late black-figure, the poorest, almost mass-produced Athenian products. Standards improve a little in the fifth century. I illustrate here one Greek *objet d'art*, rather later in date, which had passed to Al Mina, because it has not hitherto been published and is of some intrinsic interest. It is the fragmentary statuette of a seated sphinx (now in Oxford), carved in fine white marble (Plate 2a). The work and finish are exquisite. Comparisons with similar statuary in Greece, such as the rather later sphinx from Aegina or the rather earlier sphinx vase by the potter Sotades suggest a date about 470. It may have been in Al Mina only to delight a Greek resident agent, but the Persians had already acquired a taste for Greek works of art, for all the poverty of much of the Athenian pottery which was brought to Al Mina.

Few Greek coins have so far been found on Near Eastern sites before 480 B.C. Most are Athenian or Aeginetan issues of the later sixth or early fifth century, but an important hoard from Ras Shamra has a preponderance of Thracian issues, and Thracian coins are otherwise more common than one might expect. The same phenomenon is true of finds in Egypt of this date (see p. 147). There are also a few Ionian and Cypriot coins. At Persepolis a number of coins were found in association with the foundation deposits for the Hall, or 'Apadana', of Darius (511 B.C.); there are eight Lydian staters (of Croesus), and in silver one Aeginetan, one Thracian, and three Cypriot pieces.

We shall have no more to say of the fortunes of the Greeks in Syria and Palestine in the fifth century, except in so far as Greek relations with the Persians affect this area. It was the Greeks of Ionia who first had to deal with the Persians and it is to them and to their experience of the native kingdoms in Anatolia that we shall return later in this chapter.

EASTERN INFLUENCE IN GREECE

To complete the picture, something must be said of the effects in Greece of this lively intercourse and trade with the Near East, at least as they are seen by the archaeologist. The part the east played in inspiring new ideas in religious, literary, or scientific matters cannot be discussed here. Nor, in summarizing the often superficial influence of oriental motifs in Greek art, can we pay adequate attention to the native Greek contribution, and to the way the Greeks translated and adapted what they borrowed into an art unparalleled in any Near Eastern land. The account is thus bound to be unbalanced, and the reader must bear in mind the steady evolution of the Greeks, their institutions, and their art, which the east may have accelerated or conditioned, although it can never be said to have provided the initial impetus or inspired the native genius.

This, then, can be no more than a survey of the likely media and motifs in which the archaeologist can observe the influence of the east in Greece – an influence stimulated in the first place by the Greeks themselves in their visits to the east, and not vice versa. There are three aspects of the problem: the actual imported objects; the apparent influence of eastern artists who came to Greece, worked and taught there – the foreign *demioergoi* mentioned by Homer; and the Greek copying and adaptation of eastern objects and decoration. Somewhere, at some time in the long history of the Near East, a parallel can be found for any artistic motif under the sun, be it naturalistic or abstract. Comparisons can only profitably be drawn if a plausible relationship in time and a means of transmission can be demonstrated. Sometimes vital links are missing, although the debt seems direct and certain. At all times it must be remembered that this was not Greece's first contact with the east, and that some motifs or forms may well have survived from the Bronze Age or have been rediscovered.

The different sources of the oriental influences upon Greece are more complicated than the geography of the area might suggest. The following may be distinguished:

1. *Neo-Hittite*. Several sites in North Syria and Cilicia bear

witness to an art which seems to owe more to Anatolian Hittite styles than to those of the east. It is best known from its relief sculptures, and the most important sites are Carchemish, Zinjirli, Sakjegözü, and Malatya. Most of the relevant works were executed before or in the eighth century B.C. but were still visible in the seventh.

2. *Urartian*. Armenia was an important centre of metal-working, and the rich finds from sites near Lake Van often have close kin in Greece. Urartu controlled North Syria for a while in the eighth century.

3. *Assyrian*. The art of Assyria is better known from works of sculpture, especially reliefs, than bronzes or other minor objects. An important source of Assyrian decorative motifs for the Greeks may have been textiles, which have of course perished. Assyrian influence cannot be earlier than the seventh century; indeed, most is of the mid or late seventh century.

4. *Phoenician*. The ivories from Phoenician sites, and those carried off as loot to Assyria, reveal an amalgam of Near Eastern and Egyptian forms. The ivories and some bronzes are the most important products for us, but the other minor objects reflect the same often ill-welded mixture of motifs.

5. *Cypriot* art offers much that was more at home on the mainland to the east, and little of notable originality. The island was in continuous contact with Greeks in the Early Iron Age. This is reflected by minor imports and unimportant borrowings, for Cypriot influence was never profound.

The Phrygian, Lydian, and later Persian contributions will find their places later in this chapter.

Ivory work

Eastern ivories have been found in Greece on Samos, Crete (Fig. 12a), Rhodes, and in Athens. Most may have arrived before 700 B.C. Syria was still an important source of elephant ivory at this time, and the tusks found at Al Mina may reflect the trade in the raw material which served the many Greek schools of ivory-workers of the seventh century.

In a grave at Athens, which can be dated by the pottery found in it to the third quarter of the eighth century, was a group of five nude female figures (the largest, Plate 1a) which clearly imitate the eastern 'Astarte' type of the nude fertility goddess (Fig. 12d, from Nimrud). They are imbued with a strength and sense of form which reveals a Greek hand, working still within the confines of Geometric convention but in a technique learned from an eastern craftsman – and from a craftsman working in

12. (a) Ivory from Idaean Cave, Crete; (b) Ivory from Sparta; (c) Ivory seal from Ephesus; (d) Ivory from Nimrud.

Athens, as likely as not. This will be the earliest of these new schools. In the Peloponnese others supplied votives in ivory and bone for the temple of Artemis Orthia at Sparta and the temple of Hera at Perachora (near Corinth). The figurines are more hellenized adaptations now, and some new forms appear. Ivory seals, with their backs carved as recumbent animals (Fig. 12b), resemble eastern ivory groups (not, however, used as seals) as well as some Bronze Age Cretan seal forms. Disc seals were worn as pendants or perhaps on bracelets. These are to be found in other parts of Greece too, from Ithaca to the Aegean islands. Among the minor objects in bone and ivory we may pick out plaque inlays and the 'spectacle'-shaped brooches which imitate a metal form (Fig. 64a, p. 241). These are decorated with simple compass-cut circles or more elaborate cable patterns of exactly the types which we met on eastern ivories and plaques.

In East Greece there were other ivory workers who had learned from the east. Among the minor finds at Ephesus we find again the small couchant animals, and there is a ring seal of Hittite shape (Fig. 12c) which may not, however, be Greek work. The finest work appears in statuettes of the seventh or earliest sixth centuries (as Plate 1c). These match their eastern counterparts in technique and perhaps excel them in artistic quality. There are several from Ephesus, a few on Samos, Chios, and at Smyrna. With them may be associated the schools of ivory workers in Lydia, and perhaps some stray finds in mainland Greece, like a fine head from Perachora near Corinth (Plate 5a) and the god with a lion from Delphi (Plate 1b). The last is very like some Assyrian Gilgamesh groups in composition, although in nothing else.

Bronze work

Here the material is bewildering in its variety, but some sources or connexions are clear.

We have already noted the bronzes of Cypriot type which reached Crete early in the Iron Age, and the stray ninth-century bowl in Athens.

The metal-working centres of Armenia, Urartu, and even beyond concern us first. Already in the Geometric period of the eighth century we find some strange echoes of Caucasian metalwork in Greece, especially in openwork bronze pendants and some bird figurines on openwork stands. Their date in the east is not assured, nor is the means of transmission to Greece clear. They have equally obscure connexions with bronzes from Central Europe.

Some time in the eighth century it seems likely that Urartian or Assyrian metal workers came to Crete, set up shop there, and established a strong tradition for beaten metal work, which in its beginnings is quite oriental but becomes progressively more hellenized. One of the earliest works, surely by an eastern hand, but, it seems, made to serve or illustrate a Cretan cult, is a bronze tympanum (like a tambourine) from the Idaean Cave in Crete (Plate 4b). The scene on it shows a god striding over a bull and swinging a lion above his head. At either side winged men clash cymbals. The style is eastern, so are the god on a bull and the winged figures, but the latter clash their cymbals in a Greek manner and the god wears non-oriental (though perhaps Cypriot) bloomers. The piece was dedicated in a cave where the infant Zeus was said to have been hidden from his father, and where his attendants clashed shields and – no doubt – cymbals (his mother Rhea's instruments) to drown his cries. In the same style are some scraps in Olympia and Dodona in Greece, and two fine cauldron stands and a bowl found in Etruscan graves. We cannot say whether these last were brought there from Crete, or whether Urartian craftsmen travelled farther still. The former is the more probable. Although the style of these objects is wholly eastern, no work from the same school has yet been found outside Greece and Etruria.

In a related style are the great conical shields with animal-head bosses which were also made for the Idaean Cave (as Plate 3a), but have been found elsewhere in Crete, and travelled even to Delphi, Dodona, and Miletus. These span the second half of the eighth century and the first half of the seventh, and they show well the progressive hellenization of the style and motifs – generally animal friezes or groups with monsters. This type of shield was known in Assyria and in Urartu, for we see it in a Urartian temple at Musasir, which was shown on an Assyrian relief depicting the sack of the town. In the same Cretan workshop and in the same technique was made the bronze head-vase shown in Plate 6a (in Oxford; the lip and handle restored in the drawing). The conception is Greek, the execution and details eastern.

Bronze cauldron attachments, and no doubt the cauldrons themselves, also reached Greece from Urartu or Assyria in the first half of the seventh century, and perhaps a little earlier. These too were widely copied and adapted to Greek standards and taste. There are two main types: (1) bulls' heads, which have been found in Olympia, Delphi, Athens, Rhodes, Samos, Cumae (Fig. 13a), and Cyprus. These are fastened either below the rim of the cauldron or at joints in the struts which formed the tripod supports for them. And (2) sirens (Plate 4a), whose spread wings clasp the bowl beneath the rim while their heads peer within. They, and their Greek derivatives have been found at Olympia, Delphi, Athens, Boeotia (Ptoon), Argos, Delos,

13. (a) Bronze cauldron from Cumae; (b) Bronze cauldron from Gordion; (c and d) Bronze sirens' heads from Olympia.

Rhodes and in Etruria. An example from Phrygia (Gordion) is drawn in Fig. 13b. With such attachments can also be associated the bronze lion's paw feet for tripods which are found on many of the same sites. These cauldrons reached Phrygia also, as we have seen, but it is unlikely that the motif or object first became known to the Greeks from that quarter. Fig. 13c and d show an

14. (a) Hammered bronze griffin's head from Olympia; (b) Cast bronze griffin's head from Olympia; (c) Bronze griffin-bird from Olympia.

eastern siren head beside a Greek imitation which has rejected, or 'geometricized', the soft oriental features.

Other attachments, animals or monsters, are found at Olympia, Argos, and on Samos, and are eastern imports. Griffin heads are found on Greek cauldrons of the seventh and sixth centuries on very many sites (as Fig. 63, p. 228). They may represent a Greek adaptation of the oriental monster to this purpose. There were Greek workshops producing them for Olympia and on Samos, the earliest hammered (Fig. 14a), the later cast (Fig. 14b). No early griffin-head cauldrons have yet been found in the east, but it is possible that some small cast griffin-bird attachments which reached Olympia (Fig. 14c) suggested the motif. Already the Greek artist is exercising choice and originality in handling these new ideas and techniques. It may be that all the early hammered (not cast, like the bulls' heads and sirens) griffin and lion heads on cauldrons found in Greece and Etruria were made in Greek lands, though perhaps by eastern craftsmen at first who had been trained in the same centres as those who came to Crete and introduced the shields.

It is interesting to note that the 'orientalizing' workshops in Greece preferred at first to beat out the metal and trace (hammer) details on to it, while the Urartian products are usually cast and

15. (a) Athenian red-figure fragment; (b) Persian bronze phiale; (c) Device of a stone seal from Crete.

have their details incised. It may simply be that the metal was scarcer in Greece, but the difference in technique is a real one, and might prove significant in determining the source of eastern craftsmen in Greece and the degree to which they had to adapt eastern models and techniques. It may, for instance, be shown that the technique practised in Greece is more Assyrian (as for Plate 2c) than Urartian.

Of other bronze vases we should mention *phialai* or bowls, some with a central boss or navel (mesomphalic). The type is eastern, met in Phrygia, Assyria, and Phoenicia. Decorated examples, generally of Phoenician type and probably of the eighth century, reached Athens, Delphi, Olympia (Plate 3b), Delos, and Crete. Those with ribbed floral patterns were often copied in Greece, in bronze and clay. The Persians still used them, and a peculiarly Persian type (Fig. 15b) is figured on an Athenian vase fragment of the late sixth century (Fig. 15a). In Greece the shape was generally used for ritual libations, and at Perachora some two hundred thrown into a small pool had probably served some rite of divination and gave omens by sinking or swimming. Animal-head cups are seen on Assyrian reliefs. Bronze examples reached Phrygia (Plate 2c) and Samos, but the motif was not copied until the fifth century, then in imitation of Persian models. Arched handles with a floral knob appear on Assyrian bronzes and were copied all over the Greek world. I illustrate a Chian variant on the theme, in which the central bud is replaced by a bearded head peering between the petals, as over a wing collar (Plate 5b). The ring handles on metal vases (as Fig. 28a, p. 106) may be derived from Urartu, Assyria, or Phrygia.

16. (a) Bronze relief from Olympia;
(b) Bronze harness from Miletus.

Some other imports or borrowings can be noted. There are North Syrian bronze plaques (Fig. 16a) and part of an incense burner in Olympia, and on Samos an Assyrian mace head and a figurine which may be Assyrianizing Greek work. In Crete, North Syrian bronze figurines were imported and inspired a small group of local bronzes at the end of the eighth century. On Samos and Rhodes, and at Miletus (Fig. 16b) and Eretria (in Euboea), are pieces of relief-decorated harness which seem peculiarly Phoenician, and it was an Assyrian type of bit which was adopted in Greece in the seventh century. From farther east,

17. Detail from a bronze shield from the Idaen Cave, Crete.

from Persia and especially Luristan, may have come a vase in Samos, a piece of harness in Rhodes, a pendant in Crete, and a belt buckle in Perachora. None are securely dated, but most are likely to be of the seventh century, some of the eighth.

Other Greek bronze work may reflect eastern types. Some cut-out plaques in Crete are reminiscent of plaques from Assyria in their technique. For armour the Greeks seem to have invented for themselves the all-bronze corselet, while other pieces – helmets and greaves – throw back to Bronze Age forms rather than reflect contemporary eastern equipment. The helmet type with a crest fitted close to the crown seems anticipated in Urartu, but the resemblance may be superficial, and the Greek helmets of this type are not like the Urartian 'caps', but cover the ears and cheeks. Finally we should remark that the incised technique for figures on bronzes – as on the imported bowl, Plate 3b, or the Cretan shields (Plate 3a, Fig. 17) – probably inspired the incised black-figure technique on Greek vases, which lent a new range of detail after the simple Geometric silhouette styles.

Minor arts and objects

Here we are led into a great pot-pourri of subjects and materials.

Greeks began engraving seal-stones again in the eighth century, but only some crude Rhodian stones copy eastern forms at all

18. Incised tridacna shell and details.

closely. One class of stone scaraboid (the shape of the Egyptian scarab-beetle seals but without the animal carved) seems to have been made in Syria or Cilicia at the end of the eighth century, perhaps largely for the Greek market. Examples have been found in the west at Ischia (Pithekoussai) and in Etruria, on very many mainland Greek and island sites, in Cyprus, and on Near Eastern sites. The example with the device shown in Fig. 15c is from Crete. These, and imports of Egyptian and Phoenician faience scarabs, encouraged the production of Greek seals, but in shape these are often copies of Greek Bronze Age types and carry Greek orientalizing motifs. The scarab and scaraboid forms were copied, and the cylinder very rarely. One Assyrian cylinder seal reached Olympia, and what may be a North Syrian one Delos. The production of ivory seals we have already discussed.

Great tridacna shells from the Red Sea were incised with elaborate floral and animal designs, like gorgeous ashtrays or scoops (Fig. 18). The distribution of these in the Near East

19. (a) Stone relief from near Khania, Crete; (b) Detail of a bronze belt from near Knossos, Crete.

points to Assyria as the source, although the style is perhaps more Phoenician. They may be no earlier than the second half of the seventh century. In Greece they reached Aegina, Smyrna, Samos, Rhodes, Cos, the Greek site at Naucratis, as well as other Egyptian towns with Greek connexions, and Cyrene, and Vulci in Etruria. They provoked no imitations, and resemble nothing more than the gaudy gew-gaws sold to tourists in Levantine bazaars. Ostrich eggs, invariably shattered, have been found on several archaic Greek sites, and were certainly brought from the east.

In stone, there is in Samos a censer with a lion-head duct of North Syrian type. The east's main achievements in major sculpture are in relief work, usually disposed in friezes and used architecturally. Crete follows this practice, and one of the earliest examples (Fig. 19a), still of the eighth century perhaps, has many affinities with Assyrian work: notably the disposition of archers one above another, a motif met on a Cretan bronze of the same period (a belt, Fig. 19b). Cyprus produced many undistinguished statuettes in soft stone which were carried to East Greek sites and to Delos. In Rhodes and Naucratis they seem to have encouraged local imitations, sometimes in a better style. Some might be the work of immigrant Cypriots. Most are of the later seventh century but the style lingers through the sixth century, becoming more thoroughly hellenized – as indeed were the native Cypriot products.

There were many workshops for gold jewellery in Greece from the eighth century on. Some techniques (wire, granulation) and forms (crescents, inlays) in Crete and Attica are close to Phoenician types, but much more than simple imitations, and the Greek schools soon outstripped their eastern models in the quality of their work. By the middle of the eighth century in Athens, and a little later in Crete, Euboea, and Rhodes, gold diadems were being decorated by pressing them on to intaglio moulds. The animal designs seem eastern (Fig. 20a), with some

20. (a and b) Impressed gold plaques from Athens;
(c) Lead disc from Ephesus;
(d) Silver disc from Zinjirli.

more Greek Geometric (Fig. 20b), but the application and development of the technique is Greek. Two glass amulets in the form of a man's head have been found in Athens; one in a closed deposit of the eighth century. The type seems likely to be Phoenician, but had a long life and appears on Greek sites in later contexts at Selinus in Sicily and Naucratis in Egypt.

Some small *lead* discs from Sparta and Chios closely resemble Assyrian pendants – and indeed gold-work at Ephesus and, long before, at Mycenae. The cast lead figurines like toy soldiers found in such quantity on Peloponnesian sites, especially at Sparta, are equally close to Assyrian lead figures and groups, often obscene, from Assur, and others from North Syria. The connexion seems obvious, but all the eastern comparisons seem to be of the Late Bronze Age, some 500 years earlier than the Greek. Here the transmission or survival of the form still has to be explained by orientalists. Rather later, in the sixth century, there are some lead medallions from Samos, Ephesus, and Chios showing a goddess standing on a lion's back (Fig. 20c), such as appears often in the east, notably on a very similar medallion in silver from Zinjirli (Fig. 20d).

21. (a) Near-Eastern clay plaque; (b) Clay plaque from Corinth.

In clay the eastern Astarte plaques, showing the naked god-dess frontal, with hands to her breasts (Fig. 21a) and loins, had a profound influence on Greek art. An imported example may be recognized at Corinth (Fig. 21b), and the type was copied for Aphrodite figures, although the Greeks soon preferred to clothe their goddess, while retaining the suggestive position of her arms. More important was the use of the mould, which revolutionized the production of clay figurines and relief plaques (Plate 2b). The mould is used also for decorating coarser vases

a   b

22. (a) Clay mask from Sparta; (b) Clay mask from Ur.

(the so-called relief-pithoi). For this purpose too stamps were used from about 700 B.C., and this usage finds both eastern (Nimrud) and Bronze Age Greek parallels. Whole-figure moulds for plaques became common on mainland Greece and in Crete. In East Greece a different use of the mould – for the heads alone – was inspired by the many Cypriot figurines which were im-ported from the beginning of the seventh century. These have been found on many East Greek sites, and on Aegina and Delos. The rounded, puffy, oriental features were translated (as with the bronzes, Fig. 13c, d) to the more angular alert forms which Greece had developed through her Geometric art. For all that the early Greek attempts at relief and other minor statuary may owe to the east in technique or composition, the proportions and line of the figures remain profoundly non-oriental. This can be seen as early as the ivory girls from Athens (Plate 1a). A more bizarre example of copying appears in the grotesque clay masks found on Samos and in considerable numbers at Sparta (as Fig. 22a), which are closely modelled on eastern masks of the demon Humbaba (as Fig. 22b). The only eastern clay vases to reach Greece are Cypriot. In Crete they had some superficial effect on shapes and decoration. In East Greece they reached Rhodes and Cnidus, and (in the islands) Thera, Delos, and Aegina. There are trivial reflections of Cypriot in some Athenian Geometric vases, and the rows of concentric circles on the lip of Euboean cups (as Fig. 9d, p. 64) may have been picked up from Cypriots (? at Al Mina).

Decoration

From the surviving bronzes and ivories of the sort the Greeks brought back from the east we can get some idea of the impression that eastern decoration made on Greek artists, but we should remember too the patterning there may have been on textiles or embroidery, which have perished. There is certainly great similarity between Assyrian and archaic Greek representations of dress patterns. In Greek work the medium which tells us most about the way the artist used oriental motifs is not the one in which they were ever much employed in the east, but vase painting. The richly decorated vases of Corinth, Crete, Athens, and East Greece will tell us much about those eastern patterns which caught the Greek eye.

Animal figures were particularly common. Few Greeks could ever have seen a lion. When the creature is first shown on Greek vases at the end of the eighth century it is distorted to suit Geometric canons (Fig. 23a), but soon the square-headed neo-Hittite lion with its lolling tongue (Fig. 23b) is copied, especially on the vases of Corinth (Fig. 23c). After the mid seventh century it is superseded by the Assyrian type of lion, with pointed nose, folded ear, and heavy mane (Fig. 23d: Assyrian; Fig. 23e: Corinthian). On lions and many other animals in seventh-century Greek art we see also the odd 'boxed-in' way of drawing the shoulder which appears on many neo-Hittite and some

23. Greek (a, c, e) and Near-Eastern (b, d) lions.

24. (a) From a Protocorinthian vase;
(b) Stone relief from Carchemish.

Assyrian creatures. In the later eighth century, cocks and hens found their way into Greek art – and into Greek farmyards – for the first time, and they came from the east. Sphinxes and griffins had already lived in the Greek art of the Bronze Age, but they reappear in their new Near Eastern form, the sphinx sometimes with misunderstood Egyptian apron and crown (turned into a helmet), the griffin with long ears, forehead knobs, and a tendril crest – not the mane of the Bronze Age griffins. Of other *monsters* there is the lion with an extra human head (Fig. 24a), closely matched in neo-Hittite reliefs (Fig. 24b). Similar surgery produced the Greek chimaera: a lion with a goat's head growing from the small of its back and a serpent

25. (a) Stone relief from Tell Halaf; (b) From a
Corinthian vase.

tail (as on Plate 20a). Eastern lion-headed demons may have helped the Greeks determine on the lion mask for their own bogy, the Gorgon, for she is no copy of any one oriental creature. Another Assyrian and neo-Hittite demon or deity, half man and half fish (Fig. 25a), suggested the Greek Tritons (Fig. 25b). Of other mixed creatures, the goat-fish Capricorn may also derive from Assyria, and winged horses (like Pegasus) and lions are eastern; but many owe their forms to the artist's native wit and invention.

Compositions with animals in friezes were already common in Geometric Greek art, but from the late eighth-century heraldic groups become just as common, and these derive from eastern art, although they were well known also in the Greek Bronze Age.

In human-figure decoration the stimulus of eastern narrative art came at the same time as the spread of the Homeric poems, and led the Greeks to develop an individual idiom of narrative art which was still acceptable in Rome and at the Renaissance, and to a lesser degree is still acceptable today. Some particular groups or scenes may have been taken over directly by the Greeks, or lightly adapted to suit Greek stories. On late eighth-century and early seventh-century vases and sometimes seals we see horses with fish or scorpions beneath them. These are close to scenes in eastern glyptic and sculpture. The elements of the formal banqueting scene of Ashurbanipal reappear in Greek banqueting scenes from about 600 B.C., representing secular and divine occasions, but this resemblance might be fortuitous. Again, the common eastern scene of a worshipper being introduced to a seated deity by a priest or another god seems echoed much later in Greek scenes of Athena introducing Heracles to Zeus enthroned, but the lapse in time is great and again the resemblance may be a chance one. Ritual scenes of seated figures on either side of a table resemble some Late Geometric scenes in which the impedimenta and some of the furniture are changed. Even the eastern winged sun disc over a palm tree attended by demons seems to have been copied, and misunderstood, on a Cretan bronze of the mid seventh century, and winged disc and tree appear on a Melian gem of about 600 B.C. Eastern lion fighters like Gilgamesh modelled for Greek heroes, and eastern heroes had already met a monster very like Heracles' hydra, flocks of birds like the Stymphalian, and a horrific lady like Perseus' Medusa–Gorgon. The goddess standing on a bull appears on a Late Geometric bronze disc from Tegea (Peloponnese), and must be explained in terms of similar eastern scenes. The list might easily be lengthened, but many resemblances – including some cited here – are superficial or may be imaginary, and even the certain borrowings are more adaptations than copies.

Eastern *floral* decoration played a most decisive part in determining the character of the subsidiary ornament in Greek art. Nothing floral had been admitted in the Geometric period. The eastern 'tree of life', with volute-coiled branches and often a palmette at the top, was a favourite motif, especially for the centrepiece of a heraldic group. In Fig. 26a I show the device from a North Syrian silver cup, and in Fig. 26b the free Greek adaptation of the motif on a Protocorinthian vase of about 700 B.C. It becomes easy to find eastern 'trees of life' everywhere; the least happy attempt would derive both the form and significance of the floral finials on archaic Greek gravestones from the eastern motif. Floral friezes were yet more commonly copied. The lotus, once an Egyptian motif, is the most important single

26. Florals: (a) From a Syrian silver bowl; (b) From a Protocorinthian vase; (c) from an Assyrian relief (Nimrud); (d) From an East Greek vase; (e) Incised inscription on a Geometric vase from Athens.

element, and may alternate with buds, palmettes, or rarely pine cones. The fan-shaped Assyrian lotus retains its shape on the earlier Greek vases of the seventh century, and far longer in East Greece, but in the later seventh century in mainland Greece it is squared off to make a better-packed frieze, and a palmette is induced to grow from the centre. The structure of the lotus and bud was also changed by the Greeks, who omitted the invariable eastern calyx for each (compare Fig. 26c and d;

Assyrian and Greek). Less common are pomegranate friezes, also Assyrian. The filling ornament in the background of figure scenes on vases in part derives from Greek Geometric patterns, in part from the east, particularly tapestry patterns like rosettes.

Some features of eastern *furniture* were copied directly by the Greeks, like animal feet – especially lions' paws – and figures supporting the seats and arms of thrones. Other details – the finials of supports or balusters in the form of volutes or a girdle of pendent leaves – were copied in a different way. When the East Greeks were led by the example of Egypt to develop an order of monumental stone architecture, such as was never known in eastern lands, they enlarged these eastern motifs and adapted them to make the stone capitals of their Aeolic and Ionic columns. They wedded the Egyptian conception to oriental patterns, and bred a new architectural form. The last of the progeny of this union are the marble lions' paws used as anta-bases by Chian architects (Plate 5d). Perhaps the only direct architectural borrowings are more simply constructional: drafted masonry, the use of clamps, and 'Palladian' stairways on to a terrace, which appear in a sanctuary on Chios and were long popular in the east.

It would be wrong not to mention here also another borrow-ing, which although not of a material form or object is attested by archaeological evidence in the beginning: this is the *alphabet*. The Mycenaean Greeks had written their palace accounts in the clumsy syllabary adapted for them by the Minoans from their own script. When the palaces fell, the need for writing dis-appeared and the script was forgotten. Greece remained illiterate until, on the Syrian coast, her traders met a people using, not a syllabary, but an alphabet. This they borrowed, adapting it a little to suit their tongue, and at home admitting some regional preferences for certain letter forms which only became stan-dardized as writing was used more and more for inter-state business. From Semitic inscriptions it seems that it was the letter forms current in the late ninth or early eighth century which the Greeks copied, and this is exactly what our knowledge of the Greeks in North Syria would lead us to expect. The earliest examples of the Greek use of the alphabet appear scratched on vases and painted on a clay plaque, the earliest of the extant inscriptions being perhaps of the third quarter of the eighth century (Fig. 26e). Some of them are in verse, and it may even have been this new alphabet which enabled Homer to compose and set down his great poem(s), drawing on the rich oral tradition of poetry which had survived the Dark Ages.

The occasion for the carriage of these imports and ideas into the Greek world was the Greek initiative in reopening relations overseas, in the east, and we may suppose that the carriage was largely in Greek hands, although in early days the Phoenicians may have been welcomed at Greek ports. We have suspected immigrant craftsmen too, in the eighth century. By the sixth century there was little that the east had still to teach Greece – except power-politics; but in the Athenian potters' quarter we find a painter who signs himself 'Scythian', another 'the Lydian', a Phintias (an eastern name), and in the early fifth century a potter Brygos (? a Thracian or Phrygian). No few of the artists in Athens may always have been 'metics' (resident foreigners) whose work would enrich the strong tradition, itself once quickened by just such support and inspiration from overseas. By the end of the sixth century, when part of the Greek world already lay within an eastern empire which we have yet to describe, easterners must have become frequent and familiar visitors to Greek cities and ports. Perhaps residents too, to judge from the statue-base in Athens which at the end of the sixth century was inscribed for a Carian in both his native script and in Greek.

PHRYGIA AND LYDIA

In the eighth and seventh centuries, the Greek hold on the coastline of Asia Minor became stronger. The older cities of Aeolis and Ionia outgrew their walls and local resources of land, and new settlements were made, often at the expense of the native population. We have first to say something of this expansion.

In the north, several new settlements are of this period and owe their origins to the Aeolians of Lesbos or other long-established Greek communities. TROY, after its famous siege and sack by the Greeks under Agamemnon, revived briefly in the settlement known archaeologically as Troy VIIb1, and was then occupied for perhaps a century by intruders from Thrace or the upper Balkans (Troy VIIb2). In the eleventh century the site was completely abandoned, and the next signs of occupation are finds of Greek pottery of what may broadly be termed 'Aeolian' character. These show that the town was resettled by Aeolians in the second half of the eighth century.

Much farther south, in the valley of the River Hermos which leads into the heart of Lydia, there is a good acropolis site which has been identified (perhaps wrongly) as the Greek Larisa. There is one scrap of pottery from it which seems Mycenaean, but in the early Iron Age it was occupied by Anatolians using grey unpainted pottery. Some Greek sherds show contacts with the Greeks in the eighth century, but at about 700 it seems that the natives were ejected and their place taken by Aeolians who fortified the site and from it were able to overlook if not command the important route inland as well as the overland route between Smyrna and the coastal cities of Aeolis. In the sixth century the town was graced by semi-palatial buildings and some interesting stone buildings of the 'Aeolic' order.

Of the islands, TENEDOS may have been occupied about this time. In SAMOTHRACE there was a native Thracian population in possession when the Aeolian Greeks arrived about 700 B.C. The survival of pre-Greek pottery forms, language, and religious practices shows that the natives were peaceably absorbed by the Greek invaders, who were themselves profoundly affected by the indigenous culture. The earliest Greek vases made on the island (above, Fig. 7b) show an appreciation of the shapes and the plain wares which preceded them, and which, indeed, were probably still being made there.

Offshore islands seek new land by settlement on the mainland opposite them, in districts then known from their positions opposite their mother-islands as *peraiai* (*pera* = opposite). Thus Methymna in Lesbos founded ASSOS, probably by the end of the eighth century, although nothing Greek has been found there earlier than the sixth century, when there was built a Doric temple, unusual for Asia Minor. There are other foundations from Lesbos on the coastline south of Troy with surface pottery which suggests that they were established by about 700.

The story of LEMNOS is somewhat different. It was an important island, which could command access to the Hellespont, had good harbours and two main towns – Myrina and Hephaistia. In the Bronze Age it had close connexions with Troy, and in the *Iliad* we hear that the Lemnians provided wine for the Greeks besieging Troy. It is doubtful whether there was ever a true Greek settlement on the island in the Late Bronze Age or Early Iron Age. The archaeological evidence amounts to a Mycenaean gem found in a later tomb and what may be a Protogeometric vase, once in Smyrna, alleged to be from the island. Early in the Iron Age the 'Tyrsenoi' from the mainland were said to have occupied Lemnos. It was peoples of the same stock and origin who were thought to have sailed to the west, where they became known as the Etruscans. In 513 B.C. the Persians occupied the island, which was still peopled by the 'Pelasgians' (our Tyrsenoi); but it may have won its independence again, for it was Pelasgians who were in possession when the Athenian statesman and general Miltiades, who was established on the Hellespont, took the island in about 500. Of the Tyrsenian occupation we have the evidence of a cemetery at Hephaistia and some other finds in the island. Nothing seems obviously earlier than the eighth century, and at all times the painted decoration of the pottery is strongly influenced by Greek Aeolian fashions, although shapes may be closer to native models. East Greek fibulae (bronze safety-pins) are already imported in the eighth century, and Corinthian pottery appears from the mid seventh. In fact the culture seems to have been fairly thoroughly hellenized in all but speech. A link, perhaps, between the Anatolian origins of the Tyrsenoi and the stories of the origins of the Etruscans is afforded by the famous sixth-century stele from Kaminia which carries an inscription in letters which are related to the Phrygian and in a language which may be related to the Etruscan.

In Ionia a similar expansion continues through the eighth and seventh centuries. The islands develop *peraiai* on the mainland opposite them – Chios on the Erythraean peninsula, Samos on

Mycale and perhaps at the expense of other Ionians (of Priene). Inland, Ephesus occupies Magnesia in the seventh century, an important station on the routes along the Maeander valley and to the north. But most of our evidence for these is literary so far. Farther south, Dorian Cnidus occupies coastal areas which are later to form part of Rhodes' *peraia*. The penetration of LYCIA begins about 700 to judge from recent finds of Greek pottery at Xanthus.

In all these operations the Greeks are immediately concerned with the people occupying the coastal areas, and not the major power of the hinterland – Phrygia – which was more occupied with its southern and eastern frontiers. The natives met by the Aeolians shared generally in the west Phrygian 'grey-ware' culture. Those of the south are not archaeologically distinguishable, until their pottery, of which some has been recovered in recent years from various sites in south-west Asia Minor, shows the clear influence of Greek painted vases. This hardly happens before the mid seventh century. At Sinuri, a native Carian temple site near Mylasa, a quaint local style of figure-decorated pottery has been identified.

But the Greeks, especially the Ionians, were fully aware of the Phrygians and the archaeological evidence for their relations is full and varied. From the literary record, we may note in passing the marriage of a Phrygian king, Midas, to the daughter of a king of Aeolian Kyme, Agamemnon – probably in the eighth century; and that a Midas, perhaps the same man, was the first eastern monarch to send a dedication – a throne – to the Greek sanctuary at Delphi.

The probable origins of the Phrygians, and their appearance in Asia Minor, are likely to have been connected in some way with the movement into Greece in the Early Iron Age of Greek-speaking tribes from the north. In two archaeological matters there are correspondences between Greek and Phrygian products which have been thought to require an explanation going beyond the simple matter of Ionian–Phrygian relations in the eighth century or later. They are :

1. *Pottery*. The fine Phrygian painted pottery is distinguished by some distinctly oriental metalliform shapes and a rather banal

repertoire of Geometric ornament (Plate 7a). Many of the decorative motifs recall Greek Geometric patterns so closely that it seems unlikely that the resemblances are fortuitous, or even perhaps explicable by reference to a common model. There is very little Greek pottery in Phrygia in the late eighth century, and not much more from the mid seventh century on. There are Phrygian scraps in Samos. But there is no question of Phrygian influence in Greek Geometric styles, for the points of resemblance come late in the Greek Geometric series, and are largely confined to the Eastern Greeks. For the relationship with Macedonian wares see below, p. 242.

2. *Bronze fibulae.* The distinctive fibula (safety-pin) type in Phrygia has a semicircular bow, with heavy symmetrical mouldings on it, and often an elaborate form of 'safety catch' (Fig. 27a).

a   b

27. Fibulae: (a) Phrygian; (b) East Greek.

It is closely related to East Greek forms (as Fig. 27b), but in many ways more involved than they are. Yet it seems hard to believe that the type came to Phrygia otherwise than from the Aegean world. The elaboration of the Greek form may be due to Phrygia's more profound experience in metal working. The only known mould for a fibula of Phrygian type has been found at Greek Smyrna.

In about the middle of the eighth century, the Phrygians copied and adapted the Greek alphabet (itself only recently 'invented' – see above) for their own language, but at this time it seems to be the Greek cities of Ionia who are more often in receipt of Phrygian ideas. In metal work we find the most profound influence of Phrygian crafts. The Phrygians themselves imported and used Assyrian decorative metalwork (Plate 2c), but it was probably not through the Phrygians that the Greeks came to learn of such things, as we have seen. It is only those objects which seem peculiar to the Phrygian workshops that the Greeks of Ionia thought to copy or adapt:

1. *Cauldrons* or *dinoi* with ring handles set in spool-like attachments at the rim (Fig. 28a). These are found in the royal Phrygian tombs from the eighth century on. An iron ring handle

28. Bronze vases from Gordion.

in a bronze mount found in Chios seems to be a Phrygian import. Otherwise this type of vessel is not represented in early Ionia although the form reached other parts of the Greek world and is copied in clay in some East Greek and Cretan vases, and in Aeolian *bucchero* from Troy and Larisa. The ring handle and spool attachment appear again on another Phrygian vase (see below, 2) and on various Greek bronze vessels, but Phrygia may not have been the only source of inspiration for this sort of handle in Greece, and a related type is found at Al Mina.

2. *Shallow dishes* with ring handles set in spool-like attachments at the rim, and with horizontal strengthening bands

having spool-shaped members. The Phrygian examples are from tombs at Gordion (Fig. 28b, inscribed) and Ankara, and there are two from Magnesia (on the Hermos), the earliest of them being of the late eighth century. Exactly this type of dish is held by the little ivory statuette of a priestess found at Ephesus (Plate 1c) and dating to the second quarter of the sixth century, and there is another example, in bronze, from Cyprus. Fragments of similar bowls have been found in Greece at the Argive Heraeum and Olympia. Dishes with the ring handles, but without the strengthening band which is the more distinctive feature, were imitated in clay in Phrygia, and there are intimations of the same form in seventh-century clay vases from Larisa, Samos, and Chios (where they are on high conical feet). But it must be repeated that there are other possible sources in the east for ring handles.

3. *Bronze belts*. In the Princess's Tumulus at Gordion, which was opened by American excavators in 1956, were found two bronze belts. They were formed of a continuous strip of metal with a long hook at one end which engaged in one of three loops cut in a separate sheet of bronze fastened to the other end. Behind the hook there was a fibula-like attachment fastened rigidly on to the belt, making a sort of handle which would have helped in taking it in a notch. There was incised decoration on the belt-strip, not shown in Fig. 29a. Fragments of a more elaborate openwork belt strip had been found at Ankara, but with no 'handle'. In the year before the Gordion discovery, British excavators on Chios found a series of belts of this type, which had been dedicated in a sanctuary there from the later eighth century to about 600 B.C. From these more complete examples it was possible to recognize parts of similar belts which had been found elsewhere in Chios (at Phanai), in Samos, at Ephesus, and Smyrna. The Ionian belts (Fig. 29b) are in some ways more elaborate than the Phrygian. There is greater variety in the form of the 'handles', which may have animal-head terminals, and it is possible to discern independent centres for their production in Ionia. The hooks are made separately and riveted to the belt, and they engage in one of many holes in a long tongue which is actually hinged to the other end of the

belt. The strip was probably backed by linen or leather, rolled over the edges and stitched through the holes at the edge of the bronze. The earliest are perhaps as early as the Phrygian examples, but there can be little doubt that the latter are the inspiration for the Ionian versions. In Ionia it seems that they may have been worn by women, and dedicated at adolescence or on marriage. That they were still being worn in the sixth century is shown by the representation of one worn by a winged Artemis

29. Bronze belts: (a) From Gordion; (b) From Emporio, Chios.

on an East Greek bronze relief which was found at Olympia. The belts are unknown outside Ionia (but see p. 226, below, for possible imitations in the west).

These belts are a clear example of a Phrygian form adopted by the Greeks. It seems not to have been introduced to the Greeks by imported models, but immigrant craftsmen could have set the fashion in the eighth century.

The Phrygians had been driven from their southern Anatolian provinces by the Assyrians in the late eighth century, and in the early seventh they were overwhelmed at home by the Cimmerian invaders from the north and east. The same Cimmerians, displaced from their homes by the Scythians, swept on and past

he Greek cities, which they raided. Ephesus was attacked, and
here are records of Thracian 'Treres', who seem to have par-
cipated in these raids in the seventh century, occupying
ntandros in the Troad, and sacking Magnesia. The Cim-
erians – and the Scythians – are identified by a form of bronze
rrowhead with socket and barbs, found on various sites but
ter used also by the Greeks.

30. Clay relief plaque from Pazarli, Phrygia.

Phrygia lost her position of power in Asia Minor, but her
ities revived after the Cimmerian raids and became part of the
great Lydian empire. We can now detect a change in relation-
hips with the Greeks. From the mid seventh century a little
East Greek and Corinthian pottery appears on Phrygian sites,
nd the bronze dishes with ring handles are being made and
copied by Greeks. But now, more and more, it is Greek ideas
nd motifs which are penetrating Phrygia. The painted pottery
dmits motifs copied directly from archaic East Greek vases. In

various parts of Phrygia we find clay relief plaques, which served to decorate the façades of buildings. The style and inspiration of these revetments seems purely Greek, as are many of the motifs, although they are often much distorted (Fig. 30). We are also meeting here for the first time the phenomenon of 'orientalizing' Greek motifs being returned, translated, to the east. The revetments are of the sixth century. In these years too more Greek pottery is imported – Athenian and Corinthian for the most part – and other more exotic articles, Egyptian alabaster and northern amber, may have been carried there by the Greeks. Of more monumental work there is a stone basis (Fig. 31),

31. Phrygian stone basis in Ankara.

oriental or Anatolian in shape, decorated with relief motifs which, though orientalizing, are wholly Greek in their form. Thus the lotus and bud appear in the Greek manner, without the calyxes at their bases which always appear in Assyrian and other eastern examples of the motif. Another pattern on the basis is clearly derived from the Greek Ionic capital. The piece is in Ankara and has no certain provenance, but is likely to be from one of the Phrygian towns and to be of the end of the sixth century. At Midas City were found the lower parts of two limestone statues which appear to be Ionian of the mid sixth century, and the figure on a rock relief not far away owes much to Greek models.

At this time too there is even clearer evidence for the work of Greek artists in Phrygia. Fresco wall paintings have been excavated in Gordion (Plate 7b) which are wholly Greek in their style – Ionian Greek, or, in the opinion of one scholar, specifically Chian. It is interesting to note that one motif which appears in them, a crown or circlet of small griffin protomes worn by a woman, has its counterpart in Chios, where at Emporio some small lead griffin protomes are thought to have decorated the helmet peak of a cult statue of Athena in the mid sixth century.

It was perhaps from Phrygia that the Greeks adopted the worship of Cybele, the Anatolian Mother of the Gods. Most of the evidence for her worship in Greek lands is of later date, but one of the earliest Cybele monuments, perhaps even of the sixth century, is a rock-cut model of the goddess's shrine – again on Chios. The setting and technique are strongly reminiscent of sixth-century Phrygian rock-cut thrones, which served as cult-places. Cybele was particularly popular in East Greece. There too the many goddess-cults associated by the Greeks with a Hera or an Artemis may owe their origin in part at least to Anatolian cults, perhaps even pre-Phrygian. The Artemis at Ephesus is a particularly good example, and representations of her or her attendants as bees may well reflect a Hittite cult. The bee-goddess is shown on gold plaques from Rhodes, as Plate 5c.

In the sixth century Phrygia was no longer a great power, and we have to retrace our steps a little to pick up the story of the Greeks and their neighbours, to the mid seventh century and the rise of the kingdom of Lydia. Lydia may have been a province of Phrygia, but its heart lay nearer the sea, in the valley of the Hermos, with its capital at Sardis. The site is dominated by the massive acropolis, but the Lydian town was probably at its foot, near the later temple of Cybele. Recent excavations promise to tell us something of its history. We already hear of the finds of some Mycenaean pottery, and later local wares, but the first pottery to be influenced by Greek fashions looks no earlier than the eighth century (if so early), and Greek vases only begin to appear in the seventh. Out in the plain stood the massive tumuli of the cemetery, dominated by the Tomb of Alyattes, some 70m. high and 1,000m. in circumference.

Lydia came into her own after Phrygia had fallen to the Cimmerians and with the new dynasty established by King Gyges. Gyges himself fell in battle with the Cimmerians (in 652), but he and his successors generally dealt successfully with the raiders and kept them at bay, perhaps with the help of the Assyrians. He took a more active interest in the coastal cities than did the Phrygians. He may have controlled much of the south coastline of the Hellespont, and we hear of him allowing Miletus to send settlers to Abydos there. Miletus, however, was attacked by him, as was Smyrna, and he took Colophon. His son, Ardys, continued the attacks on the Ionians, took Priene and again attacked Miletus, which the Lydians seemed to regard as a particular menace. In his reign the Cimmerians attacked again, and even sacked the lower town at Sardis. Sadyattes and Alyattes continued the attacks on Miletus without success, although Alyattes sacked a temple at Assessos in Milesian territory, stormed and sacked Smyrna soon after 600, and even moved against Clazomenae. Only the islands escaped the fury of the Lydians, but of these Chios at least is recorded as going to the assistance of the Milesians. Alyattes eventually came to terms with Miletus.

Croesus succeeded Alyattes, and continued hostilities against Ionia with an attack on Ephesus, followed by others in which he seems to have forced the acquiescence of all the mainlanders of Ionia. The islanders too fell under his sway, although Herodotus says that he was dissuaded from naval action against them. Under Croesus the Lydian kingdom seems to have embraced most of the western coastline of Asia Minor and the offshore islands, although the Greeks were clearly left a considerable measure of independence and on Chios an inscription shows that some form of democratic constitution had been set up. For the first time the East Greeks found themselves owing allegiance to a native kingdom – a barbarian one, for all the hellenization and enlightenment of Croesus' court. 'Before Croesus' rule all Greeks were free,' comments Herodotus, and at another point he speaks of the enslavement of Ionia by the Lydians in the same terms as their position under the Persians later. It seems a tribute to Greek and especially Ionian resilience and opportunism that despite this their general prosperity and trade flourished as never before.

The archaeological record of this period is rich and varied. For the Lydian attacks on Ionia, the recent Anglo–Turkish excavations at Smyrna have given vivid evidence of their method and effect. By the end of the seventh century the city was enjoying its greatest prosperity (see Fig. 5, p. 50). Its walls had been newly rebuilt and stood in mudbrick on a stone base, at places some eighteen metres thick. Within the walls the houses were laid out on a regular rectangular plan, but it is clear that by now a large part of the city's population was living outside them, on the hill-slopes and shore facing the compact peninsula site of the city. A new sanctuary for the city goddess had been laid out, with an entrance court and ramp up to the temple platform. A new temple too had been planned, one of the earliest monumental stone temples in the Greek world, but as yet only its platform had been laid and some of its members carved. The votives in the sanctuary reflected the city's wealth and importance overseas – pottery from the other Ionian states and from Corinth, clay figurines and stone statuettes from Cyprus, the finest orientalizing ivories and bronze work. This was the city which faced the army of Lydian Alyattes.

The excavations have shown how thoroughly the Lydians sacked Smyrna, but they have also shown exactly how the city fell. The highest point of the low hill which now represents the site is formed today not by its natural summit but by the mass of a great siege-mound which had been thrown up against its north-west wall. This technique of attacking a walled town is an eastern one, and this was probably the first time that the Greeks had to face it. The mound was composed of earth and building materials from the houses outside the walls, and was strengthened with timbers. Some light is thrown on armaments too by the finds of bronze arrowheads respectively within and outside the walls. The Lydians used triangular heads with three flanges and a socket – a type associated with the Scythians. The Greeks used leaf-shaped, socketed heads, some squat ones with four flanges, and even some of iron. The thoroughness of the Lydian sack is shown by the utter overthrow of all the seventh-century buildings and the fact that the town seems to have been left desolate for some twenty years.

Of Greeks in Lydia itself we know little. The kingdom was fabulously rich, according to ancient authors, and 'golden Croesus' passed into legend. The Lydian culture is still barely known, although we hope for much from the excavations at Sardis. Its art seems partly dependent on the later Phrygian styles, but it is soon thoroughly permeated by the influence of East Greek art; and for all that Lydian influence was blamed for degenerate or effeminate habits learned by the Greeks, the 'enervating' luxury must have been very Greek in appearance if not in character. The poetess Sappho comments, complains rather, about her girls who have gone to grace high society in golden Sardis – a 'Hollywood' of opportunity and wealth; and elsewhere in her poems she acknowledges Lydia as the home of luxury and comfort – and formidable armies. Both Lydia and Phrygia were said to have introduced to the Greeks various musical novelties and indoor games. The seven-string lyre, one of the Lydian innovations, is shown on a seventh-century Greek sherd found at Smyrna (Fig. 32a), and on a vase from Pitane. The Lydian alphabet, like the Phrygian, was adapted from the Greek, probably about the middle of the seventh century. The more elaborate Lydian pottery is distinguished by the use of a heavy white slip and figure decoration in low relief. The content of the decoration seems derived from East Greece, while the technique may owe something to Anatolian styles of long before. The plainer vases resemble East Greek, and some, with multiple circles and hooks, are akin to the sort of pottery made and met by East Greeks at home and in Cilicia and North Syria. The fine Wild Goat style of vase painting, as practised in Rhodes and Ionia, also appears in a very provincial manner, rather like that of some Aeolian cities. A distinctively Lydian style of vase decoration is the 'marbled' ware, with massed wavy strokes in thinned paint. This has been thought to be in imitation of glass, but it is perhaps more like beaten copper work. It appears especially on perfume pots (Fig. 32b), which may have held the famous Lydian perfume *bakkaris*, and were themselves known as *lydia*. They were carried to Greece, even to Etruria, and were imitated – the shape at least (Egyptian originally) – in East Greece, Sparta, and Etruria. But this is a rare instance of Lydian ceramic influence in the Greek world. Some fine ivories from Sardis are close to Greek orientalizing work, and, again at Sardis, gravestones with palmette finials, like those made in East Greece, were set up before some tombs. Of the other arts we still have much to learn, also of the extent of Greek influence on the local craftsmen, or perhaps the

a   b

32. (a) East Greek vase fragment from Smyrna;
(b) Clay vase (*lydion*).

presence of Greek craftsmen in Lydia. We shall see that the finest dedications sent by Lydian kings to Greek sanctuaries were made for them by Greek artists. One independent find may be noticed – some gold jewellery from Aidin (Tralles) on the southern periphery of the Lydian empire. There is much in its technique and something in the motifs to remind one of archaic Greek work.

The kings of Lydia seem to have cultivated relations with the Greeks, however harsh their treatment of the Ionians. Gyges was the first barbarian king, after Phrygian Midas, to send offerings to Delphi, notably six golden bowls weighing thirty talents. Alyattes sent a golden bowl and a remarkable iron stand, which was the work of an Ionian artist, Glaukos of Chios. The Lydians could offer bullion more easily than works of art, from their native resources. To Alcaeus they offered the colossal sum of 2,000 gold pieces to help his party overthrow the government of Lesbos. Croesus was particularly generous to Delphi, and won from the oracle the ambiguous answer that he would 'destroy a great empire' by marching against Persia, without admitting that the empire might be his own. He sent the sanctuary a gold lion set on ingots of gold and electrum, and among other things two great bowls of gold and silver, which were again the work of an Ionian Greek, Theodorus of Samos. Even the Ionian cities enjoyed something of his benificence. At Branchidae, near Miletus, we hear of gold offerings matching those at Delphi. At Ephesus a new great temple for Artemis was being built, in emulation of the temple of Hera which had just been built on Samos, but larger – indeed one of the largest ever to be attempted by a Greek architect. Croesus paid for many of its columns, and scraps of columns bearing the record of his gift – 'King Croesus dedicated ...' – were excavated there in the last century and are now in the British Museum. Herodotus says too that several Greek sages visited his court, notably the Athenian lawgiver Solon; and that Ionians fought for him on his campaign against the Persians, Thales of Miletus serving as a military engineer. The Lydians probably employed many Greek mercenaries, and it has been thought that it was Gyges who sent Ionians and Carians to help the Egyptian king Psammetichos I (see Chapter 4). In Croesus' army against the Persians were 'Egyptians' – perhaps Greek mercenaries sent by the Egyptian king – who acquitted themselves well and were settled in Lydia (at Larisa and Kyllene near Kyme) by Cyrus after the defeat of the Lydians. On a more domestic-political level, we hear of marriages between Lydian princesses and members of what may be one of the royal houses at Ephesus. An Athenian father paid Croesus the compliment of naming his son after him.

The Greeks were profoundly impressed by the wealth of Lydia, especially in gold. The dedications made in Greece by the Lydian kings were spectacular, showy, and golden. Alcmaeon of Athens was supposed to have made his family's fortune by making the most of Croesus' offer to give him all the gold he could carry on his person:

He crammed it into his boots, all up his legs, as much as they would hold, filled the baggy front of his tunic full, sprinkled the dust all over his hair, stuffed some more into his mouth, and then staggered out, scarcely able to drag one foot after another [Herodotus].

The Spartans sent to buy gold from Croesus for a cult statue, and were given it. They had been courted by the Lydian king, who was trying to make the Greeks like him. In return for the present, the Spartans sent a bronze cauldron (of the same type as our Plate 16b), which was intercepted by Samian pirates. The Samians had already intercepted another gift to Lydia, 300 Corcyrean boys sent by Periander of Corinth to Alyattes to serve as eunuchs.

A more profound and salutary effect of Lydian gold, however, was the beginning of coinage in Greek lands. Our most important sources of information for this are the foundation deposit and other finds in the temple of Artemis at Ephesus. The associated finds show that the coins were deposited about 600 B.C. All are of electrum – a mixture of gold and silver, 'white gold' – but there are also some more primitive pieces, simple dumps of metal, mainly of electrum but some of silver. Some dumps have striated surfaces and have been punched, so that the striations are clear and can indicate the degree of wear. When the dump is punched over an engraved or cut die we have something we can recognize as a coin. Lydia was clearly the source of the electrum, which could, for instance, easily be panned from the River Pactolus which runs through Sardis. The primitive dumps are presumably Lydian, then, and were made to guarantee weight; or, it has been suggested, to provide a ready means of paying mercenary soldiers. The coins from the Ephesus deposits are all on roughly the same standard. Some with lion's head or paw devices must be Lydian. One bears the name of Alyattes, and although others are in a somewhat different style, there is no good reason to suppose that any of them were struck before, or at least much before, Alyattes' reign. Others have other devices – animal heads etc. – and must be Greek. A seal's head may suggest Phocaea (it was later the canting device on her coins), but we cannot certainly attribute any of them to individual Ionian states. Two other electrum coins of about this date, or soon afterwards, are inscribed 'I am the device of Phanes' and (a smaller coin) 'of Phanes', which suggest a private merchant's mint. Herodotus implies that the Lydians were the first to mint coins, and the material of the early dumps makes this seem most probable. Whether it is the Lydian lion heads or the Greek animal heads which are the earliest *devices* on coins is a different question. In later seventh-century Greece the cognate art of seal engraving – in ivory or stone – was at least as well developed in Greece as it was in Asia Minor. The idea of a figure device for a coin might well have been Greek. We cannot say whether it was applied first in a Lydian or a Greek mint.

THE PERSIANS

King Croesus of Lydia challenged the empire of the Persians and Medes, with whom his father Alyattes had already once joined battle. Croesus was defeated and Sardis was taken. Herodotus tells of the immediate effect on the Greeks who had paid allegiance to the Lydian king. They sought from the Persian Cyrus the same terms that they had enjoyed under Croesus, but only Miletus was thus favoured. The other cities looked to their defences, as the Persian general Harpagus moved against them. He took all the mainland cities, although the populations of Phocaea and Teos escaped to settle elsewhere. The islands too submitted, and may even have suffered invasion, for on Samos the great temple of Hera is burned down and a cemetery by the town pillaged at about this time. When Harpagus turned his attention to the south, against the Carians, Caunians, and Lycians, he marched with Ionian and Aeolian Greeks in his army. And when Cyrus returned home he took with him Croesus and various Ionians, the first of many Greeks to take the road to Persia in the Great King's service.

Under Persian rule, Ionia formed a department of a province or satrapy whose administrative centre lay at the old Lydian capital of Sardis. The Persians were generally tolerant rulers, although they sometimes interfered in the affairs of the Greek states, establishing 'tyrants'. Samos prospered under Polycrates, whose ships ranged freely, sometimes piratically, in the waters of the eastern Mediterranean. He supplied manned ships to serve the Persians. But before the end of the century the Persians had to visit the island with fire and the sword for a second time.

In general, however, the Greek cities seem to have flourished. Much of their trade lay in places which were already, or were soon to be, within the Persian empire – Al Mina, and Naucratis in Egypt. Only when they had taken Lydia did the Persians become aware of the attractions of 'civilized' life, and the Greeks were to serve and instruct the Persians in these matters as they had the Lydians before them; although it was sometimes the 'effeminate' eastern powers who were held responsible for the over-fondness for good living shown by the Ionians. Herodotus, at least, says that it was *from* the Greeks that the Persians first learned the vice of paederasty.

There are many stories about the Greeks who visited or were entertained in the Persian court. Darius, for instance, had a Greek physician whom he especially favoured. We are here concerned more with the artists who worked in Persia and the archaeological evidence for the influence of Greeks there. Documentary evidence is afforded by an inscription of King Darius, who came to the throne in 522, at Susa. In it he says: 'The ornamentation with which the wall was adorned, that from Ionia was brought. ... The stonecutters who wrought the stone, those were Ionians and Sardians' (i.e. of Sardis); and it was Carians and Ionians who carried the timber from Babylon to Susa. Again, Pliny mentions an Ionian sculptor, Telephanes of Phocaea, who worked for both Darius and Xerxes.

Tangible evidence of Greek taste and artistry is afforded mainly in stone-carving, both architectural and sculptural. The Ionic order of monumental stone architecture, with volute capitals, disc bases, and elaborate mouldings, had already been developed in the islands and East Greece by the mid sixth century. We have had occasion to remark how much the appearance of the new architectural decoration relied on eastern patterns, and how little the conception did so. Now we find the new idea of monumental stone orders of architecture being planted in eastern countries by the Greeks, and with it the return to their homeland of certain eastern patterns which the Greeks had made their own and had sometimes adapted out of recognition.

King Cyrus' palace lay at Pasargadae, in Persia. When he died, in 529, he was buried in a small temple-like mausoleum raised on a stepped base. The gabled monument is not readily explained in terms of the traditional forms of burial in Persia, but we are concerned with one detail only rather than its general resemblance to Greek buildings; this is the *cyma* moulding which runs round the top of its walls and is wholly Greek in type. Also at Pasargadae are cylindrical stone columns – themselves innovations in the east – standing on cushion bases with horizontal flutes of exactly the Ionic type. There is a suggestion too of the deliberate use of different-coloured stones to pick out various architectural members – again an Ionian Greek and not an eastern practice.

It is at Pasargadae too that we first see a sculptural innovation which can also be assigned to Greek influence. This is the semi-naturalistic representation of folds in drapery: a sort of surface patterning which eastern sculptors had never much cared for, but with which the Greeks had been experimenting since early in the sixth century. This is the sort of novelty which Greek artists working for Persians could well have inspired, or even executed. Fig. 33 shows the developed form of drapery at Persepolis, exactly like a rather earlier Greek fashion.

Darius (522–486) built the palace at Susa of which we have the inscription mentioning Ionian craftsmen. He also began work on the great complex of buildings at Persepolis which marks the culmination of Achaemenid (the Persian royal house) architecture, and is the fullest expression of the influence of Greek craftsmen both in Darius' reign and under his successors who continued his work there. We need not dwell on the details which betray Greek inspiration – the bead-and-reel mouldings, the orientalizing (not oriental) Greek patterns, the fluted columns. The capitals, like Greek Ionic, are no more than furniture writ large, but the motif of double opposed volutes is less well suited to monumental architecture. What is more important

s the now complete acceptance of what had already been fore-
hadowed at Pasargadae – the significance of the column as a
decorative as well as (and sometimes rather than) a structural
unit. Egyptian architecture had already discovered this, and the
Greeks had learned from them. There are several Egyptian

33. Relief from Persepolis.

motifs in the architecture of Persepolis, but the Persians who
had earlier built at Pasargadae in the same manner had at that
time no very intimate dealings with Egypt itself.

Some minor objects at Persepolis also attest the interest there
in Greek works of art, and the presence of Greek artists. On the
foot of a colossal stone figure an artist lightly incised drawings
of heads and animals, in such a purely Greek style (Plate 7c)

that he must himself have been a Greek and trained in Greece.
Comparisons with Greek vase paintings of the end of the sixth
century make this quite clear. The sketches themselves would
finally have been covered with paint. On another piece of stone
is a sketch of a Heracles, again certainly from a Greek hand.
The Greek coins in a foundation deposit at Persepolis have
already been mentioned. In his great inscription, Darius said
that the Ionians also made the ornamentation for the walls of
Susa; not, it seems, the famous glazed reliefs, but perhaps other
decorative work. Certainly the lotus patterns which appear on
fragments from Susa are of the Ionian rather than the Assyrian
eastern type.

Back at home, the East Greeks who now found themselves in
the Persian empire had at times to serve in their masters' army.
Quite soon after their submission to Cyrus, the Persian general
Harpagus led Greeks against native tribes in the south, and
Lesbian ships were used to take the islands of Lemnos and
Imbros in the north.

In other parts of the Persian empire, but nearer the Greeks
themselves and in areas already permeated by their influence,
the presence of Greek artists is even more obvious. The built
tombs of Lycia, some of which belong to this period, are decorated with reliefs in a purely Greek although somewhat provincial
manner. But they are so much part of the history of Greek sculpture that they warrant no more than a mention here, and only
some of the motifs seem eastern (piles of dead bodies). From the
middle of the sixth century too both Athenian and East Greek
vases appear with growing frequency in Caria and Lycia. In
Cyprus both the influence of East Greek art and the import of
Greek pottery grow apace, and now for the first time we may
seriously believe in new Greek settlements in the island.

Although trade, particularly with other parts of the Persian
empire, prospered at first, the East Greeks felt some setback to
their business in Egypt when that country too fell to the Persian
Cambyses in 525. But it was probably not only commercial
considerations that led the Greeks to look for an escape from the
Persian yoke, and already in 511 some Greek states on the north-
west fringe of the empire attempted to revolt. The Persians too

were beginning to covet mainland Greece where Sparta was championing the cause of her enemies. They had already met the Athenians at Sigeum, near the Hellespont (Dardanelles), and given refuge to an exiled Athenian tyrant, Hippias. In 499 the Greek tyrant of Miletus and the Persian satrap attempted to take the island of Naxos; but in the same year the East Greeks revolted, burned the capital of the Persian satrapy, Sardis, and enjoyed an uneasy freedom for some five years. The Persian counter-attack in 498 on the Greek cities in Cyprus is well illustrated by the recent excavations at Paphos, which have shown that the city fell to a siege mound of the sort the Lydians had thrown up against Smyrna (p. 113) a century earlier. In 490 Darius's generals sailed against Greece to punish those who had supported the rebels, and in their fleet were Ionian and Aeolian Greeks. Eretria in Euboea was sacked, and her folk deported to Arderikka, near Susa in Persia, where they were still living as a community in Herodotus' day. On the plain of Marathon the Persians were thwarted of their next and prime objective, Athens, and sailed away. Ten years later, their last hopes of adding a satrapy of Greece to their empire were dashed in the waters around Salamis and on the battlefield of Plataea. Even then, many eastern Greeks and many mainlanders served in Xerxes' army and fleet, and the exiled king of Sparta, Demaratus, was among Xerxes' advisers. The Eretrians were not the first to be deported. Darius had already taken back with him the men of Branchidae (near Miletus), who had surrendered their temple to the Persians and feared the consequences from their fellow Greeks. He settled them in Sogdiana, but their descendants suffered for this treachery at the hands of Alexander. Other Milesians were deported and settled at Ampe on the Persian Gulf, near the mouth of the River Tigris. Many Greeks travelled or were taken to the east in these years. Darius had threatened to carry off the Ionian maidens to Bactria, but in the event sent them to his own court.

There are many archaeological reflections of these events, mainly of course in Greece herself, and notably on the Acropolis of Athens, which was despoiled by the Persians. Loot from the victory over the Persians was to become a feature of the state treasuries there; and we may mention briefly the most recently found (1960) memorial of the ultimate Persian defeat – a Persian bronze helmet from Olympia inscribed simply 'The Athenians to Zeus, having seized [it] from the Medes.' In Persia itself there is loot from the Ionian cities – like the inscribed bronze knucklebone which had stood as a dedication in a sanctuary near Miletus (Didyma) and was found at Susa; the griffin protome from a cauldron of the Samian type, also found at Susa; part of the relief decoration from a Spartan bronze mixing bowl of the later sixth century, from Persepolis; and the scrap of bronze relief decoration from a shield of the earlier sixth century, found at Persepolis. A golden crater, the work of Theodorus of Samos, was said to stand in the royal palace, and may have been either a present to the Persian king or loot from Ionia or Lydia.

Whether or not Persian architectural forms also had their effect in Greece it is hard to decide, but some have seen them in the round 'tholos' building in the Athenian market place – like a monumental eastern parasol; in the forest of columns of the Periclean Music Hall (Odeion) at Athens; even in the re-planning of the Acropolis itself. Certainly Greek artists still worked for Persians in the fifth and fourth centuries, and con-tributed a very great deal to what we know as Achaemenid art. Gem stones in particular, often oriental in subject, shape, and material, are worked in the best classical Greek manner. In return, types of oriental animal head cups already met in Assyria, and most popular with the Persians, were copied by Greeks in clay and metal.

The details of the history and the archaeology of the Persian Wars and their aftermath cannot concern us here, but they mark an important stage in Greece's relations with the 'barbarians'. Greek ventures overseas had at last brought them face to face with a major power which was stimulated or goaded by their presence within its territory to march against the mother coun-try. That power was repulsed, and the Greeks pursued with even more vigour and freedom their trade with eastern countries and interest in eastern affairs. Exactly a century and a half later Alexander the Great was to compass the fall of that very empire and march beyond it; his soldiers burned Persepolis and liberated 800 Greeks there, and the lands of the Hittites, the Assyrians, the Babylonians, and the Persians were embraced in a new and Greek empire.

Bibliography

An excellent introduction is Dunbabin, *The Greeks and their Eastern Neighbours*, 1957. A selection of studies on Greco-oriental relations and relevant matters: Akurgal in *Anatolia*, IV, 1959, for Urartian bronzes; Amandry in *Syria*, XXXV, 1958, and *Ét. d'arch. class.*, I, 1955–6; Barnett in *Journ. Hell. Stud.*, LXVIII, 1948, for ivories, in *The Aegean and the Near East*, 1956, in *Syria*, XXXIV, 1957, and in *Éléments orientaux dans la religion grecque*, 1960; Birmingham in *Anat. Stud.*, XI, 1961; Boardman in *Ant. Journ.* XXXIX, 1959, for architecture, in *Cretan Coll.*, Oxford for Crete, in *Anatolia*, VI, 1961, for belts, and *Island Gems*, 1963; Brown, *The Etruscan Lion*, 1960; Frankfort, *Cylinder Seals*, 1939; Grace in *Amer. Journ. Arch.*, XLVI, 1942, for sculpture; Jantzen, *Griechische Griefenkessel*, 1955; Kunze, *Kretische Bronzereliefs*, 1931, in *Ath. Mitt.*, LV, 1930, and LX–LXI, 1935–6, for ivories, and the Olympia publications; Maxwell-Hyslop in *Iraq*, XVIII, 1956; Payne, *Necrocorinthia*, 1931. A good general book, J. M. Cook, *Greeks in Ionia and the East*, 1962.

AL MINA: Woolley in *Journ. Hell. Stud.*, LVIII, 1938, and briefly in *A Forgotten Kingdom*, 1953. For the Greek pottery Robertson in *Journ. Hell. Stud.*, LX, 1940, and Beazley, ibid., LIX, 1939; for the Euboean and local Greek wares Boardman, *Brit. School Ann.*, LII, 1957, and *Anat. Stud.*, iX, 1959; for the local pottery Taylor, *Iraq*, XXI, 1959.

TELL SUKAS: Riis in *Ann. Arch. de Syrie*, VIII–XI, 1959–61.

Some Greek pottery on Near Eastern sites is listed by Dunbabin, op. cit., and by Clairmont in *Berytus* XI, XII, 1955, 1956–7, and there is more in site publications.

The Penguin publications on *Iran* by Ghirshman (1954), and *Early Anatolia* by Seton Lloyd (1956), are good general introductions to these regions, as is Frankfort's *Art and Architecture of the Ancient Orient*, Pelican History of Art, 1954, for the Near East in general. For the historical background, Olmstead's *History of Assyria*, 1923, and *History of the Persian Empire*, 1948; *Cambridge Ancient History*; Wiseman, *Chronicles of the Chaldaean Kings*, 1956.

PHRYGIA and LYDIA: Akurgal, *Phrygische Kunst*, 1955. Hanfmann, *Sardis und Lydien*, 1960. Work at Gordion and Sardis is reported annually in *Amer. Journ. Arch.* For the fall of Smyrna, *Brit. School Ann.*, LIII–LIV, 1958–9. For Samothrace, Lehmann's 1961 *Guide* to the excavations; *Larisa am Hermos*, I–III, 1940–2. On Greek and Persian art, Frankfort, op. cit., and Richter in *Amer. Journ. Arch.*, L, 1946.

CHAPTER 4

THE GREEKS IN EGYPT

In many accounts, especially archaeological ones, of Greeks overseas, Egypt is grouped with the states of the Near East in a single oriental 'bloc' whose effect on and relations with the civilizations of the Aegean are treated as part of a single story. This leads only to confusion and complication. Whatever the relationship of the two great valley civilizations – of Mesopotamia and the Nile – in their earliest days, their subsequent development and history are quite distinct, and the records and fortunes of the Greeks who travelled east to Syria or south to Egypt are quite different. So too is the nature of the reciprocal influences of the east and Egypt upon the Greeks themselves. Here only one source of confusion and error is found, for one of the main routes from Egypt to Greece followed the coast of Palestine, Phoenicia, and Asia Minor, and Egyptian objects which reached Greece thus were probably passed by eastern traders for much of the way. Egyptian influence was also strong in Phoenicia, whose art is deeply tainted by Egyptian fashions, while even in the North Syrian neo-Hittite monuments which we mentioned in the last chapter, Egyptian motifs can often be found. It is certain, then, that much of what seems Egyptian in Greece may have been derived at second hand through the countries of the Near East, especially Phoenicia; but it is equally certain that much was brought direct from Egypt by the Greeks, and it is often possible to distinguish this 'pure' material. But our primary concern is with the Greeks in Egypt itself.

The only part of the complicated story of Egyptian–Greek relations in the Bronze Age which is of relevance here is its end. In the Near East we have seen how the spread of Mycenaean culture or peoples set a pattern for later Greek settlement. In Egypt the character of the Mycenaean Greek contacts was quite different, and has no bearing on the course of Greek interest in

Egypt in later centuries. Late Mycenaean pottery has indeed been found in some quantity on over a dozen different Egyptian sites as far up the Nile as Thebes, and isolated finds are reported as far south as Aswan and Nubia. The vases are generally stirrup jars of a type made in Rhodes and Cyprus. They attest no more than a brisk trade, probably in oil, and can nowhere be taken to

represent any regular Greek community, although many Greek traders were no doubt temporarily resident in the country.

The 'Peoples of the Sea' who so disrupted the countries of the eastern Mediterranean in the late thirteenth century, and who may have included Greeks, were with difficulty, but with complete success, kept from Egyptian territory. But, despite her success in keeping at bay the troubles which heralded the beginnings of the Iron Age in the Aegean and Near East, Egypt also suffered a long period of comparative decline after the brilliance of her New Kingdom dynasties. A brief rally in the later tenth century brought an Egyptian army again into Palestine, but in Egypt itself these are barren years archaeologically.

It is not until the later eighth century that the course of Egyptian history begins to be of much more than local interest. In the far south, in Nubia (Sudan), was a flourishing kingdom, worshipping Amun, as did the great cities of Egypt, and with kings related to the Egyptian royal line. The Nubian king Piankhy invaded Egypt in 730, and fifteen years later the 'Ethiopian Dynasty' (Dyn. xxv) was established. The Nubian kings ruled Egypt until 664, often threatened by the growing power of the Assyrian kings, whose invasion fleets were partly manned by Cypriots. It was the Nubian King Shabako who surrendered the Greek 'Yamani', who had stirred up revolt in Ashdod against the Assyrians in 712. In 671 Lower Egypt fell to the Assyrians, and the Nubian kings' hold on the Nile delta was never fully regained. We hear of a free Egypt again under Psammetichos (Psamtik) I (664–10), the first king of the new dynasty (xxvi), and now too, for the first time, we hear of numbers of Greeks in Egypt.

Up to this time Greek awareness of Egypt seems to have been slight, but some Egyptian objects were reaching Greece, and from them it seems possible that at times there was some more direct contact. We may briefly review these imports before coming to the question of Greeks in Egypt, but unfortunately for most we can say no more than that it is likely that they antedate the mid seventh century. The earliest objects – beads, figurines, vases, scarab seals of faience, and some stone seals – appear occasionally on Greek sites throughout the early Iron Age, and represent no more than casual imports, perhaps via the Near East. They are found in Crete, at Sparta, Argos, Sunium, Athens, Aegina, Thera; at Eleusis (some in Geometric tombs); in an eighth-century tomb at Corinth; in a Geometric context at Perachora near by; and in East Greece on Rhodes and Chios. It is possible, however, that already in the earlier seventh century there was a workshop producing very similar faience trinkets on Greek Rhodes, as there was certainly later in the century. Some minor objects were even carried west, and in the Euboean colony of Pithekoussai (Ischia) and in Etruria a seal and a faience vase bearing the name of the Egyptian king Bocchoris (720–715 B.C.) have been found. Of isolated finds of Egyptian bronzes, we may mention a bronze vase (situla) from Pherae in Thessaly in what seems a Geometric context; a bronze mirror from Perachora certainly earlier than 650; a Horus figure in Argos (the Heraeum); two bronze women and an ornament in Rhodes; and an ibis statuette at Miletus. Small bronze flower pendants have been found on various East Greek sites, and may well be from Egyptian earrings or diadems, in their turn inspiring the floral or fruit pendants on East Greek jewellery.

There are, however, two places in the Greek world which attracted a different class of Egyptian objects – fine bronzes – certainly straight from Egypt itself with no eastern intermediaries. These are Crete and Samos. Understandably so, for

34. Egyptian bronze vase from Idaean Cave, Crete.

Crete was the first stop on the direct sea route to Greece, and there is good evidence for Cretan interest in North Africa, in Cyrenaica; and it is a Samian captain whom we will first hear of trading with Egypt just after the middle of the seventh century. In Crete, as well as the minor faience objects, we find a bronze bowl and fine bronze jugs with openwork handles in the form of an Egyptian lotus (Fig. 34). Five of these have been found in the Idaean Cave, two in tombs near Knossos, and one at Amnisos. The finds at Knossos suggest that they are likely to be of the years before the middle of the seventh century. There are also Egyptian ivory plaques from the Idaean Cave and Knossos. Crouching lions holding a bowl between their forelegs are found – in faience in the Idaean Cave, and Cretan clay versions at various places. One from Afrati (Plate 8b) is of the mid seventh century, and the type is wholly Egyptian, although it was copied also in Palestine. On Samos the dating evidence is less sure, but certainly some of the rich series of Egyptian bronzes found there will also be of this earlier period.

Our first literary evidence for Greeks in Egypt is in Herodotus. First there is the mention of the Samian merchant captain Kolaios who was on his way to Egypt when he was carried off course to the west. The story implies that the Egypt run was nothing out of the ordinary for him, and it seems that his spectacular voyage (see below, p. 220) happened in about 638. So we have here the suggestion of at least casual trade visits by East Greeks about the middle of the seventh century.

Another incident concerns not Greek traders but Greek soldiers – mercenaries. Psammetichos I – to give him the name by which the Greeks called him (as I will the other Egyptian kings) – had been encouraged by an oracle to enlist the aid of 'brazen men' to regain his throne. At that time Ionian and Carian pirates were forced on to the Egyptian coast by bad weather. They had bronze armour – either the Greek 'hoplite' corselet of sheet bronze, or perhaps 'scale armour', made up of many scale-shaped pieces of iron or bronze sewn on to leather in the eastern fashion. With their help, Psammetichos prevailed; he rewarded them with two pieces of land – known as the Stratopeda, or Camps – on either side of the Pelusian branch of the Nile (the sites have not been certainly identified). Herodotus says that they were well treated and respected by the king, who even founded a school of interpreters. 'They were the first foreigners to live in Egypt, and after their original settlement there, the Greeks began regular intercourse with the Egyptians, so that we have accurate knowledge of Egyptian history from the time of Psammetichos onwards.' The historian Diodorus adds that Psammetichos also encouraged the Greeks in trade with Egypt. In Herodotus' story the Carians and Ionians arrive by accident, but it is possible that they were sent by the Lydian king Gyges.

In Necho's reign (610–595) we have no direct evidence for the use of Greek mercenaries, but the king was moved to dedicate the armour in which he fought in his Syrian campaign in 608 to Apollo at Branchidae (near Miletus), and this may imply the welcome participation by Greek soldiers. Later, in 605, he suffered defeat at the hands of the Babylonians at Carchemish. In ruined Carchemish, in a house well furnished with Egyptian objects including sealings naming King Necho, was found a Greek bronze shield (see p. 75, Plate 6b). Its find-place suggests it might well have been carried by a Greek soldier in the pay of the Egyptian king. Necho also made 'trireme' warships for service in the Mediterranean and the Red Sea, and it may be that here, as under Psammetichos II (see below), we have evidence of Greek nautical experience – never a strong point of the Egyptians – being exploited.

For some later activities by Greek mercenaries in Egypt, we can enlarge considerably on Herodotus' bald statement that Psammetichos II (595–89) made an expedition to Nubia. The Egyptian monuments show that this was a considerable expedition, made in 591 B.C., against the Nubian kingdom which was again threatening Lower Egypt. Eloquent testimony to the part played by foreign mercenaries is paid by the inscriptions cut on the legs of the colossal rock-cut statues at Abu Simbel (Plate 8a), some 700 miles up the Nile, the greatest of the monuments now threatened by the new Aswan Dam. The inscriptions are by Greek and Carian soldiers who accompanied the king and it seems held important commissions in his army. The longest Greek inscription says:

When King Psammetichos had come to Elephantine, this was written by those who sailed with Psammetichos, son of Theokles, who went as far upstream as they could – to Kerkis. Potasimto led the foreigners and Amasis the Egyptians. This was written by Archon son of Amoibichos and Pelekos son of Eudamos.

Psammetichos son of Theokles was, it seems, in charge of the river force, with Egyptian generals in charge of the Foreign Legion and the Egyptians. Potasimto is styled 'General of the Greeks' on Egyptian monuments. The other inscriptions are hardly more than the idle exhibitionist scratchings with which soldiers and others can always be relied upon to deface any convenient wall or monument; but some are important, for they reveal the home city of the men. We have Elesibios of Teos, and Pabis of Colophon, both Ionians, and a Dorian, Telephos from Ialysos in Rhodes. It is not certain whether we can argue from the Egyptian forms of some of the names that the men were born in Egypt, perhaps children of the mercenaries who had served Psammetichos I. In this same period we read in Egyptian inscriptions of an Egyptian Admiral Hor, 'commander of the foreigners and Greeks' (perhaps Cypriots), and there were Greeks at the southern fortress of Elephantine which had been established by Psammetichos I and housed a Jewish garrison also.

Returning to Herodotus' account we find little more that concerns the Greek mercenaries. King Apries (Ua-ha-bra; 589–570) led a mercenary army of 30,000 Carians and Ionians against Amasis (A-ahmes) in 570. They acquitted themselves well, but were defeated, and Amasis became king (570–26). A version of the episode is preserved on a stele in Cairo. Despite his encounter with the Greek mercenaries of Apries, Amasis too came to favour the Greeks, and seems to have used them early in his reign against an attack by the Babylonian king Nebuchadrezzar. He married a Greek princess from Cyrene. He is said to have moved the mercenary camps from Stratopeda to Memphis to 'protect him from his own people', but there is archaeological evidence too (see below) for a fort at Daphnae, in the area of Stratopeda, partly manned by Greeks throughout his reign. But the most important of the privileges which he accorded the Greeks is reported by Herodotus and concerns Naucratis:

He gave them Naucratis as a commercial headquarters for any who wished to settle in the country. He also made grants of land upon which Greek traders, who did not want to live permanently in Egypt, might erect altars and sanctuaries. Of the latter the best known and most used – and also the largest – is the Hellenion; it was built by the joint efforts of the Ionians of Chios, Teos, Phocaea, and Clazomenae, of the Dorians of Rhodes, Cnidus, Halicarnassus, and Phaselis, and of the Aeolians of Mytilene. It is to these states that the sanctuary belongs, and it is they who have the right of appointing the officers in charge of the port [*prostatai*]. Other cities

claim a share in the Hellenion, but without any justification; the
Aeginetans, however, did build a temple of Zeus on their own
initiative, the Samians one in honour of Hera, and the Milesian
another in honour of Apollo. In old days Naucratis was the only
port in Egypt, and any one who brought a ship into any of the
other mouths of the Nile was bound to state on oath that he did so
of necessity, and then proceed to the Canopic mouth; should contrary
winds prevent him from doing so, he had to carry his freight to
Naucratis in barges all round the Delta, which shows the exclusive
privilege the port enjoyed.

We should perhaps here mention too the account by Strabo of
a raid by Milesians, and a fort built by them in the Delta before
they founded Naucratis.

The archaeological evidence shows clearly enough that Naucratis was founded long before Amasis' reign, but we may
understand Herodotus' words as an indication of some reform
or regularizing of its status. But it is time to consider in more
detail what is known of this great Greek trading town in the
Nile Delta.

NAUCRATIS

The site

The town of Naucratis lay on the east bank of the Canopic
branch of the Nile, some fifty miles from the open sea and the
later Hellenistic capital, Alexandria, and only ten miles from
Sais, the capital of the XXVI Dynasty kings. Petrie discovered
the site at the mounds of Kôm Gi'eif, some two miles from the
village el-Niqrâsh, which preserves the ancient name. He dug
there in 1884–5, and his work was followed by that of Gardner,
Griffith, and finally Hogarth, in 1899 and 1903. The excavations
were not conducted under the happiest conditions. To a great
extent the excavators were digging around or through the work
of their predecessors, and Petrie's technique of publication, if
not of digging, left much to be desired when quantities of decorated pottery and minor objects, whose dates could be controlled
by finds elsewhere in the Greek world, were involved. Recent
attempts to resurrect the stratigraphy of parts of the site have
proved inconclusive.

Much in the principal buildings of the town was dug piecemeal in this way, but hardly any of the houses, while the cemeteries of the earlier period were not located. Nor is the student today helped by the way the finds have been scattered through museums and private collections throughout the world.

There were two centres of archaeological interest in the town as excavated, in the northern and southern quarters. The history of their main buildings has been made much clearer by the late Baron W. von Bissing, but there are some problems of identification and date which may for ever remain obscure.

In the southern part of the town, one of the dominant buildings was a stout structure which Petrie took for a fort and von Bissing has understood as a treasury or storehouse of Egyptian type which may have been built before the end of the seventh century. Just to the north of this lay the Greek temple of Aphrodite, a simple two-roomed building with a stepped altar before its door, standing within a small walled enclosure. The temple itself was rebuilt at least twice, but always to about the same size (about 14m. × 8m.) and plan, and of the same material – mudbrick. The offerings excavated in the temple clearly belong to its earliest period. Among them we should pick out particularly the mass of Chian vases, some certainly as early as 600 B.C., and remark that a Chian pottery established at Naucratis (see below) devoted much of its time to producing votives for dedication there. Otherwise there is a fair proportion of East Greek and Athenian pottery from the earlier sixth century on, and some objects of Cypriot type. The dedications painted (as Fig. 36, p. 140) or incised (as Plate 9b) on the vases give us the name of the goddess. Herodotus does not mention a temple of Aphrodite, but a later reference attributed to a local writer implies that the cult may have been of some antiquity there, and alleges that the cult statue was brought from Cyprus. The finds might suggest that the Chians had something to do with the foundation. The stepped altar is an interesting and important construction, if it does indeed date to the earliest years of the sanctuary. It consists of a flight of four steps, about three yards wide, leading to a flat platform for the sacrifices. The type bears some resemblance to Egyptian stepped altars, which are generally higher and with narrower steps, and it has been suggested that Ionic architects adopted it from Egypt.

East of the temple of Aphrodite was a small factory for faience scarab seals, which was active mainly in the earlier sixth century, and to which we shall have occasion to refer later.

35. Sketch plan of Naucratis.

The temples in the northern part of the town are hardly better known than those in the south. A temple to Hera, which must be the Samian one, is attested by inscriptions on scraps of sixth-century pottery, and the outlines of a sanctuary and perhaps of the temple itself. Next to it lay the Milesian temple of Apollo, also in a defined sanctuary enclosure. The pottery dedications here show that the cult goes back to the early days of the settlement. Of the temple buildings we have only architectural fragments, some preserved, some merely described. For instance, the only fragment of a stone capital which Petrie saw was smashed before he could fetch his camera to it. There seem to be several pieces from a fine limestone temple with Ionic columns, built about the middle of the sixth century, if not earlier. One feature of the columns was a necking carved with a floral pattern, such as has been found on Samos. The temple was replaced by a marble one, with similarly elaborate mouldings, perhaps early in the fifth century.

The sanctuaries of Hera and Apollo lay side by side. Near them – to the north, but in a separate enclosure – was a smaller shrine, to the Dioscuri, which is identified by the inscribed pottery dedications, some of them earlier than the mid sixth century; but the building is not mentioned by any ancient author.

To the east of these three sanctuaries, Hogarth digging in 1899 found another and larger sanctuary which could certainly be identified as the Hellenion mentioned by Herodotus, the joint foundation of several East Greek states. Again the site is architecturally disappointing, but the inscriptions on vases name several deities, the most significant being simply 'the gods of the Greeks'. None of the votive pottery found here need have arrived earlier than the reign of Amasis, so it may well be that the Hellenion was founded as the result of his reorganization of the status of Naucratis, while the independent sanctuaries – of Milesian Apollo, Samian Hera, Chian Aphrodite (if rightly identified by the Chian finds) and Aeginetan Zeus (mentioned by Herodotus) are of the earlier years of the town, and indicate the identity of the major interests there. Unfortunately the Aeginetan sanctuary has not been found. If we could read 'Dioskouron' instead of 'Dios' in Herodotus, the sanctuary of the Dioscuri might be given to Aegina, but the twin gods have no home in the island, where there is, however, an important shrine to Zeus Hellenios, also met at Naucratis (in the Hellenion).

The finds

It is the finds at Naucratis which betray to us the date of the first Greek settlement, and give the lie to what might otherwise be deduced from Herodotus, that it was founded in Amasis' reign. The earliest pottery from the site which is datable is, as usual, Corinthian: one scrap of 'Transitional', made about 630–620, and rather more 'Early Corinthian' of the later years of the seventh century and earliest sixth. As it was largely an East Greek venture, we might expect the earliest pottery to be East Greek, and indeed there is much which certainly still belongs to the end of the seventh century. But in the present state of our knowledge of vase chronology, we cannot tell how early the earliest pieces might be, and we are left with the Corinthian as our only sure evidence. This suggests that there were Greeks at Naucratis by 620, but is equally compatible with the view that they were there some twenty years before. It should, however, be remarked that von Bissing argues a later date for the foundation – to the reign of Psammetichos II (595–89) – because of the absence at Naucratis of scarabs bearing the name of any earlier Egyptian king. The positive evidence of the pottery, which indicates a substantial Greek settlement before 600, seems to outweigh this argument *ex silentio*, but there may still be room for some adjustment.

It would be satisfactory if we could assign the classes of pottery found at Naucratis to the various states known to have had dealings there. This can be done to a limited extent. Herodotus says that of the Ionians, Chios, Teos, Phocaea, and Clazomenae were represented; of the Dorians, Rhodes, Cnidus, Halicarnassus, and Phaselis; and of the Aeolians, Mytilene (Lesbos). These shared the Hellenion, but besides there were the sanctuaries built by the Aeginetans, the Samians, and the Milesians. He is speaking of the period of Amasis, but it is likely that most or all of these states were active in Naucratis from the early days of its Greek history.

Most of the vases and fragments which were kept by the excavators are finely decorated votives from the sanctuaries. The East Greek pottery may be considered first:

1. Much of it, including pieces datable to the late seventh century, is *Rhodian* in origin, or of Rhodian type. It seems to have been in general use in all the Dorian states of East Greece, and it is likely too that Miletus used or perhaps produced pottery of the same type: the problem of Milesian pottery in this period we have already met at Al Mina. 'Rhodian' vases were also used in the more northerly East Greek towns, but many of these were producing their own vases either in a style which it is still hard for us to distinguish from Rhodian, or in a peculiarly local style which we can fortunately pick out among the finds at Naucratis. Such are the vases of Chios, Samos, Clazomenae, and Lesbos.

2. *Chian* pottery is readily distinguished by its most popular shapes (especially the chalice and kantharos), the fine white slip on the vases, and a distinctive style of drawing. So much Chian pottery was found at Naucratis, before it had been recognized in the island of Chios, that the ware was for long called Naucratite. This gives a quite false indication of the home of the vases and their style, but the name is not wholly misleading, as we shall see. The earliest Chian vases at Naucratis are still of the seventh century; this we know from the early shapes of some chalices and the decoration. Some of the most spectacular vases at Naucratis are of this ware (Plate 9b), which although it never seriously competed in the pottery markets of the Greek world was still prized far from home – as in Etruria. Among the Chian vases at Naucratis, there are some classes which have not so far been recognized in excavations in Chios itself, and it is legitimate to ask whether they might not have been made in Naucratis by Chian potters. Only votives are involved, which could have been turned out fairly easily for the rich local market, even with imported potters' clay brought as ballast in the corn ships. The most distinctive are fine chalices with decoration in a polychrome style which reminds one more of Egyptian murals than of any contemporary (second quarter of the sixth century) Greek vase decoration. Somewhat earlier are some other fine chalices with animal scenes, also executed with a lively sense of colour. Somewhat later, of the middle of the century, is a host of small fine cups (mostly *kantharoi*) which are completely plain except

for a painted dedication, which must have been bespoken by the customer *before* the vase was made (Fig. 36). The only places outside Naucratis where vases of these classes have been found are Cyrene, Aegina (where there was a dedication of a man who made similar offerings at Naucratis), and Athens (one piece). We should recall that Cyrene, in North Africa, must have been in close touch with Naucratis, and that Aegina was the only non-East-Greek power with a stake in Naucratis. The probable existence of a Greek pottery in Naucratis recalls the work by Greeks, over a century before, in similar circumstances at Al Mina. Of the second half of the sixth century are some other

36. Chian votive cup from Naucratis (reconstruction drawing).

fragments which can be recognized as Chian, but the decoration of these is much influenced by Athenian fashions. Before we leave Chios, we may also note the presence at Naucratis of examples of Chian wine jars, the earliest being of the earlier sixth century.

3. *Samian* pottery of the early years of Naucratis cannot yet be identified with certainty. Of the mid sixth century is a small class of exceptionally fine black-figure cups which were probably made in Samos. Some plain one-handled cups with inscribed dedications to Hera (her temple was a Samian foundation) may be from the island; some are said to have been painted before the vases were fired, and so were bespoken. It is possible that

these, like the Chian-Naucratite, were made in Egypt, but they name only the goddess, not the dedicator, and could as well have come from a Samian shop serving the Heraeum at home.

4. Samos has also been considered by some as one of the sources for the *Fikellura* vases. These are generally large vases, amphorae, and *hydriae*, decorated in a style which owes much to Rhodes and a little to the Samian black-figure school. Their floruit was the middle and third quarter of the sixth century, and although the style probably lingered to the end of the century, the last phase is not represented at Naucratis. The style may have originated in Samos, with daughter-factories later in Rhodes. They are named after a cemetery in Rhodes.

5. An important school of black-figure vase painters has been attributed to the North Ionian town of *Clazomenae*. The vases are well represented at Naucratis, and date to the third quarter of the sixth century. The style seems to be at home on the mainland sites of North Ionia, and some of the Clazomenian vases at Naucratis, or at least those – and there are several – which seem related to 'Clazomenian' in various ways, might well be from towns like Phocaea and Teos, said by Herodotus to have traded at Naucratis.

6. The most typical vases of Aeolis, particularly *Lesbos*, are in the plain pale grey *bucchero*. There are several pieces at Naucratis, none closely datable, although many are certainly not later than the sixth century in date.

We are left with three other main classes of Greek pottery found at Naucratis which were not made in any of the states named by Herodotus. These are:

7. *Spartan* vases. Fine black-figure vases, generally cups, of the style now certainly attributed to Sparta, are found in some quantity. All are of the first half of the sixth century, the earliest are of its beginning. They are intrinsically fine, and in the Etruscan market, for example, could compete with Corinthian and Athenian. Their numbers at Naucratis are noteworthy, but the fact that the other major foreign market for them was in Samos may in part explain their popularity. They may, on the other hand, reflect Spartan interest in another part of North

Africa where they are found – Cyrene (where some once thought they had been made).

8. *Corinthian* vases. The earliest, of the later seventh century, have already been mentioned. They continue to arrive until the middle of the sixth century, although not in quantity.

9. *Athenian vases*. The earliest at Naucratis is of about 620 B.C. In the sixth century they appear in fair numbers, and the quality is of the best. Both quantity and quality are maintained until about 525, when there is a sharp falling off. The imports pick up again in the early fifth century. Also of the sixth century are some plainer Athenian storage jars (as Fig. 3b, p. 32).

The Corinthian and Athenian vases remain to be explained. Both were fine wares which in this period were being carried for their intrinsic worth as decorative pottery; and the Corinthian and Athenian coins found in Naucratis may suggest a strong if indirect interest in the trade there by the issuing cities. But there remains one state in Herodotus' list whose archaeological presence at Naucratis has yet to be tested. This is Aegina. We have already had cause to remark that Aegina had no painted vases of her own, but used Corinthian throughout the seventh and in the earlier sixth century. Now add that already in the seventh century she was beginning to use the best Athenian vases, and we have perhaps the explanation for the appearance of Athenian vases in quantity at Naucratis some time before they appear in comparable numbers on any other overseas market.

There are other classes of finds to be mentioned which may throw some light on trade at Naucratis and the identity of the merchants living in or visiting the town. There are a number of stone statuettes – of limestone, and a few of alabaster or marble – which are clearly of Cypriot type. The earliest and best of them are equally clearly not of Cypriot origin, but produced by East Greek artists inspired by the generally dull but numerous products of the Cypriot workshops. The material of some – alabaster – suggests that they may have been working in Naucratis itself. But beside them there are many stone and clay statuettes of certain Cypriot origin. These are not, generally, so early, and need not imply any very important Cypriot element in the merchant classes at Naucratis. All may in fact date to the years in which the island was held by the Egyptians, in the second and third quarters of the sixth century. Some other stone statuettes, of horsemen and of women reclining on couches, are executed in a crude Egyptianizing style and seem to be largely of some local cult significance.

Petrie found in the southern part of the town a factory for faience scarab seals which was active for part of the sixth century. This introduces us to an important class of objects – distinguished by their material rather than their form – which presents a number of important questions about Greco-Egyptian relations in the world of art (if they merit the term) in the

37. Faience pendants from Emporio, Chios.

seventh and sixth centuries, and which is best considered here. It should first be made clear that what the archaeologist calls faience bears no relation to the celebrated products of Renaissance Faenza. Ancient 'faience' is of a sandy composition and covered with a heavy lustrous glaze. It had long been used in Egypt for beads and various decorative trifles, and in the period which concerns us it is most often employed for scarab seals, small figure pendants, beads, and miniature vases. Such minor objects travelled far in the ancient world, and some time before the middle of the seventh century a factory for them was set up in Rhodes, possibly by Egyptians, but certainly intended to serve Greek markets. Some of the products have a strongly Egyptian appearance – small vases in the shape of a woman or a monkey holding a pot, flat circular flasks and bowls with figure patterns,

pendants in the shape of cats, naked girls, or some minor
Egyptian deities. Others are more wholly Greek types – flautists
and lyre players. These little figure pendants (Fig. 37), with
their whitish glaze and slight added colour, are perhaps the most
common and distinctive. They appear in Rhodes, of course, but
also on most other East Greek sites, and many mainland and
western Greek ones. Most of them still belong to the later years
of the seventh century, but the Rhodian factory still flourished
in the sixth, producing spherical flasks and elaborate figure
vases in forms already familiar in clay. One example, a flask in
the shape of the head of the river-god Achelous (Plate 12a),
found its way deep into Egypt, to Nubia. There are some faience
flasks which bear the names of Egyptian kings, and might also
be Rhodian, although they are not generally considered so. One,
in Paris, is in the purely Greek form of a helmeted head, was said
to be from Corinth, and carries the name of a king (Psammetichos I, or possibly Apries). The others are *aryballoi* which
compromise between the Greek shape for perfume flasks and the
Egyptian kohl or mascara pots : two with the name of Amasis
are in Cairo; two with the name of Apries, his predecessor, may
both be from Rhodes; and there are two apparently with the
name of Necho (610–595), one from the Lipari islands (Plate 12b;
in Oxford), the other from the Milesian colony of Panticapaeum
in South Russia.

This production on Greek soil of Egyptianizing faience was
challenged in the early sixth century by the factories at Naucratis,
which may have been manned by Egyptians but were certainly
producing for the Greek markets. Scarab seals were popular – the
old Egyptian form of seal with the back carved as the sacred
scarab beetle – but there were others in the form of a human or
a ram's head, and hundreds of small clay moulds for these good-
luck charms – they were hardly more – were found in the scarab-
factory. Moulds for the backs of these seals are shown in
Plate 12c. The devices are generally rough hieroglyphic mottoes
or names. Other Naucratite products in the sixth century are
hedgehog vases and minor statuettes. They are more poorly
executed than the Rhodian faience, mass-produced, and travelled
far in the Greek world. One better specimen, a 'New Year's

a Ivory from Athens

b Ivory from Delphi

c Ivory from Ephesus

I

a Marble sphinx from Al Mina

b Clay plaque from Crete

c Bronze vase from Gordion

a Bronze shield from the Idaean Cave, Crete

b Phoenician bronze bowl from Olympia

a Bronze siren from Olympia

b Bronze tympanum from the Idaean Cave, Crete

a Ivory from Perachora

b Bronze from Chios

c Gold from Rhodes

d Marble from Chios

b Bronze shield from Carchemish

a Bronze head-vase from the Idaean Cave, Crete

b Fresco from Gordion

c Incised stone from Persepolis

a Vase from Gordion

a Abu Simbel

b Clay lion-vase from Crete

a Relief from Abusir

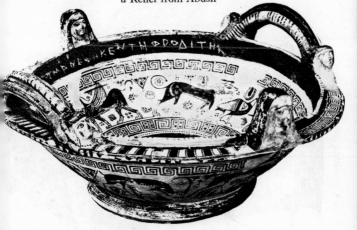

b Chian bowl from Naucratis

b Spartan Arkesilas vase

a Clay situla from Daphnae

Caeretan Busiris vase

a Faience Achelous vase from Nubia

b Faience flask from Lipara

c Clay moulds and cast from Naucratis

d Coin of Cyrene

12

a Athenian vase

b Athenian vase from Meroe

b Statue from Megara Hyblaea

a Metope from Heraeum at Posidonia

b Clay plaque from Caere

a Clay figure from Tarentum

15

a Chalcidian vase

b Bronze vase from Vix

Details of bronze vase from Vix

c Bronze horseman from Grumentum

a The 'Basilica' at Posidonia

a Coin of Syracuse

b Coins of Selinus and Zancle

c Coin of Metapontum

d Bronze vase from Grächwyl

a Plate from Thasos

b Coin of Thasos

c Coin of North Greece

a Vase from the Troad

Neck of a vase from Krivoroshie   *c* From an Athenian vase

Gilt silver mirror from Kelermes

a Gold stag from Kul Oba

b Gold stag from the Kuban

Gold fish from Vettersfelde

flask', reached Assur in Assyria. They are also, of course, well represented among the finds in Naucratis, and were probably being made through most of the sixth century. They do not command respect for any artistic qualities, and their distribution was too wide to tell us much specific about trade, but they are thickest where we would expect them, in East Greece, Aegina, the western markets (including Etruria) visited by the East Greeks, and even the East Greek colonies in the Black Sea. They afford an interesting commentary on commercial opportunism in a town whose primary function was to serve as an entrepôt, not a manufacturing town.

Among the other objects there are some stone scarab seals which have been thought the products of a local workshop, again supplying Greek markets, and there is evidence for a shop producing alabaster vases. Five fragments of carved tridacna shell were found, as well as some plain pieces. We have already (Fig. 18, p. 90) met these oriental products of the seventh century and early sixth, which were especially popular in East Greece. In Egypt they appear only at sites frequented by the Greeks – Naucratis, and one fragment each from Daphnae and Memphis. Another eastern object is a worn Assyrian cylinder seal, which – centuries old already – was carried to Naucratis, no doubt as a lucky charm; and Petrie also describes an ivory cylinder (? seal) with a man, goats, and a tree.

Trade and life

Consideration of Greek trade through Naucratis involves consideration of Greek trade with the rest of Egypt, and the evidence of finds outside Naucratis. For actual settlement in Egypt by Greeks we have first to think of the communities of mercenaries, but the story of Kolaios and the finds of Egyptian bronzes in some parts of Greece (notably Crete and Samos) show the beginnings of commercial interest as well, which actual settlement was able to safeguard and develop. There can only have been one commodity of importance which the Greeks sought – corn; although papyrus and linen may also have been carried. The East Greek states were growing fast in the seventh century, but their expansion at home was being contained both by their Greek neighbours and by the pressure of Phrygia and then Lydia. The two obvious expedients were tried. New colonies – generally founded with a shrewd eye to their value as trading posts – dispersed part of their surplus population. For those left behind who could not readily support themselves on their local resources, or whose economy was becoming specialized – as in Chios, where wine and oil were being produced rather than corn – foreign sources of grain were sought: some in the Black Sea (see Chapter 6), some in Egypt. Aegina enters the field here as the home of merchant carriers supplying central Greece, where similar economic conditions prevailed.

Payment for the corn seems to have been made in various ways. Olive oil was no doubt bartered – some Athenian storage jars can be identified. Wine was certainly carried in quantity. There is some variety of sixth-century wine jars to be found in Naucratis and Daphnae, of which the most readily recognized are the Chian. One Chian jar was re-used in Daphnae and sealed with cartouches of King Amasis (Fig. 38).

The most valuable commodity which the Greeks brought to Egypt was silver. The country had no coined money of its own, and the interest was in the precious metal as such, but it was naturally carried by the Greeks in the form of coinage. Even in the early period which is our main concern – before about 480 – a notable number of hoards of silver have been found in Egypt including both coins and the plain unminted metal. The sources of the coins can indicate which states carried the silver, or at least the source of the silver carried by the merchants. They correspond well with what we already expect of the pattern of trade at Naucratis. Aegina is prominent, with Athens (which by the end of the century was coining silver in some quantity as an export commodity) and Corinth. Of the East Greek states, we find Miletus and Chios, while Samos, Phocaea, and Teos are also represented – all of them states whose interest in Naucratis is recorded by Herodotus. A remarkable feature, however, is the very high proportion of silver coins minted in North Greece, in Thrace and Macedonia. This was an important silver-producing area, and the coins minted there could readily be carried, more or less as bullion, by other states trading in North Greece which had need of the metal for payment in places like Egypt or the east (see p. 79 above) rather than for circulation at home. Corinth had interests in North Greece, but there were Ionian and Aeolian towns there too, and it has been argued that some of the East Greeks, who had no ready source of silver at home, relied on their contacts in Thrace for supply of the metal.

It is far more difficult to see just how trade was organized through Naucratis. The archaeological evidence tells us about

38. Chian wine jar with sealing from Daphnae.

the sanctuaries, not the warehouses, and it has been assumed by some that each interested state had not only its own temple but its own trading quarter. The big independent sanctuaries founded by the Samians, Milesians, and it seems the Chians and Aeginetans, may date to the early years of the town, but the variety in the sources of the dedications and dedicators in them shows clearly that they were not separate 'nationalist' centres of worship, but in general use by the whole Greek community. The Hellenion, which may have been built in Amasis' reign, afforded a larger sanctuary area for other shrines, some no doubt founded by states trading there, others by the now established Greek community. Still, Naucratis was not yet quite an ordinary Greek town with its own 'citizens'. It was nothing like the colonies in Italy and Sicily. It owed its existence to the continued favour (and interest) of the Egyptian king, and the Greek states trading there – the same, it appears, who had already long been working side by side at Al Mina in Syria – no doubt saw to it that their monopoly of the Egyptian trade was not usurped. This in turn implies a measure of agreement between them, but not necessarily between the home states; rather between the interested merchant classes resident in Naucratis itself. From these were surely appointed the *prostatai* Herodotus mentions, the officers in charge of the port, for all that the historian seems to imply that they were posted there by the mother cities. Clearly too it was not only the founders of the Hellenion, but the sponsors of the other and independent sanctuaries, who had a share in the ordering of the life of the town, commercial and otherwise. The *prostatai* may have acted both as magistrates for the town and as 'consuls' for their kinsmen and for merchants from their mother cities.

The life of this large and rich Greek community, admitted to a country which had long mistrusted foreigners, and indeed still preferred strictly limiting their activities and settlement, must have been a very strange and varied one. It was quite unlike anything the Greeks had experienced elsewhere. It was not like a colony – an independent self-supporting town which had come to terms with the local population; nor a simple trading post, like Al Mina, where in the early period there may have been no properly organized Greek civic life, with pretentious sanctuaries and the like. Naucratis attracted the get-rich-quick merchants of East Greece, and their Aeginetan colleagues who ran the business with central Greece. It attracted poets, artists, statesmen, and historians, and in times of danger it may have become a place of refuge for professional men of East Greece who could there ply their trade again. Above all, it opened Greek eyes to the works of a great civilization, more impressive even then in its 'antiquities' than in its contemporary arts and crafts. Even the Egyptian products of these years are strongly 'archaizing'.

Later in this chapter we shall see something of how the Greeks were influenced by what they saw. For the present, at Naucratis itself, we can glean from historians and archaeology a little of the life of the town.

It seems likely that there was already an Egyptian town or village on the site when the Greeks first arrived. This, at any rate, we should expect. Its old name may have been forgotten, for the Egyptians knew the town as Piemro, which is what has been called a 'learned translation' of the Greek, although the reverse might, I supppose, be true. Certainly Egyptians always lived there beside the Greeks. There was probably a native quarter, and the labouring population would have been Egyptian, but the wretched foundations of the mudbrick houses which were excavated in the waterlogged site can tell us nothing of value about the homes of either Greeks or Egyptians there.

The dedications inscribed on vases found in the sanctuaries tell a little about the worshippers. There was Aristophanes, for instance, who about the middle of the sixth century bespoke several cups of the Chian pottery for dedication to Aphrodite, and who carried others on a business trip to Aegina, to dedicate in the temple of Aphaea there. One Rhoikos dedicated an elaborate double cup to Aphrodite some time in the second quarter of the century, and he may be the Samian architect who in these years was designing what in its day was the largest of all the Greek temples, the temple of Hera on Samos. We have already had occasion to remark on some Samian architectural features at Naucratis. The Phanes who gave a cup might be the Halicarnassian mercenary of King Amasis who deserted to the Persians, in Herodotus' story. Much later, but not lightly ignored except by the wholly sceptical, is the Athenian cup given by a Herodotus at about the time when the great historian may have been visiting Egypt. Many of the other dedications give us names only, sometimes revealing too the home of the dedicator. Several are given by women. A Doris offered a love charm to Aphrodite. Naucratis had something of a reputation for the looks and easy virtue of its women. The famous Rhodopis was brought there by a Samian procurer, Charaxes; a wine merchant dealing with Naucratis and brother of the great Lesbian poetess Sappho, bought her freedom. She stayed in Egypt and made a small fortune, one tenth of which she dedicated to Apollo at Delphi, in the form of iron spits – an early form of money. Part of the inscribed base which carried her dedication has been found there in recent years. 'For some reason or other, Naucratis must be a good place for beautiful prostitutes,' says Herodotus, and goes on to mention the famous Archedike, whose name we read on another vase-dedication found in the town. A more sober and distinguished visitor in the sixth century was the Athenian law-giver Solon, who came on a business-cum-sightseeing tour; others were the poet Alcaeus and the philosopher Thales.

These years before the Persian invasion (525) must have been Naucratis' heyday. She regained prosperity later, but an Egypt under the Persians, the vagaries of Greek politics, and a grow-ing civic conscience, combined to dull the brilliance of her cos-mopolitan life – almost the difference between the Shanghai of before and after the Second World War. When Alexander the Great took Egypt, the town was eclipsed by his new capital, Alexandria; but there were flourishing factories still there in the Roman period, and it was the birthplace of Athenaeus, the famous man of letters.

OTHER GREEKS IN EGYPT

We have yet to consider other places in Egypt where Greeks lived, or to which Greek objects penetrated. Of these the most important in our period is DAPHNAE, Tell Defenneh. The site lies between the eastern edge of the cultivated area of the Delta and the present Suez Canal, on the main route to the east, to Palestine and Syria. It was excavated by Petrie in 1886. The largest structure, roughly square in plan, had been built by Psammetichos I. Petrie reasonably took it for a fort. It is very like the large building in the southern quarter of Naucratis, which is of about the same date. It has been argued that these are rather treasuries or store-houses than military constructions, and on the whole the finds bear this out. There can hardly, however, be any doubt that the primary importance of the town was as a fortress and frontier post, and Herodotus says that in the reign of Psammetichos guards were stationed in Pelusian Daphnae against the Arabians and Syrians. Under King Apries the town afforded asylum to Jews, among them the prophet Jeremiah, driven from Judah by the Babylonians – 'and they came into the land of Egypt; for they obeyed not the voice of the Lord: and they came even to Tahpanhes' (i.e. Daphnae): Jeremiah, 43:7. The ruins of the fort are indeed still called 'Kasr el Bint el Yehudi' – Palace of the Jew's Daughter.

The earliest evidence for Greeks at Daphnae is afforded by scraps of East Greek pottery, some at least of which are of the latest seventh century. This is hardly enough to prove the presence of any substantial, or indeed any Greek force there. The mass of Greek pottery from the site belongs to the years of Amasis' reign (570–26), and this alone speaks against the identification of the site with the Stratopeda 'Camps' given to the Greeks by Psammetichos I and evacuated by Amasis. The pottery was found in various parts of the site, but there was a particular concentration in two rooms south-east of the 'fort', which have been called 'a sort of cellar or butler's pantry' – presumably for the officer's mess. The quantity of pottery is of course much less than that from Naucratis, but there are some significant differences in the classes represented:

1. '*Rhodian*'. The earliest scraps only, since the distinctive Rhodian Wild Goat style vases were no longer being made after the first years of Amasis' reign. But note:

2. *Fikellura* vases. As at Naucratis (see p. 141). Of either Rhodian or Samian origin (or both). And:

3. *Situlae*. Daphnae is the principal source of these distinctive vases. Their baggy shape (Plate 10a) may well derive from Egyptian bronze vases, and some of the motifs in their decoration – such as a hawk seated on the Neb-basket on one fragment – are purely Egyptian. The hawk and basket hieroglyphs are part of a royal title. Some half dozen vases of this general type have been found in Rhodes, but it seems probable that most of those at Daphnae were made by Greek potters, probably Rhodians, working in Egypt. And it seems likely that they were working at or near Daphnae, for not one was found at Naucratis.

The next two groups are by far the largest:

4. *Clazomenian* black-figure vases, as at Naucratis. Here again there is the possibility that some of the vases are the work of a Greek vase painter working in Egypt, for nearly all the vases of one of the Clazomenian artists, the so-called Petrie Painter, have been found at Daphnae; the rest are from Naucratis.

5. *Athenian* black-figure vases and storage jars. About as common as the Clazomenian.

Comparison with the finds at Naucratis shows a notable lack of Chian-Naucratite (one fragment is reported from near by, but there are Chian wine jars from the fort) and of Spartan, and a less notable lack of Corinthian and Lesbian, while at Naucratis there are no situlae. The differences are more likely to reflect the opportunities of the markets than any significant difference in the origins or tastes of the Greek customers.

Of the minor finds we may pick out iron weapons and iron scale-armour. One piece of carved tridacna shell was found, like the pieces at Naucratis – an eastern object brought by a Greek to Egypt, even to Daphnae, perhaps before 600. Crude stone figurines like those at Naucratis were found, but only two or three scarabs from the Naucratis factory.

The Greek finds on the site fail at about 525 B.C., and there can be little doubt that this was the direct result of the Persian invasion under Cambyses.

Elsewhere in the Delta there are scattered finds of sixth-century Greek pottery. Passing south we reach MEMPHIS, to which Amasis moved the Greek mercenary camps, according to Herodotus. But here there are pieces of Greek pottery – Corinthian and East Greek – as well as the tridacna shell fragment we have already mentioned, as early as any of the finds at Naucratis. Throughout the sixth century, Greek pottery is arriving at Memphis, mainly East Greek wares like those at Naucratis – Rhodian, Fikellura, Clazomenian – and there must certainly have been a mercenary camp there through Amasis' reign. From about 500, the Athenian black-figure vases replace the East Greek, which are no longer being made. The finds have been made at Memphis itself – in the Palace of Apries and the Temple of Ptah – and in the outlying cemeteries at Abusir and Saqqara. From the former site comes a unique monument, found in the

mortuary temple of Sahure, which may belong to our period.
It is a limestone slab (Plate 9a), apparently a tombstone, bearing
in low relief the scene of *prothesis* – the laying out of a dead
body. The scene, gestures, and furniture are wholly Greek,
although there is much in the execution of the figures which is
Egyptian; and the Egyptian winged sun-disc and *uraei* carved
above, though commonly found at the top of Egyptian stelae,
have no particular relevance here. To one side of the scene, a

39. Faience ushabti figure
from Saqqara.

poorly preserved inscription in Greek names the dead person,
apparently a Milesian. This must be the work of a local Greek
artist who had already been much affected by Egyptian forms
and techniques.

From Saqqara is a faience ushabti figure (Fig. 39) of the sort
regularly put in Egyptian tombs to serve as labourers for the
dead in the other world. But this has a Greek late-archaic head,
perhaps made especially for the burial of a Greek who had
accepted some Egyptian views about the after-life. From

Memphis again, we should mention a limestone statue of a woman, superficially just like any East Greek maiden of the later sixth century, but with some undoubtedly Egyptian features; an interesting clay sealing which carries both cartouches of King Amasis and the impression of an archaic Greek seal with the representation of a merman or Triton; and the bronze mounting for a statuette, inscribed both in Egyptian and Greek, the latter recording the dedication to 'Theban Zeus', i.e. the Egyptian Amun. At ABYDOS Greeks scratched their names on what they took to be the temple of the hero Memnon (really the funerary temple of Seti I).

South again, at Egyptian THEBES, and the great sanctuaries of Luxor and Karnak, we find more Greek pottery – Corinthian and East Greek – of the first two-thirds of the sixth century. A Karnak vase, fragments of which are in Oxford, is of especial interest. It shows the sacred ship of the Greek god Dionysus being carried and accompanied by men, some dressed as satyrs, the god's attendants (Fig. 40a). They wear loin-cloths to keep their tails on, brandish phalli, and play pipes. Processions like this were known in Athens, where the ship went on wheels, and in East Greece, at Smyrna, where the ship was carried. But they were well known in Egypt too, and particularly at Karnak and Luxor, where there was the great Opet festival each year in which the ship of the god Amun was carried (Fig. 40b). Similar processions were held at Siwa Oasis in the Libyan desert, where there was a shrine of Amun much respected by the Greeks, and often visited by them, as of 'Zeus Ammon'. Here the image of the god gave oracles by guiding the ship. That the only Greek representation of this scene should be found at Karnak seems more than coincidence, and it may well be that it was deliberately dedicated there because it was so appropriate. It may even have been painted in Egypt, for it is related to some other vases we have mentioned in like case. The success of these Greek potteries in Egypt is a noteworthy comment on the flourishing Greek communities in the country, for it is doubtful whether the Egyptians were interested in the vases in the sixth century, and most of the Greek pottery arriving in Egypt seems to have been destined for Greek tables. At Naucratis we have seen potteries turning out votives for the Greek temples there; and in the Daphnae situlae, the Karnak vase, and some others of doubtful parentage, evidence perhaps of the work of refugee Greek artists driven from their homes in Ionia by the Persian attacks of the 540s. We might even add another Karnak vase, on which another satyr leads a monster ram. The ram was the sacred animal form

40. (a) Fragments of an East Greek vase from Karnak;
(b) Relief at Luxor.

of the god Amun; but if the choice of scene on this dedication was deliberate, we can hardly applaud the tact of the dedicator.

Beyond Thebes there have been finds of Greek pottery at Edfu (Rhodian of about 600), and from much farther south, at

Sanam in Nubia, the Rhodian faience flask of Plate 12a. This is all that can so far be said of sixth-century Greek finds in Egypt. After 500, the import of Greek vases, now all of them Athenian, picked up again; but these begin to carry us outside our chosen period. One find only, of later date, I will mention for its excellence – the rhyton or figure vase in the shape of a mounted Amazon which was found at distant Meroe in Nubia (Plate 13b). It was made in Athens about the middle of the fifth century, and is now in Boston.

And what of the Carians who served beside the Greeks, and indeed the Greek Cypriots in Egypt? The Carians reveal themselves by their inscriptions – usually roughly scratched on rock or pottery. The most significant are those beside the Greek inscriptions on the rock-cut figures at Abu Simbel, cut by mercenaries in the Nubian expedition of 591. And there are Carian inscriptions too in Nubia itself, where there may have been a garrison. For the Cypriots, we have had occasion to note their presence at Naucratis. Cypriot pottery of sixth-century type has been found at Daphnae and Memphis, and in Nubia at Sanam; and their inscriptions at Gizeh, Abydos, Karnak, and Buhen in Nubia, to name only the more important.

The Egyptians were never well-disposed to foreigners, and it says much for Greek persistence, and for their fighting qualities which were appreciated by the kings, that they settled for so long and so successfully in the country. The Egyptians, Herodotus tells us, were careful to avoid Greek customs, and seemed rather to despise them :

No Egyptian, man or woman, will kiss a Greek, or use a Greek knife, spit, or cauldron, or even eat the flesh of a bull known to be clean, if it has been cut with a Greek knife.

And the head of a sacrificed animal would be cut off, cursed, and 'if there happen to be Greek traders in the market, it is sold to them; if not, it is thrown into the river'. 'A grotesque fact,' it has been called, 'that the Greeks were quite indispensable to the Egyptian kings, and at the same time the best-hated people in Egypt.' When Herodotus wrote, he described the attitude of a country at her nadir, under Persian domination, while Greece was at the zenith of her classical period. Egypt was to be prosperous again, but only as a member of the Greek empire founded by Alexander the Great.

THE PERSIANS IN EGYPT

Cambyses, king of Persia, marched against Egypt in 525 B.C. In his army were Ionian and Aeolian Greeks and Cypriots, subjects of the empire which had now spread even to the Greek islands off Asia Minor. In Egypt they faced the Ionian and Carian mercenaries of the Egyptian king, one of whose number, Phanes of Halicarnassus, had already deserted to the Persians – for which his fellows took horrible revenge on his sons. The Egyptian army was defeated, and at Memphis it was from a Greek boat, of Lesbos, that the Persian herald called for surrender. The Greeks in the Persian army then had to join in abortive expeditions to Siwa Oasis (the sanctuary of Zeus Ammon) and into Nubia, before they were dismissed home.

The archaeological evidence makes clear the effects on the Greeks in Egypt of the Persian invasion. The fort at Daphnae was abandoned. The import of Greek pottery to Naucratis and the rest of Egypt practically ceased. However, the setback did not last long, and by about 500, at Naucratis and elsewhere, Athenian pottery is beginning to arrive in some quantity, as well as Athenian silver coins. This does not necessarily mean that the East Greeks were no longer the merchants dealing with Egypt, for it could not have been until after the Persian Wars that Athens could have taken a serious and direct interest in Egypt as a source of corn.

Of the Persians themselves, we see sealings at Memphis from fine Achaemenid gems, for instance, and on many sites iron and bronze scale armour, some of which, however, might be attributed to the Ionian and Carian mercenaries. And from Memphis is a grave-stele with another prothesis scene, like Plate 9a, but less Egyptian in execution and clearly commemorating a Persian burial. But the archaeology of Persian Egypt, even of the Greeks in it, is not our concern here.

EGYPTIAN OBJECTS AND INFLUENCE IN GREECE

The Greeks got to know Egypt well over a century after they had reopened relations with the countries of the Near East. The impression made by the civilization of the Nile valley was no less forceful than that made by the east, but by that time the Greeks had matured in the 'orientalizing' phase of their culture and art, and were yet more discriminate in the foreign motifs or ideas which they admitted or adopted. Even so the example of Egypt prompted them to experiment in two new fields hitherto ignored by the Aegean peoples and yet to produce the most characteristic work of Classical Greece – monumental sculpture and architecture in stone.

For all the part played by Greek mercenaries in Egypt from the later seventh century on, it is not until the reign of Amasis that we find the Egyptian king taking a serious interest in the Greeks at home. Before his day Necho had dedicated armour at a Milesian temple, probably acknowledging the services of his Greeks, and the brother of a tyrant of Corinth, Periander, named one of his sons Psammetichos after the Egyptian king. Amasis was yet more generous to the Greek cities, and we read of his dedications in Cyrene, Rhodes (Lindos), and Samos, and a gift to Sparta of a figure-decorated linen corselet or belt, which the Samians intercepted as usual. The Samian tyrant Polycrates seems to have enjoyed an alliance with Amasis for a time, while the Egyptian king's benevolence to Cyrene was expressed by an alliance and his marriage with a Cyrenaean princess. Perhaps more remarkable was his contribution to the building of a new temple of Apollo at Delphi.

For the actual import of Egyptian objects to Greece after the foundation of Naucratis – earlier imports we have already mentioned – we have a mass of minor objects which were probably manufactured in Naucratis, and so are at least half-Greek rather than purely Egyptian works. The Naucratite faience scarabs and seals are found in plenty on many East Greek sites. They are hardly less common in central Greece, especially at Aegina, Sunium (en route to Athens), and Perachora (near Corinth), and were carried to the western colonies and Etruria. In general the distribution follows the pattern set by the states with a serious trading interest in Naucratis. To the small objects in faience we should perhaps add the glass flasks and alabaster vases which were becoming popular in Greece and for which we know there was a factory at Naucratis. Of more individual interest is the little basalt Egyptian figure brought to Rhodes by a Greek in the mid sixth century and dedicated by him after he had written his name on it in Greek. The typical alabastron shape in stone was soon copied in clay by East Greek and Athenian potters.

When we come to speak of Egyptian *influence* rather than objects, the material evidence is no less decisive. In non-material affairs the influence of Egypt was slight, or at any rate difficult to assess. Influence in religion was negligible, for all Herodotus' claims, although in myth and representations of myth there were certainly borrowings, as we shall see, and the Dionysiac processions with ships carried or wheeled are certainly most like Egyptian processions (see p. 154, above). Animal parodies of religious heroic action – like the Greek 'epic' of the Battle of the Mice and Frogs – had also long been at home in Egypt. In geometry and mathematics too the Greeks may have found something new. But in architecture and sculpture they certainly found much to impress them and lead them to new things, and these are matters which the archaeologist can investigate.

It was not until they visited Egypt that the Greeks saw colossal buildings constructed entirely of stone and featuring stone mouldings and columns with elaborately carved capitals and bases. At home they were used to mudbrick and wood, and less pretentious styles of masonry. In the Near East too brick was the main medium, columns were never of stone and were of comparatively little importance, and stone mouldings and capitals were virtually unknown. By the end of the seventh century Greek architects were moved to emulate the Egyptian manner, although not to imitate it in detail but to adapt it to local traditional architectural forms. In mainland Greece the result was the Doric order of architecture. Here the column capitals are like round cushions and their form seems to owe at least as much to the old Mycenaean Greek capitals as to Egyptian ones. Details of the upper works were more a translation of wood into stone, but one moulding, the hollow cavetto, was borrowed straight from Egypt, and was also put at the top of the gravestones in Athens. In East Greece the same interest in building all-stone temples was awakened, but here the decorative forms chosen for the parts – the capitals, bases, finials – were derived from the artist's repertoire of orientalizing forms, not Egyptian, many of them seemingly once employed in the east, on a smaller scale and in different material, for furniture. After some experiment, the Ionic order was evolved in the second quarter of the sixth cen-

a   b

41. (a) Egyptian palm capital; (b) Palm capital from Afrati, Crete.

tury, with nothing Egyptian in it beyond the guiding principle or idea which inspired its early stages. Indeed, the only architectural form which was borrowed straight from Egypt, the palm capital (Fig. 41a), was little used. There is a single seventh-century example from Crete (Fig. 41b), then others, East Greek, of the sixth century and later. For the possible Egyptian origin of the Ionic stepped altar see p. 136 above.

At about the same time as, or a little earlier than their first experiments in monumental stone architecture, the Greeks began to make monumental stone sculpture. The inspiration was again Egypt, where colossal stone statuary was commonplace. Hitherto the Greeks had made only small figures, in soft stone and in the orientalizing style ('Dedalic'). Now they exploited their resources of fine white marble and made lifesize or larger figures. Some, like the Nicandre dedication on Delos, were still in the old form, but in the new material and to the new scale. Others, the great statues of nude youths or *kouroi*, were much closer to the Egyptian models. But again the Greek artist, in accepting a new idea, a new technique, declined to copy blindly. The Egyptian figures like the *kouroi* stand back on their heels, back leg and spine straight and often supported by a pillar; and they are

a   b

42. (a) Egyptian stone figure;
(b) Greek *kouros* at Delphi.

clothed (Fig. 42a). The *kouroi* stand squarely on their two feet and convey a feeling of imminent motion; and they are naked (Fig. 42b). They clench their fists, like the Egyptians. From the beginning they are artistically finer and more sensitive (though less accurate) studies of the human form than any Egyptian work, although some observe even in detail the new canon of proportions worked out by the Egyptian artists. The Greeks soon broke with this canon, but there are memories of its use in Greece in Diodorus' story of the two sons of Rhoikos of Samos (see p. 149) who made the two halves of an Apollo statue in different places, but effected a perfect join by observing canons of proportion like the Egyptian. A further example of the changes wrought by the Greek sculptors is the group of marble scribes from the Acropolis at Athens, which are wholly Greek in their execution and dress, although as subjects they are quite Egyptian. Within a generation the Greeks had given new mean-

43. (a) Faience toilet dish from Sanam, Nubia;
(b) Clay copy of the same type from Rhodes.

ing and life to an art form which in Egypt had lain sterile for centuries.

For the moment still keeping to objects in the round, we may pick out a number of particular forms or conceptions in sixth-century Greek art which seem to owe something to Egypt. The great avenue of marble lions on the sacred island of Delos must surely have been inspired by Egyptian avenues of lions, sphinxes, or rams; and near Miletus a processional way flanked by massive seated figures seems to have been conceived in much the same spirit. Herodotus himself compared the round sacred lake before the lions on Delos with Egyptian sacred lakes. In smaller objects some favourite Egyptian forms seem to have been copied: the crouching lion with a bowl between its paws copied in clay in seventh-century Crete (Plate 8b); the naked swimming girl as

44. (a) Egyptian bronze mirror in Cairo; (b) Greek bronze mirror from near Odessa.

a handle to a flat dish copied in clay in sixth-century Rhodes (Fig. 43). A girl, again, as handle to a bronze mirror (Fig. 44a), becomes a most common motif in Greek art (Fig. 44b) from the mid sixth century on, appearing first at Sparta. Some of these motifs may perhaps have been transmitted via the Near East, but hardly all, and certainly not those picked up in the sixth century. The ultimate origin of all is quite clearly Egyptian. Representations of lions in Greek art have already occupied our attention for their relationship to eastern types, but we have also had cause to note one Egyptian lion-motif copied in Crete (Plate 8b), and again in the sixth century a peculiarly Egyptian lion is adopted by Spartan bronze-workers and appears on the handles of bronze vases. Other Egyptian leonine characteristics, not derived from the Near East, are displayed by East Greek stone statues and statuettes and some mainland Greek works of the latest seventh and sixth centuries.

The number of Egyptian traits in sixth-century Spartan art

45. (a) From a Spartan stone relief;
(b) From an Athenian vase of about 650;
(c) From an Egyptian painting.

which we have already remarked – and there will be more – may be due to her close relations with Cyrene in North Africa, but we must also remember Amasis' present, her vases at Naucratis, and the fact that for a time at least Sparta seems to have been on good terms with pro-Egyptian Samos.

The small faience artefacts – vases and statuettes – made in Rhodes and probably elsewhere, naturally reflect many motifs from the country in which the technique was learnt. The grotesque figures of the god Bes, a distant cousin of the Greek satyr but certainly not more closely related, are perhaps the most typical. In Rhodes too, some limestone statuettes are found

ather like those at Naucratis, but of seated figures with rams'
heads – the Egyptian Amun. Scarab seals copying the Egyptian
form are already being made in Greece in the seventh century,
and an Egyptian type of gold ring is also adopted.

46. From an Athenian black-figure vase in Florence (François vase).

Some new forms of wooden furniture which first become
popular in sixth-century Greece seem to copy Egyptian models
very closely, and no doubt the original pieces were imported
as well. The best examples are the thrones with animal legs (not
just feet) such as are seen on Spartan votive reliefs (Fig. 45a) and

vases, and elsewhere. There is much too in the subject of these
Spartan reliefs – hero and consort receiving offerings – to remind
one of Egyptian reliefs.

Strangely enough it seems that Egyptian wall painting made
almost as profound an effect on Greek artists and visitors as did
the sculpture and architecture. Here was decoration of a sort
virtually unknown to them at home, and certainly uncommon
in the Near East. The finest examples of Egyptian painting
which we possess belong to the New Kingdom, some 500 years
earlier than the foundation of Naucratis, but such was the con-
servatism in technique and subject in Egyptian art that it is not
unreasonable to look to them for an idea of what our Greeks

47. (a) From an Athenian black-figure vase;
(b) From an Egyptian painting.

saw, since extant examples of painting of the seventh and sixth
centuries in Egypt are so few. These major paintings had their
effect in three ways: by their colour, their style, and their subject
matter. It is just possible, too, that the effect was felt as early as
the middle of the seventh century, as soon as we have any evidence at all for regular visits by Greeks to Egypt. Already on some
Corinthian, and particularly on Athenian and island vases, we find
attempts at polychromy and the laying on of broad masses of
colour within painted outlines in the Egyptian manner. Already
too there may be intimations of Egyptian scenes or motifs in the
appearance of the battles of pygmies and cranes (Fig. 46),
which were also known to Homer, and in the little palmettes
which grow from the foreheads of figures on Athenian (Fig. 45b)
and island vases, like the Egyptian lotus headbands (Fig. 45c).

In the matter of style the effect was more subtle. The Greek artist was interested only in representations of men, gods, and animals, and not in the natural settings for his scenes or in landscape. When a tree or a vine is admitted it makes its way as best it may in the background or around the figures. In Egypt the natural proportions are more often observed, and on some sixth-century Greek vases the same principle is to be seen in striking contrast with the normal Greek treatment. We may mention the East Greek cup with a man dancing between two trees; the vineyard scene on the Karnak vase whose Egyptian provenance and subjects we have already discussed; a vintage on a votive plaque; an olive harvest; and a flock of birds which fly

48. From an Athenian
black-figure vase by
Exekias (London).

before Heracles as they might before Pharaoh on one of his Nile fowling parties.

Some individual scenes too are copied or adapted. On a Spartan cup (Plate 10b) the Greek king of Cyrene supervises the weighing and packing of wool in a scene which is very close to Egyptian representations of an overseer and the weighing and stacking of goods. On a vase made by an East Greek in Etruria (a 'Caeretan' hydria; Plate 11) the Greek hero Heracles copes with a flock of cowering Egyptians, servants of King Busiris who had hoped to maintain his record of sacrificing all foreigners who came his way. Heracles grasps and tramples his foes like the Pharaohs whose personal successes against hordes of adversaries were celebrated on many paintings and reliefs. The North African settings of both these scenes – on the cup and the hydria – add point to the Egyptianizing attitudes.

Other scenes or figures are inspired by contact with Egypt rather than copied. Such are those of the battle of the pygmies and the cranes. One famous version, on the François Vase painted about 570, shows the pygmies grappling the cranes with walking sticks and riding against them on goats (Fig. 46). A

49. (a) Clay alabastron by Amasis in Athens; (b) Egyptian stone alabastron; (c) Athenian clay alabastron.

strange scene on an Athenian vase shows three men doing obeisance before what appears to be a mummy (Fig. 47a). Their attitude is not one which we meet again on Greek work, but is purely Egyptian (Fig. 47b) and appropriate for such a scene of mourning. The 'mummy' looks rather like a Greek herm (a pillar with a head of Hermes), but not quite: it has no arm stumps or phallus (like a herm), but a criss-cross pattern which resembles the bandaging of a mummy. Although there is literary testimony about bowing to herms, it is perhaps easier to see here a Greek copy of a common Egyptian scene than to take it as a unique version of a Greek one. These isolated Egyptian scenes of course reflect no deeper awareness or influence of Egyptian practices or beliefs.

Negroes appear more often now in Greek art (Plate 13a; no doubt many Greeks took them for Egyptians) and monkeys; even a camel. Memnon's Ethiopian followers at Troy are shown on vases as negroes. The great Athenian vase painter Exekias names two such, Amasis (Fig. 48) and Amasos: after the Egyptian king, we might think – but there was an Amasis in Athens too, a colleague and rival potter-painter to Exekias himself. Perhaps he was dusky-skinned and had been born in Egypt, to pick up his foreign (though Graecized) name. In a city like Naucratis he could have seen the finest work of eastern and mainland Greek potters and painters and might there have informed his style with those almost exotic characteristics which make his vases so attractive. We should note too that it was he who, with one of the earliest of his vases to have survived (Fig. 49a), introduced the clay version of the Egyptian stone alabastron (Fig. 49b) to Athens. There are some rather later clay alabastra made in Athens which advertise the history of their shape by the figures of negroes painted on them (Fig. 49c).

The other borrowed scenes which have been mentioned must also have been inspired by artists who had themselves visited Egypt, for they could not have been readily transmitted on any portable Egyptian objects. Greeks, and artists, are inveterate travellers. The more so, then, Greek artists; and no less in antiquity than today.

GREEKS IN LIBYA AND CYRENAICA

Greeks settled in Cyrenaica as soon as they did in Egypt; but while the Greeks of Naucratis were merchants, the Greeks at Cyrene were farmers. A severe drought at home had driven them to seek new homes overseas. The way was made easier by traders who had visited North Africa before them, and the establishment of colonies there had a considerable commercial value. But the prime attraction was the fertile land of the Cyrenaican plateau and seaboard, an area whose climate and geographical position made it a logical extension for any Aegean civilization. Crete is no farther from Cyrene than it is from Athens.

Herodotus' story of the colonization of Cyrene presents an interesting account of the way these communities were dispatched, not always willingly (one adult male per family chosen by lot, in this case), but the constitutional background to the sending of a colony concerns us less than the physical reasons and results of it.

The colonists came from Thera, a relatively barren small island formed by the lip of the crater of a great volcano. It was occupied by Dorian Greeks, and lay to the south of the main group of the Cyclades, towards Crete. The island had seen some prosperity in the later eighth and seventh centuries, shown by the excavations there, but it could never support a large population. Soon after the middle of the seventh century the Theran party sailed for North Africa, and were guided by a Cretan to the offshore island of Platea – which may already have served for some time as a trading point with the mainland tribes, and is still a favourite resort of Greek sponge fishers. A temporary settlement was established there – we are told that the Samian skipper Kolaios put in on his famous voyage. Herodotus says that after two years the Therans moved to a site on the mainland opposite Platea, to Aziris, 'a charming place with a river on one side and lovely valleys on both'. After six years there, that is about 630 B.C., the native Libyans persuaded them to move to a better site inland, and showed them Cyrene, a well-watered and easily defensible hill in good country on the high plateau. The men took native wives, and in Herodotus' day the womenfolk still observed native restrictions about the eating of certain meats.

The community prospered, and in the sixth century invited new colonists from the Peloponnese and from the Dorian islands. In the years before the middle of the century, dissentients founded Barce, to the west on the plateau. Euhesperides (Benghazi) was established on the coast farther west, and, some 40 miles north-east, Taucheira. The latter at least was dependent on Barce. The access of prosperity enjoyed by the newcomers alarmed the native Libyans, who invited the Egyptians to help them against the Greeks. Apries sent an army in 570, but it was heavily defeated. His successor Amasis was kindlier: he married a Cyrenean princess, and sent dedications to the city. Later dynastic troubles in the royal family at Cyrene provoked other engagements with the native Libyans in which the Greeks did not fare so well. When the Persians took Egypt in 525, the people of Cyrene and Barce submitted and sent presents. Further dissents led to the intervention of the Persian governor of Egypt. He took Barce, and marched as far as Euhesperides before retiring, harried by the Libyans. Men of Barce were taken as slaves to Bactria (the present Afghanistan-Russian border) and settled in a town given the name of their old home, where they still were in Herodotus' time. From about 515, Cyrene formed part of the Persian empire; but the archaeological evidence shows that if anything it enjoyed increased prosperity, for to these years can be attributed the finest sculpture and tombs, the greatest of the temples, and probably its first coinage.

The material evidence about the early Greek cities in Cyrenaica is rather scrappy, but Italian excavations in Cyrene and recent British ones in Euhesperides can tell us something.

At Cyrene the early town lay on the heights overlooking the sacred spring which the Greeks called Apollo's fountain. In front of this, and so outside any walled circuit there may have been, a sanctuary area was laid out. The earliest building we can recognize, perhaps of the early sixth century, is a simple shrine about 8.5 m. square, with two interior columns. The sixth-century votives found in it included some fine jewellery and bronzes as well as decorated pottery. Beside it, nearer the fountain, was the temple of Apollo. The earliest form of it is a fine Doric building of the mid sixth century or earlier, measuring some 16 m. by 30 m. It was rebuilt on the same foundations in the fourth century. The first temple on the heights, though still outside the old town, is that of Zeus – Zeus Ammon, as a compliment to the respected oracle in the Libyan desert, which the Greeks seem almost to have adopted. This was an immense Doric building, some 69 m. by 30 m., built before the end of the sixth century. In later times it held a marble copy of the famous

Zeus made by Phidias at Olympia. In fact by 500 Cyrene was as well equipped with major temples as any of the more important cities in Greece, and it could clearly vie with them in wealth.

Of the early tombs, the most important – apart from the probable tomb of the founder, which became a cult-place – are rock-cut, with architectural façades of two or more columns. The earliest of them may belong to the last quarter of the sixth century. The type is non-Greek, but such tomb façades are well known in the east, and it may be that they were introduced to the Greeks at Cyrene after their submission to the Persians, although it seems that the Persian governors of Egypt took little direct interest in the city's affairs.

The sculpture from the sanctuaries and town matches the excellence of the architecture. There are several figures of the mid sixth century or just before which betray a strong island Greek style, some clearly Samian, and other figures, *kouroi* and *korai*, of the late sixth and early fifth century which are closer in style to the work of the Dorian Peloponnese.

The little pottery from Cyrene reflects the city's history and overseas relations. The earliest piece alleged to be from Cyrene is an eighth-century cup in Berlin, made in Athens or perhaps Sparta; but it is difficult to believe in its provenance, and nothing else so early has been found in controlled excavations. Other and better authenticated finds show that the Peloponnese is well represented and East Greece only slightly; quite different from Naucratis. The earliest, perhaps still of the seventh century, is Corinthian, and towards the middle of the sixth century there is some Spartan. Athenian is already appearing at this date. The only East Greek is some Chian of the type which we have suspected (p. 139) was being made in Naucratis rather than in the island of Chios itself. But the yield of early pottery from Cyrene has been disappointing. A piece of incised tridacna shell may have arrived from the east by 600.

Cyrene started minting her own coins in the last quarter of the sixth century, on the standard used by Athens, Corinth, and Samos. One device on them was the silphion plant (Plate 12d). This was a wild vegetable which resisted attempts at transplanting and flourished only in Cyrenaica. It completely disappeared, probably through bad husbandry, early in the Roman period. Its leaf could be eaten like cabbage and its root pickled, but its main value lay in the sap, which was prized as a medicine or a flavouring. It must have been an important export, and contributed no little to the prosperity of the Greeks in Cyrenaica; but it was certainly not the only export of a land rich in corn, fruit, and horses.

At Barce nothing early has been excavated. Aziris is located but not explored. At Euhesperides and Taucheira the excavations have yet to be fully published. At the former the earliest pottery goes to the mid sixth century, and includes a little East Greek and Athenian; at Taucheira there are now finds of the early sixth century.

The Libyan natives, nomad tribesmen, are archaeologically

50. From an Athenian red-figure vase by
Euphronios.

unknown, or at least inaccessible, and their culture – described so vividly by Herodotus – had no material influence on the Greeks who had settled among them. The Greek hero Heracles was said to have encountered a Libyan giant, Antaios, and wrestled with him. A fine Athenian vase painting of little before 500 (Fig. 50) renders Antaios in a manner in which Libyans are often shown in Egyptian art; in sharp contrast with the sleek civilized Heracles.

Some degree of 'native' influence can be seen in the worship of Zeus Ammon in Cyrene. The cult derived from the famous oasis shrine of Amun in the Libyan desert, whose oracle came to share the reputation accorded to those of Dodona and Delphi in Greece. The head of Zeus wearing Amun's ram-horns appears on coins of Cyrene (Plate 12d). There is brief mention by Herodotus of another oasis in which some Samians were living in 525; it is probably Khargeh Oasis. They had called it the Isle of the Blessed, and were probably veteran mercenaries who had settled down to a quiet life: surely one of the most unusual and appealing of the remote Greek communities in this period.

Bibliography

There is no handy archaeological history of Egypt in these years, but the political background is well summarized in Drioton and Vandier, *L'Égypte*, 1952, and in more detail in Kienitz, *Die politische Geschichte Ägyptens*, 1953.

NAUCRATIS: Petrie, *Naukratis*, I, 1886; Gardner, *Naukratis*, II, 1888; Hogarth, *Brit. School Ann.*, V, 1898–9, *Journ. Hell. Stud.*, XXV, 1905; *Brit. Mus. Cat. Sculpture*, I : I; R. M. Cook, *Journ. Hell. Stud.*, LVII, 1937; von Bissing, *Bull. Soc. Arch. Alex.*, XXXIX, 1951.

DAPHNAE: Petri, *Tanis*, II, 1888; Cook, *Corpus Vas. Ant. Brit. Mus.*, VIII.

CYRENE: Chamoux, *Cyrène sous la monarchie des Battiades*, 1953; for the tombs, Cassels, *Pap. Brit. School Rome*, XXIII, 1955; Paribeni, *Cat. delle sculture di Cirene*, 1959.

For Greco-Egyptian faience: von Bissing, *Zeit und Herkunft*, 1941; Greek vases in Egypt: Boardman, *Journ. Hell. Stud.*, LXXVIII, 1958, *Brit. School Ann.*, LI, 1956. A useful though now dated survey of Egyptian influence in Greece is von Bissing's *Der Anteil der äg. Kunst*, 1912. For Egyptian finds in Greece: Pendlebury, *Aegyptiaca*, 1930; Porter and Moss, *Topographical Bibliography*, VII, 1951; Boardman, *Cretan Coll. Oxford*, 1961; Samos, *Ath. Mitt.*, LXVIII, 1953; *Perachora*, I and II, 1940 and 1961.

CHAPTER 5

ITALY, SICILY, AND THE WEST

GREEK colonization on the shores of the western Mediterranean is well documented and forms an essential part of any history of the Greek world. It was with the western Greeks that the growing power of Rome first had to deal, and so to them in large part are due the continuity and transmission of Greek culture through Rome to the later western world.

The Greek cities in the west were prosperous, *nouveaux riches*; their temples were that little bit bigger than those at home, their art that little bit more ornate. Artists and philosophers could readily be tempted from Greece by commissions or lecture tours, and their work did not always suffer. And in more recent times these cities were more readily accessible to excavators, whose experience on other Italian sites had led them to appreciate sources of major architectural or sculptural work. In all this the archaeology of the earliest years of the colonies has generally come off second best, except where the early cemeteries gave promise of yielding Greek vases as handsome as those from the Etruscan graves.

The evidence in ancient historians for the foundation and early history of the colonies is well set out in other works, and this is no place for an account of their internal politics and wars. Here our main interest is in the physical history of the colonies in their earliest days, their relations both with native populations and rivals like the Phoenicians, and the characteristics of the arts which they derived from homeland Greece and then developed independently. It is in these matters that the archaeologist can hope to fill out the literary record, and for some problems – of relations with foreigners and even relative dates of foundations – his evidence may sometimes claim priority; remembering, of course, how much his chronology still depends on the ancient historians' dates for some colonial foundations (see p. 27 above). Where exact dates are given in this chapter, it will be realized that they are derived from ancient writers. But first something must be said about the colonists – who they were, where they came from, and why they went where they did.

It is not uncommon today to read that trade did not play a very important role in early Greek history in general or in the founding of colonies in particular; that for the latter land-hunger and overpopulation were more pressing motives. Two chapters already in this book have been largely devoted to overseas trading enterprises by the Greeks, in the east and in Egypt, and it would be idle to pretend that considerations of trade did not provide some part of the motive in founding many colonies, and the major part in a few. Certainly, knowledge of possible sites for colonial development could only have been won from the reports of merchants who had already explored the shores of the western Mediterranean. The earliest colonies in the west were founded by Euboeans, not on the nearest good farmland, but in a position which gave the most immediate opportunities for trade with Etruria, and they were supported by foundations safeguarding the passage to them through the Straits of Messina. They may even have done some preliminary exploration in South France and North Africa, as we shall see. As in the east, the commodities most sought after were metals – iron, copper, and (from remoter sources supplying Etruria) tin. And as in the east, the Greek states who initiated these trading settlements were the Euboean cities of Eretria and Chalcis, with the difference that here our evidence for their identity is literary as well as archaeological. Much later, Marseilles too was founded primarily as a port for trade with Gaul, on the tin route from the north; and once her routes were closed to her, new towns on the North Adriatic took her place.

For most of the colonies, however, the choice was more simply strategic and economic. First, to find a defensible position – steep acropolis, peninsula, or offshore island – the last being the sort of site which merchants dealing with the natives would already have sought out. Secondly, to see that they had at hand good cultivable land to support a growing community. There were not many such sites, and most of them were already occupied, so that the native population usually had to be dealt with, by diplomacy or force; and very soon Greek met Greek, and the interstate quarrels which form the pattern of early Greek history grew as lively and as vicious in the new foundations as they were at home, and could only be forgotten (and that only by some) in the face of a common foe – the Persians in the east, the Carthaginians in the west.

Of the cities which sent the colonies, those with an interest in trade, like the Euboeans, were prompted by the same motives which had led them to the markets of the Near East over a generation before. The others were those whose growth of population had outstripped their agricultural resources, and who were not prepared to meet the crisis by attacking their neighbours like the Spartans, or by a radical change in their home economy – an export drive – like the Athenians and the Chians. It was not only the large cities which had cause to dispatch part of their population to fend for themselves overseas, but it was generally they who had the resources and transport for mounting such an expedition, in which families from smaller towns would take part. But it was not always whole families who emigrated, nor was the move always voluntary. The Therans who went to Cyrenaica were men chosen by lot, one from each family, and they went unwillingly. Such parties, sometimes only a few dozen men, would find their wives from among the natives. Again, the Spartans sent to found Tarentum were illegitimate children, born in a time of war when the Spartans had sworn not to return until victorious, but had yielded to the complaints of their women and sent some youngsters home on compassionate leave. The children, grown up, came to resent their lack of rights, fomented revolt, and were packed off to found a colony. Elsewhere too we read of a dissident party within a city choosing (or being obliged) to emigrate. A more tragic reason might be like that of the Phocaeans, whose city was sacked by the Persians and who went to look for a new home. Once in these new homes, the colonists were politically independent of their mother city, and formed new city-states in their own right; but there were still ties of blood, religion, and, we may be sure, trade.

The colonizing cities are usually clearly identified in the historical record and from their institutions. The archaeological evidence for the earliest days of the colonies often reflects both their source and the identity of their new friends. First, however, we should remark on the ubiquity of Corinthian pottery. Corinth herself was only involved in the foundation of Syracuse in 733, but such was the popularity of her pottery that it was carried and used by many other states, as we have already observed in previous chapters. Indeed, of the colonizers, the

Achaean cities and Megara had no other fine ware. The pottery of the Euboeans, first to settle in the west, is recognized in their earliest colony, at Pithekoussai, and its style can be traced at Cumae and in early Greek vases made for Etruria. But after the eighth century the Euboeans' active interest in the west dwindles, and their pottery can no longer be recognized there, although their colonies waxed strong. Rhodes was the first of the East Greeks to send a colony to the west, but East Greek pottery is found in many other of the early colonies. This is more an indication of trading interests than of cooperation in the settlements. Sixth-century Chian wine jars can be recognized at Syracuse, Mylae, and Marseilles, and the island's finer pottery at Tarentum, Selinus, Gela, Catane, Marseilles, and in Etruria. Fikellura vases (of Rhodes or Samos, see p. 141) are found in Syracuse and Gela. And there are many fine East Greek vases, not all perhaps Rhodian, on other sites from the mid seventh century on. There is also a host of plainer striped vases from unidentified East Greek centres, among them probably Phocaea, which were widely carried and often locally imitated, as in Gaul. Crete joined Rhodes in founding Gela, but Cretan (?) flasks are found in earlier Euboean colonies, and it may be that the island shared with Corinth some of the trade in perfume to the west. The western markets, Greek and Etruscan, were the proving grounds for the selling qualities of the more ambitious black-figure vases of the sixth century. Here the Athenian wares drove the Corinthian out of the competition, but there was always a small market for Sparta's finer cups. This trade in fine pottery tells us nothing of fresh settlement or even the identity of the traders, but the consumer demand had some interesting effects on production, as we shall see.

Before we turn to the individual cities we may briefly consider earlier Greek contacts in this part of the Mediterranean. There is evidence for a lively Cretan and Mycenaean interest in the Lipari Islands and parts of Sicily – especially the south east – from about 1600 B.C. to the end of the Bronze Age. In the islands at least there seem to have been small trading settlements. In Italy itself a settlement was certainly established at Tarentum, not quite on the site of the later colony but at Scoglio del Tonno opposite (Fig. 55, p. 194). It flourished from about 1400 to 1200 B.C., and from the style of the Mycenaean vases found there it seems likely that it was used as a trading post by Rhodians. Slighter Mycenaean finds have been made in Italy – notably on the island of Ischia, where the city of Pithekoussai was later to be founded – and in Malta. While echoes of Mycenaean civilization may be caught as far away as Spain or even Britain, there is no question of direct connexions with the Aegean world. The memory of Greeks in Italy and Sicily survived in a most confused form in some myths, and especially in the stories of Odysseus' wanderings, but the break in contact after 1200 B.C. was almost complete, and the later Greek voyages to the west do not seem to have been conditioned or guided by the experience of their Mycenaean forebears as much as they were in the east, where the break was incomplete or of shorter duration.

GREEK CITIES IN ITALY AND SICILY

In this section the earliest finds in the principal colonies are discussed and their archaeological record followed down to the early fifth century. This is done in outline only, since their story soon becomes one with that of mainland Greece rather than an account of colonies on foreign soil. Indeed, to later historians, they were known collectively as Great Greece, Magna Graecia.

The strict chronological order of foundation is broken here, to keep together important groups of colonies or colonizers. We have, then:

Euboeans in central Italy	Pithekoussai, Cumae
Euboeans in eastern Sicily	Naxos, Leontini, Catane
Euboeans in the Straits	Zancle, Mylae, Rhegium
Dorians in Sicily	Syracuse, Megara Hyblaea
Rhodians and Cretans in Sicily	Gela
Achaeans in South Italy	Sybaris, Croton, Caulonia, Metapontum, Posidonia
Spartans and others in Southern Italy	Tarentum, Siris, Locri
Syracusan expansion	Acrae, Casmenae, Camarina

Colonies in western Sicily   Selinus, Acragas, Himera
The latest foundations   Lipara, Velia

PITHEKOUSSAI (Ischia). There is an ancient tradition that Pithekoussai was founded by the Euboeans of Eretria and Chalcis before they settled at Cumae, on the mainland opposite, and this tradition has been vindicated by the recent excavations. The town, on Monte di Vico at the north of the island of Ischia, has yet to be properly explored, but has already yielded pottery of the eighth century and architectural terracottas from a sixth-century temple; and there seems to have been another early settlement at Castiglione farther to the east, where some Mycenaean Greek vases had arrived long before. It is the cemetery south west of Monte di Vico which has been more fully excavated. The graves generally hold cremation burials, and are covered with low stone or earth tumuli in a fashion unfamiliar except in parts of East Greece. The earliest pottery is certainly of the years before the middle of the eighth century. There is a fair quantity of Corinthian, but some Euboean too, notably the imitations of Corinthian of the type found in Al Mina, the Euboeans' eastern trading town (see p. 63, group 2). Locally made vases are in a style which we should recognize as Euboean, and include an

51. Shipwreck on a vase from Pithekoussai.

unusual Late Geometric scene of a shipwreck (Fig. 51), which may tell of an incident on the voyage west (there *are* sharks in the Mediterranean) or be a heroic story, as of Odysseus. There is some Cretan and East Greek pottery in the early graves, including a cup inscribed with a challenge to Nestor's famous cup of which Homer sang. It reads: 'Nestor had a most drink-worthy cup, but whoever drinks of mine will straightway be smitten with desire of fair-crowned Aphrodite.' More interesting reflections of Euboea's interests at the other end of the Mediterranean are the Near Eastern seals and the Egyptian faience and scarabs which also appear in the eighth-century graves.

Strabo says that the Eretrians and Chalcidians of Pithekoussai quarrelled, and the former left – an echo of the bitter rivalry which flared up in the eighth century between the mother-cities in Euboea. He adds that the settlers left the island after a volcanic eruption and earthquakes; and Castiglione at least, where some Geometric pottery has been found, seems to have been over-whelmed. There are supposed to have been gold mines on the island.

CUMAE lies on the mainland opposite Ischia, twelve miles west of Naples. There is a good acropolis, a marshy hinterland, and a safe beach rather than a sheltered harbour. It was primarily a foundation of the Chalcidians. To the north of the town lay the early cemetery, and much of this has been excavated. A number of native pre-Greek graves can be identified, furnished with plain pottery and bronzes of Italian types. In some of them are Greek cups and Egyptian faience objects which must have come from Pithekoussai, and represent contact between the newly-arrived Greeks and the natives before ever there was a Greek town at Cumae. The earliest pottery in the wholly Greek tombs is later than the earliest from Pithekoussai. It should probably be dated little before 750 B.C., but unfortunately there is no plausible date for the foundation in any ancient author. The pottery is mainly Corinthian, but there are Euboean and local styles, probably derived from Pithekoussai, and some Cretan vases. There is one fine Cycladic vase of the mid seventh century, but on the whole there are few other imports to be recognized until the mass of Corinthian pottery, which is most common from about 600 and is then displaced by the arrival of the fine Athenian black-figure vases later in the sixth century. With them come a few Spartan. There is very little East Greek at all until the sixth century, and then mainly perfume flasks. As trade with Etruria grew, more and more Etruscan objects – pottery, bronzes, jewellery – arrived; but the artistic relations of the Euboean colonies with Etruria are best considered later in the chapter.

One find at Cumae, or alleged to be from Cumae, deserves special mention. It is a bronze cauldron with bulls-head attachments, now in Copenhagen (Fig. 13a, p. 85). It is typical of the eastern bronzes which reached the Greek world before and after 700 B.C. (see pp. 83 ff.), and its appearance in Euboean Cumae underlines Euboea's part in the eastern trade; or it might be said to support an ancient tradition that Cumae (Kymai) is named after Aeolian Kyme in Asia Minor, which had ready access to Phrygia where the bulls-head cauldrons were known. In view of the flow of Syrian and Phoenician objects to Pithekoussai and Cumae, and to Etruria beyond, the former explanation for the cauldron is probably the correct one.

NAXOS. According to Thucydides the first Greek foundation in Sicily was made by the Chalcidians at Naxos in 734. The site was the first landfall in Sicily for ships rounding the 'toe' of Italy from the east. It was a headland site, just south of Taormina, made virtually a peninsula by the stream to its south, and it enjoyed the use of a small but fertile valley inland which proved especially favourable to the vine. In recent excavations in the town, pottery from its earliest days is reported, but all that has been published is of the later sixth century – Corinthian, Athenian, and local pottery, and figurines, and terracottas from a temple. What is more important at present is that there were clear signs that the Greek settlement displaced a native one on the same site. It is now said to have been fortified in the sixth century. The town was never of first importance in Sicily, but in its early years it served as a base for the foundation of two other colonies, at Leontini and Catane.

LEONTINI. Six years after the foundation of Naxos, the Chalcidians there set out to found another colony, at Leontini. The city was occupied by native Sicels, whom they expelled. It lay on the far side of the rich plain through which the River Symaithos flows, but more than six miles from the sea, so it was primarily an agricultural community. Recent excavations have shown that the first settlement was on the hill of San Mauro, and that there was a fortified circuit built about the middle of the seventh century. The earliest pottery found so far is Corinthian, but some Euboean types are represented also, as well as a local ware with figure decoration. At about 600 or soon after, the circuit was enlarged to take in a second hill, Metapiccola, where foundations of a sixth-century temple have been exposed. No tombs earlier than the mid sixth century have been found so far. From old excavations in the cemetery comes a superb bronze bowl with rams-head attachments. There are traces of the native Sicel village below the Greek town on San Mauro, and there was another Sicel village on Metapiccola.

CATANE. Chalcidian control of the rich plain of the Symaithos was established by the foundation of Catane, on its north side, soon after the foundation of Leontini at the south. The settlers came from Naxos. Unlike Leontini, Catane was on the coast, and it had a good harbour. Eruptions of Etna and lava-flow have rendered the ancient town unrecognizable, but a pre-Greek native cemetery has been excavated, and more recently a notable collection of votive pottery has been recovered from what must be the site of the ancient acropolis. None of it is earlier than about 600, but besides the expected Corinthian, Athenian, and 'Chalcidian' there is a lot of Chian pottery, some other East Greek wares, and good Spartan vases.

At the same time as the establishment of these sites on the east coast of Sicily the Euboeans took steps to see that they could control the approach to their earlier foundations at Pithekoussai and Cumae. To effect this, Zancle and Rhegium were founded, on either side of the straits between Italy and Sicily:

ZANCLE (later Messina) was founded perhaps very soon after Naxos by settlers from Cumae (who had especial interest in free passage through the straits) and from Chalcis. The very first settlers are said to be 'pirates' from Cumae – something of a reflection on the trading techniques of Greeks in the west. Zancle lies just south of the narrowest point in the straits, but it is blessed with a superb natural harbour whose sickle shape perhaps gave the town its name. The earliest town seems to have been largely to the south of the harbour, but finds are scattered and not very informative. At the tip of the natural mole encircling the harbour there seems to have been a sanctuary, and here the earliest pottery has been found – Corinthian and imitations (? Euboean), of the later eighth century. In the seventh and sixth centuries there is the expected showing of Corinthian and Athenian wares, and a very little East Greek.

Zancle's strength lay in her position on the straits and in her harbour. She had virtually no agricultural resources, and was obliged to look for a dependency to supply her needs. This was Mylae.

MYLAE (Milazzo). Twenty miles west of Zancle, on the north coast of Sicily and facing the Lipari Islands, is a small coastal plain behind a long rocky peninsula. Mylae was founded at the base of this peninsula by settlers from Zancle, who evicted the Sicels in occupation there. Recent excavations may tell us more of Mylae than we can hope for from her mother city. The earliest datable Greek pottery is of course Corinthian, and can be compared with the earliest from Syracuse, so the foundation may be somewhat earlier than that suggested by ancient sources (716 B.C.) and nearer that of Zancle, as we might expect. From the later eighth and seventh centuries a quantity of 'Cycladic' pottery is reported (probably Euboean or of Euboean type), with a little Cretan (as on other Euboean sites in the west). In the late seventh and sixth centuries there is much more East Greek, including plain striped wares and Chian wine jars.

RHEGIUM. The Chalcidians of Zancle invited the Messenians from the Peloponnese to join them in the foundation of Rhegium. It lay nearly ten miles south of Zancle, on the other side of the straits, chosen (as was Zancle) for its strategic position controlling the passage. The date of its foundation cannot have been long after that of the city opposite. The ancient town lies beneath modern Reggio, and our knowledge of it derives largely from chance finds and sporadic excavation. Of its earliest years

almost nothing is known beyond its general location south of
the modern harbour. One early vase of about 700 B.C. is like
the Euboean and Cycladic imitations of Corinthian. From the
later seventh century on are some Corinthian vases, and in the
sixth century a growing import of Athenian and East Greek,
with some Spartan pieces and many 'Chalcidian', to which we
shall return (p. 205). The Greek pottery of Euboean type found
in native villages to the east, near the later colony of Locri, may
represent the spread of Euboean interests on this side of the
straits, which was curtailed when Locri was founded.

52. Sketch plan of Syracuse.

SYRACUSE (Fig. 52). The richest of the Greek cities in Sicily
was Syracuse. It was founded by the Corinthians, only one year
after the Euboeans settled in Naxos, according to Thucydides.
Naxos had the most opportune harbour for shipping from the
east on this coast of Sicily, but Syracuse had the best. Similarity
in place-names in Chalcis and Syracuse has led some to argue
that the Euboeans were interested in Syracuse before the Corinthians. This might seem to be supported by the presence of
eighth-century Euboean sherds in the native town of Castelluccio

not far away, and some of the earliest pottery from Syracuse itself shows affinities with the wares of the Greek islands and Euboea. But we may also remember the tradition that Archias, the leader of the Corinthian settlers, picked up some Greeks en route, from Zephyrion at the toe of Italy. The same tradition says they were Dorians, but archaeological evidence shows Euboeans near the Zephyrion promontory (by Locri, see above) at this time.

The deep bay at Syracuse was partly closed by the island Ortygia (Quail-island), which was nearly attached to the mainland at its northern edge. There was a native Sicel settlement on the island, which was replaced by the new Greek town. This long remained the heart of the colony – easily defensible, with harbours to north and south, and a good source of water, the spring Arethusa. A sanctuary of Athena there may have been one of the first to be built by the new settlers. Of the temple we know nothing until the earlier sixth century, when there is the evidence of elaborate clay revetments which adorned the brick and wood building. At the end of the century its altar was rebuilt in a more ornate form, with some Ionic decoration. The temple's fifth-century Doric form is still largely preserved in the fabric of the later cathedral. Another and earlier Doric temple on Ortygia was for Apollo. It is of the mid sixth century, 25·6m. by 55·3m., with the long plan and deep porches seen elsewhere in Sicily. An Ionic temple has now been found.

In the later sixth century the island Ortygia was linked to the mainland by a causeway, but it is clear from the finds of pottery that even in the early years of the colony the landward slopes below the cliffs of the Epipolae heights were occupied. It was here that the later market place (agora) stood, but of the early buildings only part of some sixth-century houses has been excavated. Farther south, and a little inland from the great bay, stood the temple of Olympian Zeus. Its seventh-century form again is known only from clay revetments. In its Doric stone form it is very like the Apollo temple on Ortygia, but some twenty-two feet (seven metres) longer and possibly a little older.

The early cemeteries lay to the west and north of the landward part of the city; the earliest (Fusco) being to the west. The earliest Greek pottery – from the cemetery, from beneath the temple of Athena, and from the town – is Corinthian, and this of course remains the most popular ware here. Even the sixth-century Athenian vases which won almost all other markets are comparatively rare. As a result, perhaps, other Greek wares are better represented. East Greek vases arrive from about 700 on; some are recognizably Rhodian, and in the sixth century a few Chian and Fikellura are found. Two very early fragments are more curious than important – one, of the second half of the eighth century, is Cycladic; the other, of about 700, is one of the few Athenian pieces which travelled west so early. Of the first half of the seventh century are some local vases (as Fig. 53)

53. Vase from the Fusco
cemetery, Syracuse.

decorated, it may be, by an immigrant Argive painter who had a fairly eclectic taste. Among the smaller finds we may pick out ivories – fibulae, a relief, and a seal – which are very like those found in the Peloponnese, but are almost unknown otherwise in the western colonies; and Cycladic stone lamps. The general archaeological picture shows a steady growth in prosperity through the seventh and sixth centuries, with ambitious temple-building programmes. In the fifth century the city was to become one of the great powers not merely in the west but in the whole Greek world.

MEGARA HYBLAEA. The only Megarian colony in Sicily was

not easily established. The first settlement was made on the east coast at Trotilon. The settlers were invited to move to Chalcidian Leontini, near by, but were later expelled and moved to the rocky peninsula of Thapsus. After a few months there, they were invited by the local Sicel king to occupy a site on the coast which was inevitably dominated by the greater city of Syracuse some ten miles to the south. Thucydides says that Megara Hyblaea was founded six years after Syracuse. Archaeological arguments have been adduced to reverse this order, but the Megarians' difficulties in settling down, and their final home in a poorish site so near to the magnificent harbour of Syracuse, perhaps speak more clearly than over-detailed arguments from few vases of rather dissimilar types.

There may be trace of the short-lived settlement on Thapsus in the tomb with late eighth-century pottery, which might well be that of Lamis, the Megarian leader who died there. There is nothing else Greek on the site.

The city of Megara Hyblaea lay on a small plateau by the sea, where there was no natural harbour but an adequately sheltered anchorage. Recent French excavations have told us much more about the site's early history than the earlier sporadic exploration. There was clearly no native site here when the Greeks first settled. The town, not the cemetery, has yielded the earliest pottery, which is Corinthian. From about 650, East Greek and Etruscan vases appear, and in the sixth century Athenian and one or two Spartan. Some local vases of the mid seventh century are related to Syracusan vases, but there seems to have been a flourishing local school through much of the seventh century. In the town, some early houses have been excavated, and in the north-west, traces of sixth-century temples – one Doric with fine clay revetments, another a simpler structure with plain ashlar walls. In the same area are votive deposits going back to about 700 B.C. The southern part of the later city is said not to have been occupied before 650, yet this is the part nearest to the anchorage. No graves earlier than 650 have been found. There are some unusual products of a local school of sculptors of about 550 (Plate 14b), and towards the end of the century some ornate decorative carving on tomb monuments in an Ionic style. In

483 the city was destroyed by Syracuse, and there are no other finds until its reoccupation in the fourth century B.C.

GELA. The last of the major Dorian foundations in Sicily was a joint effort by the Rhodians and Cretans. Thucydides dates it to 688. The city occupied a low hill by the sea just west of the mouth of the River Gelas on the south coast of the island, and commanded a rich coastal plain. A native settlement was displaced from the hill, but the early Greek town did not occupy the whole great area of the classical city. It may have been no more than a walled citadel with extra-mural sanctuaries to the east. The most notable early temple is that of Athena, which was decorated with a fine series of painted clay revetments. A smaller sanctuary, perhaps of Demeter, lay on the other side of the river and was founded before the end of the seventh century. Pottery has been recovered from the temple deposits and tombs. As well as the customary succession of Corinthian and Athenian vases, the East Greek wares – especially of Rhodes, with some of Chios – are quite common; and the joint-founder, Crete, is represented by a few early pieces. There was a local school for figure-decorated pottery in the mid seventh century, comparable with those of Syracuse and Megara Hyblaea. The Rhodian character of the colony remains clear well into the sixth century, with numerous imports and great similarity in burial customs – like child-burial in storage jars, etc. The extent of Geloan contacts with the natives (Sicans) has been well shown by recent excavations at Butera, fifteen miles away, where there are native tombs of the mid seventh century with several Greek vases in them. The period of Gela's greatest prosperity was at the end of the sixth century and the beginning of the fifth. It is marked by considerable building activity and a great variety of the finest bronzes, vases, and other imports from Greece.

Euboean and Corinthian colonies had established trading points close to Etruria, then commanded the Straits of Messina, and controlled the best farmland in east Sicily. The next series of colonies, sent by the Achaeans from the north-west Peloponnese, were founded in the 'instep' of Italy and on the west coast south of Cumae, in positions which could exploit overland routes between the Ionian and Tyrrhenian Seas, by-passing the Straits of Messina. These are Sybaris, Croton, Metapontum, and to the west, Posidonia (Paestum). In the same region Tarentum (Taranto) was founded by Sparta, Siris by Colophon (in Ionia), and Locri by Locris (in Central Greece).

SYBARIS was chosen for the immensely rich plain it commanded rather than for its convenient position on the west-east coastal route and its overland proximity to the shores of the Tyrrhenian Sea. It was particularly noted for the wealth of its cornlands and the excellence of its wine. The foundation is dated in literary sources to about 720 B.C. The city's size and wealth, as well as the extravagant tastes of its citizens, became proverbial (cf. our 'sybarite'). And no less famous was its utter destruction by Croton in 510 B.C., when the waters of the river Crathis were diverted to lay waste the site. The ancient city is almost inaccessible beneath a heavy alluvial deposit; although excavations have so far revealed nothing of its former glory, a serious attempt to recover something of its archaeological record is now being made. None of the occasional finds has been earlier than the sixth century.

Sybaris commanded routes to the coast on the west and to the towns of Scidrus (not located), Sirinus, and Laus, which sheltered refugees from the disaster of 510. It is said to have served as the main entrepôt for Milesian trade with the Etruscans, and when Sybaris fell Miletus declared public mourning.

CROTON was founded soon after Sybaris. It too commanded good farmland, not so extensive as its rival's, but it also had a small double harbour by the promontory on which the citadel stood. Little is known of it archaeologically, but an important temple of Hera Lacinia, which stood on another promontory some six miles to the south-west, has been excavated. The main structure is of the fifth century, but the earlier finds include a figurine of a goddess holding her breasts, of the later seventh century.

Croton's territory lay mainly to the south-east. Its most important subsidiary foundation was at CAULONIA, which is better known from excavations, at least in the period of its greatest prosperity – the fifth century. Some fragments of early seventh-century pottery suggest an early foundation date, but after them hardly anything has been found earlier than some mid-sixth-century graves. The site embraced low hills beside a straight open beach with no real harbour.

METAPONTUM is about thirty miles west of Tarentum. It had no harbour to speak of, but enjoyed good farmland and lay at the end of a route west to Posidonia. The temple of Apollo Lykeios in the town has been partly excavated and has yielded votive figurines which perhaps go back to 700. The early cemeteries have not been found. Two miles to the north, a sanctuary of Hera was built on a low hill where there had been a native settlement. The Doric temple built there about 500 B.C. measured about 16·1m. by 33·5m. Fifteen of its columns still stand, known as the 'Knights' Tables' – Tavole Paladine.

POSIDONIA (Paestum). The foundation of Posidonia on the west coast of Italy, little over fifty miles south-west of Cumae, was the first challenge to the Euboean colonies' monopoly of trade with Etruria. The city may have been founded from Sybaris. There are good overland routes to the south, which can be traced through sites like that at Sala Consilina, where many sixth-century Greek finds have been made.

Two sites are involved, both partly excavated, of which the smaller, which seems to be the earlier, may be considered first. It lies near the mouth of the River Sele and comprises a sanctuary in which several temples and treasuries have been excavated. For the earlier history of the site, some late seventh-century Corinthian pottery takes us back to near its foundation date. The main temple, to Argive Hera, was a Doric building of little before 500 B.C. Some of its sculptural decoration (relief metopes) has been found (Plate 14a). Just north of it is a 'treasury', perhaps built by some other west Greek state to honour the goddess, from which there is a rich series of relief metopes with various mythological scenes. These date to the years around the middle of the sixth century. Other architectural sculpture must be attributed to other archaic buildings, not yet certainly identified.

The city site lay some eight miles to the south-east, on a low flat plateau quite near the sea. There are traces of its sixth-century walls, and the earliest finds reported are of the end of he seventh century. No cemetery earlier than the sixth century has been found. But the town's greatest glory lies in its three great Doric temples which still stand so well preserved and have excited the imaginations of visitors and artists for so long. The temples lay to the west of the main north–south road in the town. To the south are the so-called Basilica (mid sixth century, Plate 18a) and the Temple of Hera (mid fifth century), and to the north the so-called Temple of Ceres (late sixth century) which is probably better identified as of the goddess Athena. Beside the last are the remains of a smaller temple of the earlier sixth century. An exciting find of recent years, a little to the

54. Underground shrine at Posidonia.

south of the Athena Temple, is a small stone chamber whose roof alone shows above ground level (Fig. 54). It is in the form of a tomb, with the remains of a couch or bier in the centre, bronze jars full of honey along either wall and an Athenian painted vase in one corner; but no body. It stood in a small enclosure or precinct. Its purpose is still far from clear – a 'cenotaph' for the founder? a shrine of Persephone, queen of the underworld? On a vase found in the precinct is the inscription 'I am sacred to the Nymph'. The building is dated by the vases in it to about 520 B.C.

There are many native, perhaps Oenotrian, sites and cemeteries near by. In the twin-sites of Palinurus and Molpa on the promontory thirty-five miles south of Posidonia, Greeks and natives may have lived side by side after about 550 B.C., to judge from finds in excavations around the walls and in tombs.

TARENTUM (Fig. 55). We have already had occasion to remark on the choice of settlers sent by Sparta to Tarentum

55. Sketch plan of Tarentum.

(p. 178). Literary sources suggest a date for the settlement in the last decade of the eighth century, but the earliest tomb found in the town cemetery contains Corinthian vases which look a little earlier. However, the native Iapygian site at Scoglio del Tonno, opposite the Greek town, seems to have been in intermittent touch with Greece from Mycenaean times down to the early years of the colony, and in the seventh century the native towns inland were receiving Greek vases. Closer to Tarentum, several small villages were occupied by Greeks. Of these we may mention Leporano, just east of Tarentum, where Mycenaean pottery has also been found. This may be Satyrium, where the founders of Tarentum were said to have settled first.

The Greek city of Tarentum lies beneath the modern Taranto, on a fine peninsula site which embraces a large lagoon (the Mare Piccolo). Its port is the best in South Italy, and it commands good cornlands. Except for parts of a large sixth-century Doric temple, little is known of the early buildings, but the city's art and wealth are well attested by stray finds of votive offerings and the contents of tombs. Its connexions with its mother city are reflected in the fine Spartan vases found in sixth-century tombs. There is also a little East Greek and island pottery, including Chian, as well as the usual Corinthian and Athenian vases. The city's Spartan origin is revealed in many ways – cults, and the practice of burial within the walls.

SIRIS is supposed to have been founded by settlers from Colophon, in Ionia, who had been driven from their homes by the Lydians. This must have been just before 650 B.C. It was then an isolated Ionian colony on a coast otherwise dominated by Dorian settlers. Yet it prospered for a while, and no doubt it shared the overland trade west to the coast of the Tyrrhenian Sea. There is hardly anything to show for the early town, except an early sixth-century loom weight inscribed (significantly in Ionic script) 'I belong to Isodike'. About the middle of the century the town was destroyed by its non-Ionian neighbours Metapontum, Sybaris, and Croton.

LOCRI was founded from Locris in Central Greece in 673 (according to Eusebius). Near-by native Sicel villages (notably at Canale) had already been in close contact with Greeks, since several Greek vases have been found in them, some apparently made locally by Greek potters. There was a tradition that Dorian Greeks in this area were picked up en route by the expedition which founded Syracuse (see p. 187), but to judge from the pottery in the native towns these Greeks seem rather to have been islanders or Euboeans, who elsewhere too seem to have got on better with the Sicels than the Corinthians did. The vases are of the latest eighth and early seventh centuries. When Locri was settled the natives were ejected. We know most about the town and its temples in the fifth century, but pottery of its early years is reported, and there are tombs of the mid sixth century on. The town has no natural harbour, but would have served as the last port of call in Italy on a voyage to Sicily.

Locri established some colonies of her own, especially at Medma, Hipponium, and Metaurus, at the other ends of routes across the 'toe' of Italy to the Tyrrhenian Sea. The earliest finds at MEDMA, from tombs and votive deposits, take us back to near the beginning of the sixth century, so the foundation might even be seventh-century. The other two towns might be as early, but the finds from them are slight. Graves in a Sicel town near Hipponium (at Torre Galli) contain Corinthian pottery of the late seventh century to the later sixth; and Greek contacts (and perhaps occupation) induced a change in funeral customs from inhumation to cremation.

The seventh century saw the consolidation of the earliest Greek colonies in Sicily, and their expansion in the island with new foundations. Syracuse confirmed her control of the south-east by founding Acrae, Casmenae, and Camarina. Megara Hyblaea struck farther east to Selinus. Other moves to the east were by Zancle at Himera, and by Gela at Acragas. With the foundation of Acragas in 580, the Greek colonizing of Sicily was virtually at an end.

Of the Syracusan towns, ACRAE lay in a strategic position inland, just in sight of Syracuse. It had been an important Sicel hill town before the Greeks settled there in 663 (Thucydides' date). None of the pottery from the graves seems as early as the mid seventh century. Within the town there was a Doric temple of the later sixth century, and some other architectural pieces in an Ionic style which can be matched in the same period at Syracuse – notably decoration from an altar.

A little farther inland, at Monte Casale, a fortified town was established. Excavations there have not yet been published, but it seems that the earliest pottery is of the late seventh century and that an early fortification wall, archaic houses, tombs, and a sanctuary have been uncovered. This town is perhaps the best of the candidates for CASMENAE (said to have been founded in 643).

HELORUM, on the coast south of Syracuse, has yielded nothing earlier than the sixth century. It was primarily a farming community. CAMARINA, the most westerly Syracusan town, lay on the coast less than twenty miles south-east of Gela. It was founded in 598, and tombs to the north-east together with votives from a temple in the town belong to its earliest years. In 552 the city joined the native Sicels in a revolt against Syracuse and was defeated and destroyed, but its survival as a town is proved by the many graves with pottery of the later sixth century. It had no natural harbour, and the coast here and along much of South Sicily is marked by a succession of sandy cliffs and dunes.

SELINUS. The ruins of Selinus are the most impressive of any Greek city in Sicily. The site is not naturally a very good one, but it has a harbour and it commands good cultivable land. The walled acropolis lay on a low hill by the sea with the town spreading to the north of it. There is evidence for a regular planned town grid as early as the sixth century. Within the town are four large Doric temples. (The temples at Selinus defy ready identification by deities, and are known by letters, for which two different series operate.) Temple C is of the mid sixth century, Temple D a little later, and Temples A and O of the mid fifth century. There are also traces of earlier temples going back to before the middle of the sixth century.

Outside the walls were other sanctuaries. Beyond a stream to the west lay that of Demeter Malophoros (Apple-bearer), who was worshipped by the same name in the mother city of Megara. Her temple was a simple hall, but the precinct must have been one of the first to be laid out by the settlers. There was an associated cult of Zeus Meilichios, to whom simple stelae crowned by two carved human heads were dedicated. These are odd objects (Fig. 56), and the style of some seems native, but the inscriptions on them are Greek. To the north, another small archaic temple and altar have been discovered in recent years. East of the town lay three more Doric temples. Temple E(R) is of the fifth century, but both Temple F(S) and Temple G(T) (for Apollo) were begun in the last quarter of the sixth century. The last was a colossal building measuring 50·1m. by 110·1m., only exceeded in size by the slightly later Temple of Zeus at Acragas and the Ionic, earlier temples of East Greece.

No less impressive than the site itself are the finds of architecture, sculpture, and vases which it has yielded, and which represent the best of colonial Greek art in Sicily. For the early years of the colony our evidence comes from tombs and from the sanctuary of Demeter Malophoros. The dating of Corinthian pottery of the later seventh century has long relied on the earliest finds here and on Thucydides' date for the foundation, 627 B.C. Recently some Corinthian vases from the sanctuary of an earlier style have been published, and it is still not clear whether this means that a different ancient tradition putting the foundation at 650 is to be accepted, or that the vase-chronology should be seriously revised. The latter is difficult, since the series is now better established with other fixed points. Most of the early pottery at Selinus is Corinthian, being replaced

56. Stone stelae from Selinus

by Athenian in the second quarter of the sixth century, but there is also a fair amount of East Greek (Rhodian and some Chian) of the first half of the century, a little Spartan, and an unusual and large 'orientalizing' vase of the late seventh century painted in Sicily by an immigrant artist from one of the Greek islands.

Selinus takes its name from the wild parsley (Greek *selinos*) which grew there, and which appeared as the device on the city's coinage (Plate 19b).

ACRAGAS (Agrigento) was founded in 580 by Gela, and by the Rhodian settlers there, with reinforcements from home, rather than by the Cretans. It lies less than forty miles west of Gela, and the area had certainly often been visited before the town was established. There may even have been settlement, since pottery of the latest seventh and early sixth century is reported from a cemetery between the town and the sea (Montelusa), and there is a spring-house shrine of Persephone outside the walls (San Biagio) which may also have been in use by Greeks before 580. A native Sican settlement had been displaced. The steep acropolis lies over two miles from the sea, but the town – which spreads on the terraced ground to the south – was also included within a circuit wall before the end of the sixth century. The whole area enclosed is about one and a half square miles, an extravagant piece of planning for a young colony.

The temples on the great terrace which lay within the south limit of the town are for the most part of the fifth century, but the greatest of them, to Zeus Olympios, was begun at the end of the sixth century. Its size rivalled that of the great Temple G(T) at Selinus, whose building had already started when the Acragas temple was laid out, nearly 3m. wider. But the plan and construction are quite different, and a unique feature is the use of giant figures (Telamones) as structural supports on the outer screen walls. There were smaller temples of the later sixth century near the temple of Zeus and the Temple of the Dioscuri, and one of the second half of the century, also on the south terrace (Villa Aurea). The Athena temple on the acropolis is of about 500 B.C. Some archaic houses have also been excavated in the southern quarter of the town.

Apart from the inevitable succession of Corinthian and Athenian pottery in the sixth century, there is also a fair amount of pottery from Rhodes, mainly clay figurines and figure-vases. There is some archaeological evidence for the spread of Greek interests in the rich hinterland of Acragas in the sixth century. This is the time of the notorious tyrant Phalaris, and his brazen bull in which he roasted his opponents. But the zenith of the city's fortunes was not reached until the fifth century, when it wholly eclipsed its mother city Gela.

HIMERA. Expansion westward along the north coast of Sicily was left to the Chalcidian colonies of the straits, and of them Zancle had established a colony at Himera as early as 649 B.C. It was an easily defensible site, though not over-richly endowed in natural resources – land or harbour. But it might have proved a useful post for western trade, and it was to prove a challenge to the Phoenicians in the west of the island. It saw the defeat of the Carthaginians in 480, and was itself razed by them in 408. The site has yielded some pottery of the later seventh century, but excavations have been mainly devoted to the temple built to commemorate the victory of 480.

LIPARA. The Lipari Islands had been visited by Mycenaean Greeks, and must certainly have attracted Greek attention again as soon as the new colonies were founded. One early token of interest there is the faience *aryballos* (p. 144, Plate 12b). In the same private collection as this vase and also, it was said, from Lipari, were four *ushabti* figures of Egyptian faience. Their style is late and not closely datable, but it looks as though an Egyptian, or a Greek from Egypt, had intended his tomb to be properly furnished in the Egyptian manner. But when the Greeks came to live at Lipara, the acropolis had been unoccupied for some 200 years, as the finds show. A colony was established in the 570s, and then by Cnidians and Rhodians who, led by Pentathlos, had just failed to establish themselves in eastern Sicily at Lilybaeum, in the teeth of the Phoenicians. In recent excavations in the acropolis and cemeteries of Lipara, pottery from the earliest years of the colony has been reported – mainly Corinthian and East Greek.

VELIA (Hyele). The last of the South Italian colonies was founded in about 535 by Phocaeans, whose unhappy wanderings after the destruction of their city by the Persians will be spoken of later. Posidonia is about twenty-five miles north of Velia, and the greater city seems to have favoured an enterprise which could hardly challenge her power. The small fortified hill site has been explored, and has yielded pottery of its earliest days. The mouths of the rivers on either side of the town afforded two harbours.

GREEKS AND NATIVES IN SICILY AND ITALY

The Greek tradition about the natives of Sicily was a simple one. They, the Sicels, had invaded the island from Italy some time in the eleventh century, and driven the Sicans whom they found there into the centre and south. The archaeological story is rather different, for if there were any invasions they made little impression on a culture which in the main had more in common with the Greek Aegean than with Italy. The only Italian people in this area are represented by the 'Ausonians', who lived in the Lipari Islands and in Sicily at Milazzo-Mylae, perhaps until the arrival of the Greeks in the west. In the disturbed years of the early Iron Age, the Sicels had gathered themselves for protection into large communities. One of the greatest was at Pantalica (just west of Syracuse), perhaps the ancient Hybla, seat of the king Hyblon with whom the Greeks had dealings. When the Greeks arrived, the Sicel culture had perhaps only just admitted painted pottery beside the plain incised wares. They had some skill in bronze working, and they buried their dead in rock-cut chamber tombs which honeycomb the hillsides near all Sicel towns. Almost all the sites chosen by the Greeks for their colonies had been occupied by Sicels, and in every instance the latter seem to have been ejected. Hyblon was friendly enough to the Megarians in showing them a home, but his capital did not long survive. And when, in the seventh and sixth centuries, the colonies began expanding by making new foundations, these were always at the expense of Sicel communities.

The impact of Greek ideas and culture was immediate. On many Sicel sites near the early colonies we find Greek vases, and often too vases which are native in shape but quite Greek in decoration (Fig. 57a). Where these have figure decoration, it certainly looks as though they had been painted by Greeks especially for their Sicel neighbours. The natives also learnt from the Greeks to make bronze and clay figurines, in which an interesting mixture of styles is revealed, and their bronze work in particular was stimulated and encouraged by the Greeks. They adopted a form of the Chalcidian alphabet. Whether we should also admit the possibility that Greek families lived in Sicel towns is another matter, but at one place it seems likely. This is at Grammichele, west of Leontini. Villages here received Greek goods as soon as the colonies were founded on the coast, but from about 600 on we have some evidence for sanctuaries and graves of a wholly Greek type, as well as native graves which sometimes have Greek vases in them. Here, then, there may have been a small Greek community admitted beside the Sicels.

At any rate it is clear that in most places the Greeks and Sicels got on well enough, even if only in the relationship of master and slave (there was a Sicel slave-woman in Homer's Ithaca). The natives weighed their new prosperity, brought by the

a   b

57. (a) Vase from Leontini; (b) Vase from Vulci.

Greeks, against the sites and land they had lost to them, and were generally satisfied – or at least had short memories. In the mid fifth century there was a nationalist Sicel movement, but by then the natives had been almost completely hellenized.

We might expect to find some native influence in the matter of religion or customs upon the newly-come Greeks, with whom there must surely have been intermarriage. It has been suggested that the siting of some of the extra-mural sanctuaries in Greek colonies was dictated by pre-existent native cult-places, but if so this is as far as the matter went, for the gods were always Greek and conceded nothing in attributes or function to native belief. An important concession to Sicel usage was the adoption by some cities of weights for their coinage which would suit both native and Greek standards. Farther off we find a Sikelos and a Sikanos working in the potters' quarter in Athens in the later sixth century, but they do not have to be Sicilian slaves. In the west the Greeks had nothing to learn, much to teach.

In central Sicily, the Greeks at Gela and Acragas had to deal with the Sicans, who are less well-known archaeologically but who, in the literary record, seem to have been more belligerent than the Sicels. Several native sites in this area seem to have been destroyed or taken over in the course of the seventh and sixth centuries.

In South Italy the story is much the same, but the archaeological character of the natives whom the Greeks met – Iapygians, Oenotrians, etc. – is less clearly defined. Here too, though, Greek goods and ideas rapidly penetrated. Near Locri, as in Sicily, there were Greeks decorating vases for the natives in the years around 700 B.C. Only in Apulia (the 'heel' above Tarentum) did the native tradition in vase shapes, allied to Greek geometric patterns, survive long as an independent and flourishing style. The routes across the 'instep' of South Italy are particularly rich in Greeks finds – notably the sixth-century bronze vases of Spartan type – which attracted the attention of the native villagers before they could pass on to the Greek colonies on the west coast and from them perhaps to Etruria. At Torre Galli near Hipponium it looks as though there may have been Greeks living in the native village, and this probably happened far more often than the archaeological evidence may lead us to think. In the town by the sanctuary of Apollo Alaios, on the Crimissa promontory between Sybaris and Croton, there may have been another mixed community. The sanctuary was used by Greeks in the seventh century, and a Doric temple was built there, perhaps before the end of the sixth century.

Farther north, at Cumae and Posidonia, the natives met by the Greeks belonged much more closely to the Apennine cultures of central Italy. Here too Greek goods and influence penetrated quickly. Naples (Parthenope) had already been settled by

Rhodians by 650, to judge from the reported finds; and before the end of the sixth century there were other settlements at Puteoli (founded by refugee Samians in 531) and Pompeii, where there was a small Doric temple. But of more importance is the effect which the arrival of the Greeks had upon the Etruscans, and this is better considered separately, later in this chapter.

WESTERN GREEK COLONIAL ART

The main imports to the western colonies have been mentioned in the remarks on the individual cities, and need only be summarized here. From the beginning, Corinthian pottery was in great demand, although Euboean styles can be detected in the earliest days of the Euboean colonies. By the mid sixth century, Athenian vases replaced the Corinthian; but this was a victory for the artists rather than the merchants, and the Corinthian colony Syracuse resisted the change in fashion for a while. East Greek vases travelled far, though in little quantity except to the Rhodian foundation at Gela, where the continued popularity of even plainer wares suggests continued support from home. Crete is represented only in the early years of the Euboean colonies and in her own joint foundation at Gela. Spartan vases come in numbers to Spartan Tarentum, and there are a few on other sites. Ivories of the type found in Peloponnesian sanctuaries appear in Corinthian Syracuse, and Corinth may have brought the more trivial Spartan vases which are found in Sicily. Etruria had little to offer in the way of art, but a few vases reached the Greek cities, especially those near by in Campania and Selinus, which was ever ready to fraternize with the barbarian. In other materials, there are fine stone lamps of the late seventh and early sixth centuries from the Greek islands in Selinus and Syracuse, and some pieces of archaic marble statuary. From the earlier seventh century the Sicilian colonies received Rhodian trinkets and perfume vases in faience. Later faience objects may be from Rhodes, Egypt (Naucratis), or Phoenicia. Of truly oriental imports there are Near Eastern seals brought to their earliest colonies in the west by the Euboeans, and much later some alabaster vases.

The earliest Greek settlements in the west had to be self-suffi-cient. Where they could, they made their own vases in styles familiar to them at home, and their architecture and other works of art copied forms which they remembered or their artists had brought with them. There was virtually no question of adapting these Greeks forms to native usage, although some concessions had to be made to the different materials available. Nevertheless, the more flourishing colonies came to develop individual styles and tastes independently of each other and of homeland Greece. New settlers from Greece included artists, and the flow of im-ports kept them in touch with Greek fashions. To this extent colonial art is a simple extension of Greek art, and it might have gone the way it did in any other part of the ancient world where there was no native art of a quality to invite imitation. Here I shall mention only those products of the Greek west which betray some originality of taste and an independence of the forms current in homeland Greece.

Most of the finely decorated pottery used by the western Greeks was imported, but there is some evidence for local schools also. Grave vases (craters as Fig. 51, p. 181) at Pithekoussai are local products of Euboean artists, and at Cumae in the earlier seventh century some local potters turned out extremely good copies of Corinthian vases, imitating the pale clay by using a fine creamy slip. In Sicily there was a little work for the natives, but about the middle of the seventh century, before rather than after, there were experiments in an outline 'oriental-izing' style. At Syracuse the inspiration seems Argive, but there are other related styles from Gela and Megara Hyblaea, and a still earlier style at Leontini. The famous crater signed by Aris-tonothos, which reached Caere in Etruria, may be of the same family. It shows a sea fight, and Odysseus with his companions blinding Polyphemus (Cyclops). These schools have no successors in the later seventh century. In the sixth century, isolated imita-tions of black-figure do not deserve more than passing mention, but there was one important workshop which flourished through the second half of the century. This produced the 'Chalcidian' vases (as Plate 16a), so named for the style of the lettering in their inscriptions. The painting on them betrays the influence of

Corinth, Athens, and East Greece a little; but the artists were no mere copyists, and they produced a ware which at its best rivals the best Athenian vases for finesse and composition, or perhaps excels them in general decorative effect. The finds are almost evenly distributed between Etruria and Rhegium (the Chalcidian colony), with a few in other western Greek cities, and in Aegean Greece so far only at Smyrna. The quality is far above anything made by the Greeks in Etruria, and it is tempting to suppose that the first painters of the school learned their craft in Greece – perhaps in Chalcis, although there is little there or elsewhere in Euboea to suggest that it could be the nursery of such fine artists. It is likely that they worked in Rhegium itself. After them there is nothing worthy of note until immigrant Athenian painters established workshops for red-figure vases in South Italy in the mid fifth century.

In their architecture, the western Greeks – most of them Peloponnesian by origin – preferred the Doric order. In details their temples often show a considerable lag behind models in mainland Greece, but there were ambitious and original architects in the west also. Some of the most unusual features of western Doric are, however, to be attributed to the influence of Ionic decorative forms – the elaboration of the necking on some capitals, acroteria, balustrades on altars, whole columns at Posidonia – and it may be that the 'double-fronted' plans of the great temples at Syracuse and Selinus owe something to the Ionic earlier temples of Samos and Ephesus. Most of the earlier and many of the later western buildings are especially distinguished by the painted clay revetments which encased or protected the wooden parts of their roof and gables. The models for such revetments are Corinthian, but in Sicily the type was elaborated in a manner which is not met in Greece and which can be claimed as wholly Sicilian in its development, if not in its invention.

The western Greeks had no fine marble for their sculpture, and had to use the coarser local stones, or turned more often to major works in clay. The few archaic marble statues found on Sicilian and South Italian sites were all imported ready made from the Peloponnese, Athens, and East Greece. In Sicily there was an early school of about 600 B.C. making sculptures in the archaic Greek 'Dedalic' style and using soft limestone. The main achievements, though, were in architectural sculpture, and the metope-reliefs from the Heraeum by the Sele (Posidonia, as Plate 14a) and Selinus between them tell the story of western sculpture from the earlier sixth century on. Their style has much in common with Peloponnesian work, but the artists were generally slow to admit the rapid development which characterizes the sixth century in Greece itself, and were perhaps consciously archaizing. There is an occasional 'looseness' of style and touch of realism which also stamps their work as provincial, although none the worse for that. There are some minor local schools working in a more primitive style, as that which produced the remarkable goddess suckling twins from Megara Hyblaea (Plate 14b). Perhaps a little earlier in the sixth century are the three figures from a small fountain-shrine just east of Acragas (at Montechiaro) – some of the very few examples of wooden statuary preserved from the archaic period.

For minor works in clay – figurines and other votives – it is again Corinthian models which we most often see copied, but soon distinctive local schools and types can be made out. Small clay altars with reliefs at their sides (Plate 18b) represent a type developed wholly in the west and almost unknown in Greece itself. At Gela there was a vogue for clay coffins with Ionic architectural mouldings in relief. In the later decades of the sixth century more East Greek influence is admitted. This is best seen in the fine series of clay relief plaques which were being made at Locri from the end of the sixth century on. They generally carry mythological scenes to do with the goddess Persephone, and were probably intended to hang on walls. At Tarentum there was another important school of coroplasts whose earliest work in a wholly individual style takes us back to near 600 B.C. (Plate 15a).

There was a limited production of bronzes in the west. In the later sixth century there were workshops in South Italy, although the recent claims made for the Chalcidian cities seem somewhat exaggerated. Locri and Tarentum in particular seem to have been making fine bronze vases and mirrors with figure attachments, and there have been one or two good finds in Sicily. From Grumentum, near Metapontum, comes a bronze horseman (Plate 18c) – in the British Museum – which was certainly made somewhere in the west before 550 B.C. But the whole problem of the identification of local schools of bronze workers is complicated by the presence of imports, which are largely Peloponnesian, and by our ignorance of Sybaris, which is likely to have been an important artistic centre in its day.

We hear nothing of the names of artists in Sicily and South Italy. One who did work in the west is the sculptor Pythagoras who came from Samos soon after 500 B.C. The expensive offerings made in the Greek sanctuaries by the western tyrants and kings are the work of Greek craftsmen working at home. The sanctuary of Zeus at Olympia was the obvious place for dedications from the west. On the terrace of the Treasuries – the small shrine-like buildings dedicated by the Greek states – half of the buildings were given by westerners: Gela, Metapontum, Sybaris, Selinus, Syracuse. Most were built in the sixth century, and the earliest of them, of Gela, is decorated with elaborate clay revetments in the Sicilian style.

COINAGE

Some of the colonies began to mint their own silver coinage before the middle of the sixth century, and the others soon followed suit. The silver could have been obtained from Spain – indeed two of the earliest cities to coin (Himera, Selinus) are well placed for the western trade – or from Greece. Greek coins were often overstruck in the colonial mints. The choice of weight-standard was determined by current usage and commercial convenience, but the sources of some of the standards in use are still far from clear, and for the dates of the coins there is generally little more to go on than their style.

The Euboean colonies used a light standard which could easily be related to other Greek standards and to those used in Etruria and, it seems, by the Sicels. The devices usually have some significance. For Himera ('day', daybreak) a cock; for Naxos (wine-growing) Dionysus' head and grapes; for Zancle a dolphin sporting in her sickle-shaped harbour (Plate 19b). Syracuse was late to coin (about 530), just as she was late to open her market to other than Corinthian vases. She chose the Attic standard, which could readily be adjusted to the native Sicel usage, as had Selinus for her coins bearing the canting device of a parsley leaf (Plate 19b).

The Achaean cities of South Italy began to mint on the Corinthian standard after the middle of the sixth century. They chose, or invented, an unusual type of coin on which the device which appears in relief on the front is repeated on the back reversed, in intaglio, and often simplified. This is not a style met in Greece proper; but in the west Rhegium, Zancle, and Tarentum also adopted it for some issues. Some fine examples are of Metapontum, with an ear of corn as device (Plate 19c); and there is an interesting sidelight on Sybaris' subjection to Croton after 510 in coins carrying the devices of both cities (Croton's tripod, Sybaris' bull). The same style of coin was minted at Posidonia, but here on the 'Phoenician' standard, which is met also at Cumae and seems to have been spread by East Greeks here and in the south of France.

GREEKS AND ETRUSCANS

The problem of the origins of the Etruscans is one which has vexed scholars for generations and is likely to do so for many years more. Fortunately it requires no discussion here, but it should be made clear that the following account of early Etruria is not the only possible one, although it is well supported by several recent studies. In brief, it would seem that in the early Iron Age, perhaps by 1000 B.C., an immigrant people from the west coast of Asia Minor – set travelling both by the disturbances which marked the end of the Aegean Bronze Age (to which they may have contributed) and by other setbacks – settled in Etruria. There they found adequate farmland and mineral resources. Their language was not 'Aryan' Indo-European, but their culture became much affected by that of Italy in her Late Bronze Age, admitting features from the cultures of Central Europe, and only rarely acknowledging its remote eastern home.

At about the same time, another people from the east, of different stock, settled in Rome and the Alban Hills.

Before the end of the eighth century the Etruscan culture was completely transformed by the intrusion of 'orientalizing' objects and techniques. To some this had seemed the moment at which immigrants from the east settled in Etruria, but the new 'orientalizing' features do not derive from any one eastern centre, and they share the same range and variety as the orientalizing features which Greece had accepted a little earlier and which we have already discussed in Chapter 3. Beside these new eastern forms we also observe a number of Greek Geometric ones. The source of these is easy to divine, since the earliest of the Greek colonies in the west had been deliberately planted in a position which was particularly favourable for trade with Etruria, at Pithekoussai and Cumae. Etruria admits both the eastern and the Greek at the same time, and it is worth considering whether she did not accept them from the same source. The Greeks at Pithekoussai and Cumae were Euboeans, the same folk who had opened up the east to the Greek world nearly a century before. The Etruscans were a rich but artistically immature and impoverished people, and they became ready and receptive customers for anything exotic that the Euboeans could bring them – to a small degree the forms of Greek Geometric art, and to a greater the wonders of the east, gold, jewellery, and bronzes.

If this is true, the orientalizing phase of Etruscan civilization is very largely due to trade with the Greeks. In effect they were exposed to the same new art forms and techniques of the eastern world as the Greeks had been. The difference in the reactions of the two peoples is a measure of the difference in their quality and originality. The Greeks chose, adapted, and assimilated until they produced a material culture which was wholly Greek, despite all the superficial inspiration which the east provided. The Etruscans accepted all they were offered, without discrimination. They copied – or paid Greeks and perhaps immigrant easterners to copy – with little understanding of the forms and subjects which served as models. They had their gold worked into extravagant pastiches of eastern jewellery, and gave the Greeks the metal they wanted in return for what was often hardly more than the bright beads with which merchants are usually supposed to dazzle natives. The result was 'Etruscan art': the showy blend of Greek, oriental, and barbarian taste which can still inspire or impress those who cannot come to terms with the more controlled achievements of Greek art.

What part eastern traders could have played in bringing eastern objects to Etruria we cannot judge, but it is likely to have been slight once the Greeks were established at Cumae, and it is only after the foundation of Cumae that the orientalizing phase in Etruria begins in earnest.

The full measure of the effect of eastern art in Etruria cannot be taken here, but there are some things which may illustrate the part the Greeks played as middlemen. Near Eastern seals of the latest eighth century can be traced through Pithekoussai to Etruria. Bronze cauldrons of eastern type with bull's-head or siren attachments can be traced through Cumae. Other orientalizing bronzes, cauldrons, and a bowl in Etruria (at Praeneste and Capena) are of an oriental workshop which seems to have been established at some time in Greece, probably in Crete (see pp. 83 ff.). We find Cretan vases in the early graves of the Euboean colonies, both at Pithekoussai and Cumae, and there may be some return traffic of minor Etruscan or Italic bronzes to Crete at this early date. And in a grave at Cumae is a plainer cauldron of the same type as the fine bronzes in Etruria.

We are more directly concerned, however, with (1) Greek imports to Etruria; (2) the evidence for Greeks working and living in Etruria; and (3) the influence of Greek rather than oriental models on Etruscan art.

1. The earliest imported vases, of the mid eighth century, passed through the Euboean colonies, and they are Corinthian, or imitations of Corinthian, perhaps made in Euboea or the western colonies, and a few Cretan such as we have already noted in the Euboean colonies. The Corinthian vases continue to arrive through the seventh century together with a growing number of East Greek. The sixth century sees the liveliest trade, with the fine Athenian vases gradually winning the market from the Corinthian. But the Athenian vases were not carried by

Athenians, nor the Corinthian necessarily by Corinthian ships.
Merchants' marks scratched on the bases of vases betray Ionian
hands, and much of the carrying was probably done by Phocaeans,
Chians, or others from the eastern Aegean. In effect, not very
much fine East Greek pottery was carried to Etruria – some
Chian and Rhodian of the later seventh and sixth centuries –
although figure-flasks were popular later. Of the other vases, we
may note only the vogue for Spartan cups through the second
and third quarters of the sixth century, for 'Chalcidian' vases

58. Nikosthenic amphora
shape, Athenian.

(see p. 205) in its second half, and (carried for their contents)
Chian wine-jars and Athenian oil-jars. The Greek potters were
careful to observe Etruscan taste. Before the mid sixth century,
both Corinthians and Athenians catered for Etruscan delight in
colourful story-telling on respectively their craters (wine-mixing
bowls) and the so-called Tyrrhenian amphorae. The inscriptions
labelling the figures on the latter did not always make sense, but
the Etruscan buyer was not likely to realize that. After the mid
sixth century, when the Athenian vases had won the market, the
potter Nikosthenes started supplying a vase-shape (Fig. 58)

familiar to the Etruscans, in their plain native *bucchero*, but decorated with the usual Athenian figures. This sort of ingenuity ensured a brisk market.

2. For evidence of Greeks actually working and living in Etruria there is even a literary record (Pliny). One Demaratus, a Corinthian noble, emigrated about the middle of the seventh century at a time of political crisis at home, and settled in Etruria, at Tarquinii, where he married a local lady and carried on his prosperous business. With him he brought a painter and three clay-modellers, who introduced the new technique of clay statuary to Etruria.

Greek work or influence is most readily shown by the pottery. There are geometric vases in Etruria of the late eighth and early seventh centuries whose shape and decoration are still Greek, although they are clearly not imported from Greece or necessarily from the Greek colonies. Important examples are standed craters from Vulci (Fig. 57b, p. 202) and Bisenzio, which seem likely to be the work of Euboean artists working in Etruria. Other painted vases of non-Greek local shapes may also have been made by Greeks, but it becomes difficult to draw the line here. Etruscan painters must quickly have picked up the techniques and patterns, and for over a hundred years all the vases painted in Etruria are probably the work of local artists.

After the middle of the sixth century, the Ionian 'diaspora' led many East Greek artists to look for new homes. Some came to Etruria and set up shop to supply a market whose taste for finely decorated pottery was already highly developed; and this too was no doubt the most active period of East Greek trade through Sybaris. Black-figure painters of the 'Clazomenian' school produced two series of vases in Etruria, which admit some local patterns as well as much influence from the popular Athenian styles. These are the so-called 'Northampton Group' amphorae of the 530s, and the 'Campana *dinoi*' which follow them. The work of the same artists, or at least artists from the same schools, can be traced in East Greece, and in Egypt (see p. 155), and was carried to Greek cities on the Black Sea. Of about this date is another group of vases, all of one shape, certainly made at Caere: the 'Caeretan *hydriae*' (as Plate 11). Their painter had a lively sense of humour and appreciation of how colour could be effectively employed in what was basically a black-and-white technique. The elements of his style are Ionian and Corinthian, but it is his individuality which is most impressive. He had no followers.

Another field in which we may suspect the work of Greek artists is tomb-painting. Some of the paintings on the walls of Etruscan tombs seem in a wholly Greek style (Plate 15b), and the 'Caeretan' vase-painter may even have worked in this medium also. There is no comparative material from Greece itself, where chamber tombs of this type were not built, but some fresco painting at Gordion in Phrygia (Plate 7b) seems also to have been executed by Ionian artists, and there are points for comparison with this and with Greek vases.

3. The influence of Greek artists and art on Etruscan products is quite easily recognized. The Euboean and Corinthian Geometric and early orientalizing styles which became familiar after the founding of the first Greek colonies were slavishly copied by native artists, who were especially attracted by the simple 'metope pattern' which could be mass-produced with a multiple brush.

All Corinthian styles were imitated in the 'Italo-Corinthian' vases, which can be traced at least down to the middle of the sixth century. Vase-shapes are copied, and all the elements of figure and abstract decoration, with one or two other patterns suggested by imported oriental bronzes and ivories. The mixture of patterns and disposition of the decoration is seldom quite as the Corinthian. The animals are often caricatures of their models and behave in a non-Greek way, with dismembered bodies in their mouths. Throughout the same period, Etruria developed her own plain black ware (*bucchero*) admitting Greek shapes and impressed or moulded decoration of Greek and oriental style.

As Athenian vases replaced Corinthian in the markets, so they were in their turn copied in a comparably jejune manner. One class, mis-called 'Pontic', admits more colour and variety, but was certainly developed by Etruscan artists influenced by

Athenian, Ionian, and the later Corinthian styles. And in the fifth century even red-figure was imitated, at first by painting the figures in red instead of leaving them reserved in the clay ground of the vase.

In tomb painting the Etruscans soon followed the Greek lead (see above), often distorting proportions or misunderstanding subjects, but at times inspiring their work with a sense of lively movement or of grim other-worldliness.

In bronze work they developed several types – as of fibulae – which were introduced by the Greeks but did not become so popular in Greece itself. Their metalwork was of a high quality, dependent in varying degrees on Greek models for vase shapes (though some are Phoenician or native) or plastic attachments, the latter generally inspired by Peloponnesian (often Spartan) bronzes.

Demaratus' companions were said to have introduced clay modelling to Etruria, and this was soon a craft in which the Etruscans approached the skill of the Greeks. It was one they practised more, for they did not have – or at least did not exploit – any sources of fine white marble for statuary such as the Greeks used. Finally we should remark that the Etruscans learned their alphabet from the Chalcidians, and that the earliest Etruscan ABC is inscribed on an ivory writing tablet which imitates an eastern form.

In return, the Etruscans had nothing to offer but raw materials. Some vases reached the western colonial cities, and a few *bucchero* cups were carried as curios to Greece itself in the years around 600. A bronze tripod of about 500 from the Vulci workshop was found on the Acropolis at Athens; there are bronze strainers at Olympia and Lindos (Rhodes) and a bronze attachment at Dodona. Olympia is perhaps the obvious place for us to look for Etruscan things, and Pausanias says that an Etruscan king was the first barbarian to make a dedication there. There is part of a silver diadem of mid seventh century date from Olympia which seems certainly Etruscan, and scraps of bronze shields which might also be so. The fibulae of types most popular in Italy are not necessarily imported dedications, or certainly not all of them. Even in the fifth century the occasional fine object reached Greece from Etruria, casually and not by way of trade.

Despite this record of cultural dependence, the political relations between Greeks and Etruscans worsened after the mid sixth century. The Etruscans had acquired a considerable fleet, and in 540 joined the Carthaginians in driving the Phocaeans from the seas at Alalia. In 524 they attacked Cumae, but were defeated; and when they had to face the Latin alliance against them, they found Greeks in the ranks of their enemies. The Etruscan fleet dominated the waters north of the Messina Straits, and only the overland routes to Campania remained in Greek hands. Soon after 500, the flow of Greek goods to Etruria began to fall off; but by then the Greek-trained or Greek artists in Etruria could supply all needs, and at any rate the Greeks were soon to regain control of the seas.

GREEKS AND PHOENICIANS

Ancient Greek historians believed that the Phoenicians had preceded the Greeks in trade and colonization in the western Mediterranean, and Thucydides says that they had been using promontories and islets off Sicily for trade with the natives until the arrival of the Greeks drove them to the western end of the island. The archaeological evidence – indeed a simple glance on a map at the relative positions of the Greek and Phoenician towns – shows that this was not true. There is nothing from the native sites in Sicily to suggest trade with Phoenicians. The first foreign objects there are Greek, and in their train come some of the minor oriental trinkets which the Greeks used or distributed.

While there may have been some Phoenician activity in the west when the Greeks started operating there, it cannot have been very effective. There certainly seem to have been no organized trading communities to match the first Greek colonies. But the Phoenicians obviously had or acquired some interest in the western trade, and decided to safeguard and promote their interests by colonial foundations on the lines of the Greek ones. A major attraction for traders from the East Mediterranean was the supply of metal in the west, especially tin. For tin the main source was probably Britain, even in quite early times. Trade was not, of course, the only motive for colonization, but if the Phoenicians had been interested only in land, there seems little reason why they should have taken pains to try to elbow out the Greeks on the important routes, and ignored nearer tracts of good farmland like Cyrenaica.

The tin reached the Mediterranean in two ways: (a) overland

through France, whence it could be supplied to the metal-working centres of Etruria. This route was the one the Greeks first tapped through the Euboean foundations at Pithekoussai and Cumae, safeguarded by their colonies on the Straits of Messina, and later pursued by colonies in the south of France. The other tin route (b) was by sea to the south of Spain, where there were other important mineral resources – notably silver – to be won. Once the trade routes via Etruria had been secured by the Greeks, well before the end of the eighth century, only the Spanish route was open, and this the Phoenicians sought to secure by the foundation of Carthage in North Africa, by occupying the western end of Sicily (which the Greeks had not yet touched), and later by posts in Sardinia, the Balearics, and Spain itself.

It is likely that the Greeks too would have had an interest in the route to Spain, but were ousted by the Phoenicians. There are place-names in the Carthage area which have a Euboean ring – an island called Euboea, Naxian Islands, and Pithekoussai, the last two bearing names of the earliest Euboean colonies in Sicily and Italy respectively. And there is a suggestion too in the Old Testament that Carthage lay once in the Ionian (Javan) sphere. Excavation may one day explain these records. The earliest Phoenician settlement was supposed to be at Utica, just north-west of Carthage, but the finds there do not seem appreciably earlier. Carthage itself was razed to the ground by the Romans in 146, but it has left fairly rich pickings for the archaeologist. The earliest datable deposits there are caches of vases in the Tanit sanctuary – likely to be one of the earliest buildings. Many of the vases are Greek of the later eighth century – Corinthian, or imitations of Corinthian such as the Euboeans made. At this early date such a deposit of Greek vases might suggest some direct Greek interest in this area. At least, they are hard to explain here in the early years of a rival Phoenician colony. The earliest Phoenician objects in Carthage can be dated only by their context with Greek things, but so far it seems unlikely that the city was occupied until the later eighth century – after the main Greek foundations in Sicily and South Italy. It may be significant too that some of Carthage's own early vases are decorated with the multiple brush, a technique that could only have been picked up from the Greeks.

In western Sicily the Phoenicians established cities at Motya, Solus, and Panormus (Palermo). Only Motya yields anything Phoenician or Greek obviously earlier than the seventh century. During this century the Greek cities in Sicily expanded westward, with foundations at Himera and Selinus, on the borders of the Phoenicians' territory, but the latter enjoyed the cooperation of the native Elymians and retained their hold on this part of the island.

We should expect the other Phoenician foundations in the

western Mediterranean to belong to this period also. On Malta a tomb was found to contain two Greek vases – Corinthian and Rhodian of the earlier seventh century – together with a Cypriot bronze lamp stand and Phoenician vases. In Sardinia, at Nora, a Phoenician inscription on local stone may be our earliest evidence, but comparisons with inscriptions in Phoenicia date it to the ninth century, while allowance for provincialism in the alphabet puts it some three centuries later. Other finds, Phoenician (of Carthage) and Greek, take us to the late seventh century, but we must await proper excavation. The Ionians more than once thought of emigrating to Sardinia when they were under pressure from Persia, and it is by no means clear whether Greeks or Phoenicians had the upper hand there in the early sixth century. Olbia, in the north, may have been a Greek settlement, but nothing has been found there earlier than the fifth century. In the Balearics Ibiza was said to have been founded in 654, but again has yielded nothing datable earlier than about 600 B.C., and the earliest finds are many of them Greek. The islands were supposed to have been colonized by the Rhodians at some time.

In the south of Spain itself the Phoenicians are just as elusive in the early period. It may be that we should distinguish: (a) an early period of Phoenician interest, which is not easily recognized archaeologically and might prove to be wholly illusory; (b) a period of Phocaean Greek monopoly; followed by (c) renewed Phoenician control, directed from Carthage. The same sequence could be argued for Sardinia (for (a) the Nora stone) and the Balearics.

For early Phoenician interest in Spain there is little reliable to show. Some incised and relief ivories of Phoenician type seem from their style more likely to be from early Phoenician trade, before the Greeks arrived, than of the later sixth century when the Phoenicians were again in control. But they certainly cannot be as early as some have claimed, since one of the figures on them wears a helmet of a Greek type which was not invented until about 700 B.C. (Fig. 59). One has now appeared on Samos in a mid-seventh-century context. These ivories are from sites up the River Guadalquivir. Bronze jugs of Phoenician shape from the same area are matched in Etruria, but are no earlier than the mid seventh century. Phoenician gold jewellery from Aliseda may be as early. But this, if ever, was the time of the 'grave Tyrian trader' driven west by the 'merry Grecian coasters, the young light-hearted Masters of the waves', to

> There, where down cloudy cliffs, through sheets of foam,
> Shy traffickers, the dark Iberians come;
> And on the beach undid his corded bales

– though Arnold set the encounter of Tyrian and Greek in the Aegean.

In the second half of the seventh century, the Greeks began serious trade with the south of Spain, although in their poems

59. Ivory plaque from Carmona.

they had already heard long before of the Hesperides and the Atlantic. Kolaios the Samian, blown rather a long way off his course to Egypt in about 638 B.C., passed through the Straits of Gibraltar (the 'pillars of Heracles' to the Greeks), visited Tartessos (in Cadiz Bay) and came away with such a load of silver that it would seem that the market was a new one – or at least long unvisited : 'inviolate' Herodotus calls it. There were dedications, said to be of 'Tartessian bronze', at Olympia of an even earlier date (648). The Phocaeans carried on the trade, encouraged by the native King. In the 540s they were reinforced by their kinsfolk, who had been driven from their homes by the Persians and came to live at Alalia in Corsica, founded from Marseilles in about 565. To judge from this colonizing at Marseilles in 600 and later in Corsica (and perhaps Sardinia), the Phocaeans avoided the North Africa route to the west. In the south of Spain there are several indications of Greek trade: a Corinthian helmet at Jerez, which had been made in the earlier seventh century (Fig. 60), and another of the sixth century from the Huelva; a bronze griffin protome from an East Greek cauldron of the early sixth century, and other bronze vases. The route can be traced through the sixth-century bronzes and pottery on the Balearics; in the Corinthian and Athenian vases of the earlier sixth century at Villaricos on the coast half way from the

60. Bronze helmet from Jerez.

Balearics to Gibraltar; and in the East Greek bronze vase (neck and handle, Fig. 61) of about 600 or little after from the Granada district. In the other Phocaean towns on this coast, Hemeroskopeion and Mainake, nothing earlier than the fifth century has been found, and the location of the former at the Ifach peninsula is not completely certain.

In 540 the Phocaeans provoked a naval battle with the Carthaginians and Etruscans, and although they were successful their losses were such that they had to abandon their colony at Alalia. Thence they fled to a new home in Velia (see p. 200 above). The struggle for mastery of the western seas went on for some years. We hear of a victory for the Phocaeans from Marseilles, and of a treaty between Carthage and the Etruscans defining spheres of interest. By 500 Greek trade with Tartessos was at an end, and Carthage's succession there is marked by the Phoenician settlement at Gades (Cadiz).

The clash between Greeks and Phoenicians had begun earlier in the sixth century. In the 570s Rhodians and Cnidians tried to establish a colony at Lilybaeum, a promontory overlooking the Phoenician town of Motya in west Sicily, but they were expelled and moved on to Lipara. Later the Phoenician and native (as Segesta) towns became partly hellenized and admitted more Greek goods. There seems to have been a clash with Selinus, but that city generally found it convenient to keep on good terms

61. Handle and lip of a
bronze vase from
Granada.

with its neighbours, Phoenician or native. Next comes the Phocaeans' naval battle at Alalia (540) and consequent Greek loss of Corsica to the Etruscans, and Sardinia to the Carthaginians. The direct western passage to Spain was closed and Tartessos eventually destroyed. Then a Spartan, Dorieus, set out in 514 to found a colony in Libya, at Kinyps on the coast between Cyrene and Carthage, but he was driven out by the Carthaginians and natives in little over two years. The scraps of Greek pottery of about 500 B.C. at Sabratha and Leptis Magna (where seventh-century Greek pottery is also now reported) do not indicate Greek settlement, for at Carthage itself Greek objects were always arriving whatever the political climate. Dorieus moved on to west Sicily, where he founded another city at Heraclea (probably Trapani) by Mount Eryx, in Phoenician territory. Here again he was soon assailed by Phoenicians and natives, and succumbed. Some of his followers escaped, to settle at Minoa between Selinus and Acragas.

In the early fifth century, Gelon, tyrant of Gela, sought to revenge Dorieus' death and to open Africa to Greek trade. We know little of his early campaigns, but in 480 things came to a head. He had strengthened his position by obliging most of the inhabitants of Gela, Camarina, and Megara Hyblaea to move into Syracuse, which became his new capital. His rivals in Rhegium and Himera invited the Carthaginians to send a force to Sicily and overthrow him. Selinus, it seems, sided with its Phoenician neighbours. The force arrived under Hamilcar, encamped at Himera, and was utterly routed by Gelon's army. It was said that on the very same day that he liberated Sicily from the threat of Carthage, the Greek fleet finally repulsed the Persians at Salamis and the Greeks of east and west were saved from the barbarians. The battle in Sicily was commemorated by new temples – paid for from the Carthaginian indemnity – one of which was built at Himera. And Gelon struck a victory issue of coins (Plate 19a) which take their place among the finest examples of Greek numismatic art. At Delphi he and his brothers dedicated golden Victories and tripods 'having conquered the barbarians and extended the friendly hand of freedom to all Greeks'.

GREEKS IN FRANCE AND NORTH SPAIN

An alternative route from the tin islands of Britain to that which led to the south of Spain lay overland across France. On the southern route the East Greek traders – mainly Phocaeans, it seems – had to face the competition of the Phoenicians, and not even their island bases on Corsica, Sardinia, and the Balearics were safe. As long as Etruria was friendly, though, they could push up a safe coastline to France and to the other tin route where the Phoenicians did not operate, at least in strength. In accordance with their practice elsewhere, they safeguarded their trade by founding colonies. But they were not the first Greeks to visit this coast.

Occasional finds of seventh-century Greek pottery have been

made in the south of France. These indicate perhaps trade but certainly not settlement, and unfortunately we cannot be certain about their alleged find-places. There are vases of around 700 from Marseilles (Cycladic and 'Athenian') and Hyères (Olbia – the vase might be Euboean); Corinthian from the same site; and early fibulae from near Nîmes. It might well be that this first exploration so far north was conducted by Euboeans from Pithe- koussai and Cumae – indeed this is what we should expect, although the more thorough exploration of the area was left to their East Greek colleagues. Some of the early pottery looks Euboean, and the 'Athenian' may rather be Euboean, as we have suspected similar attributions of finds in the Near East.

Clearly the most crucial point was at the mouth of the Rhône. Here, in native villages at Saint-Blaise and La Couronne, Greek pottery of the later seventh century has been found. The earliest datable pieces are Corinthian, but most of the pottery is East Greek, with some Athenian arriving after the middle of the sixth century, at Saint-Blaise. The Greek community here grew rapidly, and may have taken over the site eventually, although no ancient name is known for it. Nor is it clear which Greeks arrived there first in the seventh century. There is some literary evidence for Rhodian colonization before the foundation of Mar- seilles, probably in this region and certainly farther along the coast at Rhode in North Spain. Unfortunately there is no archaeological evidence for the date of the foundation of Rhode. Some bronze vases which passed this way about 600 and just afterwards have also been called Rhodian, but their East Greek character might just as well indicate some other centre like Samos, famous for its bronzes, or even Phocaea, which is still something of an unknown quantity in this period. At any rate it could well be that all these bronzes arrived after the Phocaeans had founded Marseilles. Certainly it was the Phocaeans who were most active hereabouts after 600, and one of these very bronze vases has been found in the other Phocaean market, South Spain (Fig. 61).

The Phocaeans founded Massalia (Marseilles) just east of the mouth of the Rhône, in about 600 B.C. The modern town has hampered excavation, but opportunities have been well taken, and the results – treated with caution – are most revealing. The Greek city lay on the hill to the north of the Old Harbour. Finds were made here and at Fort St Jean (which occupies the north side of the entrance to the harbour) early in this century; and demolitions during the last war gave the opportunity for excavation soon after it near the quayside of the Old Harbour just east of Fort St Jean.

The finds show that through the sixth century the town received a notable variety of imports from homeland Greece. As well as the usual Corinthian, then Athenian, there are some Spartan, Etruscan, and 'Chalcidian' pieces. There is a good deal of East Greek pottery, as we would expect, though little of it is certainly Rhodian. There were fine Chian vases as well as wine jars from the island. The other wares are distinctive but not easily localized. There are striped vases of a type which became much copied locally; and there is pale grey *bucchero* pottery. This is a ware common in the northern states of East Greece and it is probably rightly recognized as Phocaean by import or example when it is found in the west. There is plenty at Marseilles, and it appears wherever there is any other Greek pottery on the French coast. Indications of Marseilles' prosperity in the later sixth century are her relatively prolific coinage and the fine marble treasury built by the city at Delphi. The palm capitals of the columns in its porch are of a type met earlier at Phocaea.

A daughter foundation of Marseilles was at Emporion, modern Ampurias, in North Spain. It lies far beyond the overland tin route, and although it may have served to tap the metal resources of the Pyrenees, it is better regarded as a stage in Phocaean littoral exploration. A late Roman author, Avienus, wrote a poetical geography which seems in part based on an account of a journey from Marseilles, via Gibraltar, to Ireland and Britain. Details in it, notably its failure to mention Emporion, suggest that it may go back to an account of Phocaean voyages before the town was founded. Emporion itself seems to have been established little if at all after Marseilles. There is Corinthian and East Greek pottery from the beginning of the sixth century on, and eventually Athenian as well. The first settlement lay on an islet just offshore from a native town, but it seems that the Greeks had their cemetery on the mainland. Strabo says that when the Greek centre was established on the shore, it lay beside but distinct from the native town, but that they later combined. Excavations in the town have shown Greeks living there in the last quarter of the sixth century, and have told much about the later history, but the details of topography in the early years of the Greek colony are still far from clear.

The foundation of Marseilles was an important landmark in the history of the peoples of Gaul. Their culture was a branch of the Bronze Age 'Hallstatt' culture which obtained through much of central Europe, and for the west at least this was the first time that it was brought into close contact with the Greeks. There are some effects which the archaeologist can observe, other than simple imports. One is the production locally of vases painted

      a   b   c

62. (a) Vase fragment from Ensérune; (b and c) Belt hooks from Cayla.

freely with a multiple brush (Fig. 62a, from Ensérune). This could only have been learned from the Greeks, and began in the sixth century in the south of France and north of Spain. It may be, too, that the new type of bronze belt-hook (Fig. 62 b and c) which becomes popular in this same area at this time owes something to the bronze belts which we have already seen in Phrygia and Ionia (Fig. 29, p. 108) and which may have been introduced to the west by the Phocaeans.

The Roman historian Justinus says that 'from the Greeks the Gauls learned a more civilized way of life and abandoned their barbarous ways. They set to tilling their fields and walling their towns. They even got used to living by law rather than force of arms, to cultivating the vine and the olive. Their progress, in manners and wealth, was so brilliant that it seemed as though

Gaul had become part of Greece, rather than that Greece had colonized Gaul.'

For the Greeks' introduction of the vine and even the olive to the south of France we may still be grateful. Marseilles soon became an active exporter of her own products, and although the occasional Chian and Athenian jar was imported in the sixth century, she was soon making her own pots for wine or oil, and conducting a lively trade with the natives. The first wine to be drunk in Burgundy was Greek wine from Marseilles. With the wine jars went Greek pottery – mainly Athenian and East Greek of the second half of the sixth century. The greatest concentration of such finds is, of course, near the coast around Marseilles and the mouth of the Rhône, as at Arles, but there is much too from a number of sites in the Languedoc, to the north and south of Narbonne, notably Ensérune where there must have been a Greek settlement. To the east of Marseilles, and just west of Toulon, a new site (Mt Garou) gives a stratified picture of the archaeology of the region, with native Hallstatt settlement succeeded by a mixed level of the early sixth century containing Etruscan, Greek, and Phoenician pottery, and then Greek wares becoming dominant.

Inland, along the tin routes and to the richer Celtic 'Hallstatt' cities, the volume of Greek finds grows less, but more spectacular. There is one place, however, with enough Greek pottery to suggest that it played an important part in Marseilles' trade. This is the town at Mt Lassois overlooking the Seine, little over a hundred miles south-east of Paris. It lies at the crucial point where the river becomes no longer easily navigable and goods had to be unloaded for the journey south to the Saône, the Rhône, and Marseilles, or to the native cities to the east, or through the Swiss passes into North Italy. Some have held that it was by the last route that the Greek finds in central and eastern France arrived, but in the sixth century the Marseilles route is vouched for by the Massaliot and Phocaean pottery found at Mt Lassois, while Greek interest in North Italy and the Po valley comes only later.

In 1953 the burial mound of a princess was excavated at Vix, the cemetery of Mt Lassois, and yielded finds whose artistic merit rivals their historical importance. The offerings included the largest and finest Greek bronze crater (Plate 16b) yet known, its neck decorated in relief with warriors and chariots (Plate 17), its handles with gorgons, all its mouldings exquisitely cast and chased. It stood nearly 5′ 6″ (1·64m.) high with its lid, which was a dish with a superb statuette of a woman (Plate 17) at its centre as handle. The crater is probably Spartan work, but besides there were three Etruscan bronze vases, two clay Athenian cups, one of the 520s which dates the burial to the end of the sixth

63. Bronze cauldron and
tripod from near Mt Lassois.

century, as well as other bronzes, ornaments, and jewellery, including the gold diadem on the young woman's head.

Ninety years before the discovery of the Vix treasure, another tumulus two miles away had been excavated and found to contain a Greek bronze vessel of a very different type. It was a cauldron with four griffin protomes below its rim, complete with its tripod stand (Fig. 63). Orientalizing cauldrons of this sort have already been discussed (p. 86). This is a late example, of the first half of the sixth century, and it has been thought that it was made in the west, at Cumae; but it may well be from some other west Greek city, or even East Greece, like so many of the others. A griffin from another such cauldron was found in the Loire, near Angers. This takes us far away to the west, to one of the other possible tin routes from the Channel and Brittany, which passed along the Loire to the Rhône. And these same cauldrons can be followed yet farther afield to Sweden, where one has been found near Stockholm, missing its griffins to be sure, but with clear signs of where they had been attached.

Far to the east of Mt Lassois, in South Germany, the spread of Greek goods in the sixth century is marked by other East Greek bronze vases and a little Athenian pottery. A notable find is the Spartan bronze vase (Plate 19d), made about 600 B.C., from Grächwyl in Switzerland. The most important site so far excavated in which Greek goods and influence can be recognized is the fortress town at Heuneburg, overlooking the Schwabian Danube, just north-west of Munich. Here there is some Greek pottery of the later sixth century, but more remarkable is the possibility that the construction of its fortification walls in this period was inspired by – or even modelled on – Greek practice. Part of the circuit is built in the usual local style of rubble and timber, but there is a long stretch which is built of mudbrick on a stone socle with projecting rectangular bastions at regular intervals. Both plan and construction are quite foreign to central Europe at this time, quite familiar on archaic Greek sites. It is tempting to suppose that the chieftains who so much prized Greek works of art were also moved to invite Greek technical assistance.

About 500 B.C. events in central Europe took a turn which had a profound influence on the Greek trade through Marseilles. For the European archaeologist this is the transition between the cultures of Hallstatt and La Tène. On the ground it is represented by the abandonment of the Hallstatt fortress-towns, and a general shift of the centre of wealth and power towards the east and north. The town at Mt Lassois was abandoned. Marseilles lost her entrepôt there, and trade down the Rhône came to a halt. At Marseilles the transition is marked by a rapid falling off in imports of fine pottery, which surely betokens a lapse in prosperity. Inland, the imported bronzes and pottery are no longer Greek but Etruscan. The new routes to the south led through the Alps and Switzerland to North Italy. Within a single generation the western Greeks had lost control of the routes through the Straits of Gibraltar, and through France, but their cities were wealthy and well-established, strong enough to resist Carthaginians and Etruscans, and already other Greeks had moved up the Adriatic to meet the new routes into North Italy. These we shall meet in the next chapter.

Bibliography

SICILY and SOUTH ITALY: Dunbabin, *The Western Greeks*, 1948, gives an excellent account of the early history and archaeology of the Greek colonies. Bérard's *La Colonisation grecque*, 1957, covers the literary evidence fully, and with its first edition (1941) appeared a useful bibliography of sites. Brea, *Sicily before the Greeks*, 1957; Taylour, *Mycenaean Pottery in Italy*, 1958. A recent monograph is Vallet's *Rhégion et Zancle*, 1958. De Miré, *Sicile grecque*, is an intelligent picture book. New finds and sites are reported in *Archaeological Reports, Amer. Journ. Arch., Boll. d'Arte, Not. degli Scavi,* and *Fasti Arch.*; French excavations (*Megara Hyblaea*) in *Mél. d'arch. et d'hist.* Kraay, *Num. Chron.*, 1958, 1960. A general book, Woodhead, *Greeks in the West*, 1962.

SPAIN and PHOENICIANS: García y Bellido, *Hispania Graeca*, 1948; Carpenter, *The Greeks in Spain*, 1925, and in *Amer. Journ. Arch.*, LXII, 1958; Harden, *The Phoenicians*, 1962. Early Carthage is still under-published, but see Cintas, *La Céramique punique.* For the literary evidence for Greeks in the Carthage area Treidler in *Historia*, VIII, 1959.

FRANCE: Villard in *La Céramique grecque de Marseille*, 1960, reviews Greek and Etruscan finds in France and the tin routes. New finds are reported in *Gallia* and local journals. Joffroy, *Le Trésor de Vix*, 1954.

ETRURIA: There are many Etruscan art books; the most useful are Riis, *Etruscan Art*, 1953, and, for the pictures, Mühlestein, *Die Kunst der Etrusker*, 1929; Pallottino, *Etruscan Painting*, 1952. Good general works are Pallottino, *The Etruscans*, 1955, and Banti, *Die Welt der Etrusker*, 1960. A recent discussion of origins by Hawkes in *Stud. Etr.*, XXVII, 1959. Brown, *The Etruscan Lion*, 1960, discusses relations with Greeks and the east. Beazley, *Etruscan Vase-painting*, 1947. For Etruscan things in Greece see Karo in *Arch. Eph.*, 1937, and Kunze in *Stud. pres. to D. M. Robinson*, I, 1951.

WEST GREEK ART: Richter, *Ancient Italy*, 1955, gives a useful
survey, as does Dunbabin, op. cit. Sculpture and architecture are
discussed in the Greek handbooks. For the local vases see Cook,
Greek Painted Pottery. Jantzen, *Bronze-werkstätten*, 1938.

CHAPTER 6

THE NORTH AND THE BLACK SEA

THIS chapter will take us from the Po Valley to the shores of the Black Sea. It is a vast range, in which the history of each area is closely involved with that of its neighbour, but for convenience the following scheme is adopted. First, the progress of the Greeks up the Adriatic to North Italy. Secondly, their spread up the Balkan peninsula and along the Thracian coast. Both these moves led them to contact with the natives of Illyria and Thrace, and this situation can be considered together with problems of earlier Greek relations with the north. Then there is the approach to the Black Sea, colonization on its shores, and relations with the Scythians; and we are brought full circle back to Asia Minor, the scene of the Greek migrations of the Early Iron Age which occupied us in Chapter 2.

GREEKS IN THE ADRIATIC

The first Greek colony in the Adriatic was on the island of CORCYRA (Corfu), and it was placed less with a view to further exploitation of the seas to the north, than as a port of call on the routes to the west. This is shown in part by the origins of the colonists : first the Eretrians, from Euboea, who with Chalcis had first sent colonies to Italy and Sicily; then, in 733, the Corinthians, who evicted the Eretrians and were at the same time on their way to found Syracuse in Sicily.

The principal town on Corcyra faces the mainland and controls the narrow coastal straits. It is a fine peninsula site enclosing a good harbour. There is nothing to show as yet for Eretrian occupation, but the fortunes of the Corinthian settlement can be followed. There is a little Corinthian pottery from the town's earliest years and from later in the seventh century, but the most important finds are architectural, of the sixth century. These include the Temple of Artemis which gives us our first near-complete example of pedimental sculptures in Greek art. This is of the early sixth century. Rather later is another Doric temple, not far away, in what is now the park of the Villa Monrepos, and at the southern tip of the peninsula was a second sanctuary of Artemis which has yielded some seventh-century clay votives showing the goddess with her lion. The early cemetery lay to the north of the town, and is best known for two monuments of about 600 B.C. – one, a fine stone lion from a grave, the other the tomb of one Menecrates who died at sea. This is a round stone structure a little over five yards across and nearly two yards high.

Corcyra's early history shows that she was soon quite independent of her founder, Corinth, and at times positively hostile. For all that, her art is always wholly in the Corinthian tradition.

Although at first Corcyra played her part largely on the routes to the west, she was naturally the first to explore further the coasts of the Adriatic itself, while Corinth concentrated on consolidating her position in the northern approaches to the Corinthian Gulf. The Euboeans had, it seems, already put settlements on the mainland opposite and at Oricum, far to the north on the borders of Illyria. Of these we have no more than stray references in ancient authors.

In 627 Corcyra founded EPIDAMNUS (Roman Dyrrhachium, modern Durazzo) on the coast some 150 miles to the north. We do not know how the Illyrians reacted to this intrusion, and it seems to have taken a little while for trade to develop. Silver mines in Illyria may have been one of the attractions of the area for the Greeks.

Of the early town of Epidamnus we know nothing, but its foundation was followed shortly by another, this time by Corinth, at APOLLONIA on the coast to the south. The little pottery which has so far been found there – both Corinthian and Rhodian – shows that Greeks were there by about 600 B.C. The hill site of the ancient city is today separated from the coastline by five miles of lagoons and marshes.

The next major move up the Illyrian coast was again sponsored by the Corcyraeans, who helped their East Greek friends, the Cnidians, to settle on 'Black Corcyra' (Korčula), an island in the Dalmatian archipelago. This apparently happened early in the sixth century, and the adjacent islands were also later settled by the Greeks. We know nothing archaeologically about the early towns, beyond an early sixth-century Corinthian vase from Korčula and another, later, from the island of Issa.

On the other side of the Adriatic, Corinthian pottery appears on various sites in Apulia and Messapia on the far side of the 'heel' of Italy from the Greeks at Tarentum, but nothing to suggest settlement. There are even one or two seventh-century pieces at Bari and Brindisi which may have come via Tarentum, and we may recall the tale of Phalanthus, who led the colonists to Tarentum, was expelled by his fellow citizens, and took refuge with the natives of Brentesion (Brindisi).

The most important Greek enterprise in the Adriatic came comparatively late in the period which we are studying, and was centred on the Po Valley in north-east Italy. The last chapter has already indicated the importance of this area in the years after the decline of the tin route through France and Marseilles. When Herodotus says that it was the Phocaeans who first explored the Adriatic, it is tempting to associate this with their foundation at Marseilles and their continued interest in the northern routes, but there is little to support this archaeologically, and there are only a very few East Greek vases of the sixth century at all in the cities of the Adriatic.

The area from the Po south to Ancona was occupied by Enetians, Umbrians, and Picenes. They had already admitted some orientalizing influences in their cultures by the sixth century, at second hand via Etruria. During the sixth century, Etruscan expansion to the south was being contained by the Greeks, and they looked to the north-east. A group of Etruscan cities was founded here with their centre at Felsina (Bologna). The attraction was probably twofold: excellent farmland, and the routes from the north via Switzerland and the Alps.

A little Corinthian pottery was beginning to arrive in the new Etruscan cities by the mid sixth century, and earlier still a slave called Omrikos, presumably an Umbrian, was brought to Corinth and named on a vase (which was then exported to Caere in Etruria). In the second half of the sixth century Felsina and other sites begin to receive a quantity of Athenian vases, and in the north of the Po delta the city of Adria was serving as an important entrepôt for Greek trade with the Enetians. As in the cities of Etruria, so in Felsina and Adria there may have been Greeks, but in one new city there were certainly Greeks living beside Etruscans, and in sufficient numbers for the town to be called Greek – at least by the Greeks themselves – and it is far from clear whether it was primarily an Etruscan or a Greek foundation. This is the city of SPINA, on the southern arm of the Po delta, not far north of Ravenna. The lowlying waterlogged land of the delta is unpromising archaeologically, but the cemeteries of Spina have proved to be probably the greatest single source of fine Athenian vases in the Greek world, or outside it. From 1932 to 1935, and again since 1954, drainage work has uncovered a great part of the early cemetery of the city, with the groups of vases and other offerings lying intact in the thick mud. By 1958 the total score of graves was nearing 3,000, and the work continues. The earliest vases are of about 520 B.C., not quite as early as some from the other cities we have mentioned. Nearly all the imported vases are Athenian, and many are of the highest quality. There are inscriptions scratched on the vases in both Greek and Etruscan. A little of the town itself can now be made out also. It seems to have been something of an ancient Venice, with street-canals.

We have to think here of a Greek trading colony established in a city newly founded by the Etruscans, or perhaps even a wholly Greek foundation which admitted Etruscan families from the neighbouring cities. The Greeks, like the Etruscans, were attracted by the cornlands of the Po Valley and the routes from the north. The literary record says nothing about the origins of the Greeks in Spina. The imported fine pottery is nearly all Athenian, but it could hardly be anything else at this time. At least there is no South Italian pottery in the later years, so this is no extension of the activities of the earlier Greek colonies in the west. There is some indication, though, that Athenians were in fact taking a direct interest in Spina, at least later in the fifth century, for we find there white-ground *lekythoi*, a special type of funerary vase which was made for the cemeteries of Athens and for the Athenian community at Eretria in Euboea. A very few other examples have been found elsewhere, and we may suppose them to indicate the presence of Athenian families, since these vases never formed part of the general current of trade in decorated pottery. One reached Palestine; one Lycia; two were found in a tomb – no doubt of an Athenian – in Jugoslavia (Demir Kapija); and there are stray poor examples on a few Greek sites like Delos. A few are reported at Spina, and this probably means Athenian families there.

GREEKS ON THE THRACIAN COAST

For the Greek colonies on the northern shores of the Aegean, our evidence is mainly literary. The earliest were planted in the eighth century by the Euboeans, whom we again meet as the first of the Greeks in a new colonizing area. But here, unlike Syria or Italy, the object was simply land, and there can have been little interest at first in trade. In this respect the move was an obvious one for the islanders, up past the Thessalians (with whom they enjoyed friendly relations) to the first available lands which were non-Greek, though partly hellenized, as we shall see. Chalcis was the most active colonizer here, and the promontory Chalcidice, projecting south into the Aegean like a grotesque three-fingered hand, takes its name from her. There were several Chalcidian colonies here, the most important of them Torone. Eretria's cities were for the most part on the western 'finger' of Chalcidice, notably at Mende and Scione. The Eretrians who were evicted from Corcyra by the Corinthians in 733 came to found Methone, on the western shore of the Gulf of Salonica. About the middle of the seventh century the island of Andros was helped by the Chalcidian cities to found new towns in the east of Chalcidice. The only intrusion into this area dominated by Euboeans and islanders was by Corinth in her foundation of Potidaea about 600 B.C.

To the east the coastline was settled by other Greeks. Foremost were the Parians, who occupied the island of Thasos in the 680s and from it went on to found several cities on the mainland opposite, among them Neapolis (Kavalla). They had some trouble with the native Thracians, and the Parian poet Archilochus sings of some of the encounters. The other newcomers were East Greeks: Chians at Maroneia, Aeolians at Aenus (which lay at the end of an important overland route to the Black Sea), and Clazomenians at Abdera. The last was a short-lived venture, as the Greeks were soon expelled by the Thracians, but the city was reoccupied soon after the mid sixth century by other East Greeks from Teos, fleeing before the Persians.

To the east again lay the Thracian Chersonese – a tongue of land flanking the Hellespont (Dardanelles). Two Greek colonies (Cardia, Limnae) facing west are the only Milesian foundations on this Thracian coast. The others were sited for their strategic positions on the straits, and can best be considered in the account of the Greeks' approach to the Black Sea, later in this chapter.

The physical attractions of the Thracian coastline can be considered briefly before we look at the scant archaeological record. There are no good harbours and few reasonable anchorages. The cities are placed more with regard to defence, available land, and inland communications than with regard to the sea. The coastal plains are fertile though marshy, and until recent times have been malarial. The rich supplies of timber in Chalcidice and inland were much exploited in later days, and may have been an early attraction for the Greeks, whose homeland was rapidly becoming deforested and could not satisfy their demands for shipbuilding and architecture. The excellence of Thracian horses had been appreciated by the Greeks at an early date. The vine was introduced with notable success, especially at Torone, Mende, Maroneia, and – foremost – Thasos. The mineral resources of the region may not have been fully recognized by the earliest colonists. Gold and silver were mined around Mt Pangaeum, opposite Thasos. Here the Athenian tyrant Pisistratus owned mines to which he owed much of his wealth, and he himself had to spend some years in the north while out of favour in Athens. Later on Histiaeus of Miletus was allowed by the Persian king to found the city of Myrcinus, on the Strymon, and enjoy the revenues from the silver mines and timber there. Of the island of Thasos itself Herodotus says that part of it was turned upside down by the Phoenicians in their search for gold, but quite when this happened, and where the mines are, remains a mystery. The mines on the mainland were at first operated by the native Thracians, but were later owned by the Greeks. The resources of silver encouraged prolific coinages in many of the Greek cities, and we have already seen the way the East Greek states seem to have used silver from this area for their trade in the Near East and Egypt.

The cities most concerned with the wine trade chose Dionysiac subjects for the devices on their coins. Torone has simply a wine jar, Mende an ass beside a vine. On Thasian coins appears a lively group of a satyr carrying off a nymph. On the early coins she puts up a token resistance (Plate 20b), but later, in the fifth century, she goes quietly. On a unique coin in London which is from a yet unidentified city on this coast is the charming scene of two nymphs handling a wine jar (Plate 20c). To Abdera the Teans brought with them their civic device – a griffin – for their coins. Potidaea showed her patron Poseidon (who was also the patron of her mother-city Corinth) on a horse. Some Euboean colonies copy Euboean types, notably the cow and calf, and the same device appears on some of the issues made by hellenized native princes. Thasos may have been one of the first northern cities to mint coins, but many others had their own issues too before the end of the sixth century.

For the archaeology of the Greek cities themselves we know little enough of the early years. Abdera offers a little Athenian black-figure pottery. Only Thasos has been dug at all systematically, by the French. The city-site lay at the north-east of the island, at the point nearest the mainland, and has a fine acropolis as well as a harbour. It seems likely that it was founded from Paros by about 680 B.C., in the time of the poet Archilochus' father. The inscribed memorial to one of the foundation heroes, Glaukos, set up about 600 B.C., has been found there. The earliest pottery which can be dated is Corinthian and Rhodian, none of it earlier than the mid seventh century, but these two wares are henceforward poorly represented on the island. Instead there is a mass of pottery of the mid seventh to early sixth centuries brought north from the islands of the Cyclades. A fine example is the plate showing Bellerophon on Pegasus fighting the chimaera (Plate 20a). Paros, mother-city of Thasos, was using 'Melian' pottery at this time, and her taste is reflected in her colony. In the sixth century there is rather more East Greek pottery, especially Chian of the first half of the century, and it seems that Chian vase-painters may have worked on the island. Athenian vases arrive from about 580, but Corinthian was always scarce in North Greece. In general the pottery reflects the island's contacts – with its founder Paros, with the East Greek states which had also founded cities on the Thracian coast, and with Athens, which had other concerns in the north at this time, as we shall see. Paros' sculptural record is also reflected on Thasos: from the colossal unfinished marble figure of a man carrying a ram, of about 600 B.C., to the fine reliefs which flanked the city gate some hundred years later. An architectural oddity of about this time is the use of carved foreparts of winged horses as supporting members – a device met also in Chios.

From the Thasian town of Neapolis, on the mainland opposite, the finds of pottery have been much the same: 'Melian', Chian, and Athenian, with a little Rhodian and Corinthian. The earliest is of about 600, and there are comparable finds, perhaps not quite so early, from another site five miles to the west (Kalamitsa). The most notable find at Neapolis, on a site largely hidden by modern Kavalla, has been parts of a fine Ionic temple. This may take us a little outside our period, into the fifth century and after the passage of the Persian host through North Greece, but it is worth mentioning since its style is distinctive, and is echoed in the find of an Ionic capital near Salonica, from what may be the ancient city of Aineia. From the Salonica area there are a few Corinthian vases, the earliest perhaps of about 650 B.C., but most of the Greek finds in this region which might be associated with the new colonizing movement from Euboea are not earlier than 600 B.C. There is still very much to be learnt about these cities, from properly controlled excavations.

So far as our evidence goes, and it is not likely to be seriously misleading, the artistic centre of the northern Greek cities lay in Thasos and her cities on the mainland in the sixth century. Even there we can hardly speak of an independent colonial school of art, since all its products rely so heavily on fashions set in the Greek islands and Ionia. But in the years after the Persian Wars the most celebrated of the Greek painters was a Thasian, Polygnotus.

ILLYRIANS, MACEDONIANS, AND THRACIANS

Excavations in what are now Albania, Jugoslavia, and Bulgaria have told us much about the northern neighbours of the Greeks in the Iron Age and supplemented the scant and often imaginative testimony of ancient writers. But there is still much to be understood, and although the character of the civilization of these peoples is at times quite clear, its relationship to that of Greece itself, even in the simple matter of time, is not always so straightforward.

Not the least difficulty is the problem of knowing where to draw the line between Greek and non-Greek in the Balkans in various periods. In the days before passports it was probably not of great importance. Illyrians and Thracians at least could be treated as thoroughgoing barbarians. The Macedonians were a borderline case, but the Macedonian royal family had to invoke a largely mythical family tree connecting themselves with the old royal family of Argos; and Alexander the Great was hard put to it in his attempt to justify his ambitions as champion of the Greeks against the barbarian east.

It was from the north that the Dorians swept into Greece during the troubles that marked the transition between the Bronze Age and Iron Age in the twelfth century. We should expect to find a clear archaeological record of their arrival, or of their former homes, but this either does not exist or, more likely, has not yet been properly recognized. While European (Hallstatt) chronology is still so uncertain, it is dangerous to draw far-reaching conclusions from similarities in finds in Greece and Europe. In later centuries too there are many things which connect the cultures of Illyria and Macedonia with that of Greece, although their date and significance are not always readily understood.

Macedonia seems to have been part Greek in its culture in the early Iron Age, but there are some objects from this area which have seemed to many to point rather to close connexions with the north – for example the so-called spectacle fibulae (Fig. 64a). These are safety-pin brooches formed of wire tight-rolled in an S-spiral. They are common in Macedonia, but found too in

64. (a) Bronze spectacle fibula; (b) Bronze 'Illyrian' fibula from Emporio, Chios; (c and d) Vases from Macedonia.

Greece, especially at Sparta. The spiral motif had long been known both in Central Europe and in the Aegean world, although in Greece it forms no part of the vase painter's repertoire of patterns in post-Bronze-Age times until well on in the eighth century. But the fibula itself seems to be an Aegean invention, and there is no clear indication that the spiral fibulae in the north are the first. In Greece they are imitated in bone and ivory in the seventh century, but this does not mean that the original bronze form was foreign. In this as in other matters it may be that a Greek form or variant became more popular, and so better known to us, on the borders of the Greek world. A parallel example is given by the so-called Illyrian helmets, a type most popular in Illyria from the sixth century on, but demonstrably invented in Greece by about 700 B.C., although its popularity there was soon eclipsed by other types. Other bronzes in the north – like spiral beads – are in like case. Painted pottery from Macedonia (Fig. 64c and d) is in a Geometric style which recalls Greek work of the eighth century but is far closer to the wares of Phrygia in Asia Minor, both in this period and, for all we can as yet tell, earlier. This broaches problems of the sources of the Phrygians, and of references to Phrygians in the Macedonia–Thrace area. This 'bridge' across from Europe to Asia saw so much passage and mingling of peoples that the archaeological record of the area is one of the most difficult to understand.

Illyria is hardly simpler. Here again there is a distinctive fibula-type, apparently of the eighth to seventh centuries, which is met too in North Greece, and of which one example reached Chios (Fig. 64b). This again might as easily be a barbarian product modelled on a Greek type which had less success at home. It was through Illyria, perhaps, that the Greeks received their supplies of Baltic amber in the eighth century and later: some to the south, along the coast into the Peloponnese, some via Macedonia and the Greek colonies into East Greece and the islands. This is the route by which the Hyperboreans were said to have sent their mysterious presents (perhaps amber) wrapped in straw to Delos. There are plenty of amber beads in East Greece, but in general the Greeks were not greatly impressed by the material, and they seldom carved it with the care which we see lavished on it by the Etruscans. In Illyria itself there are some carved amber statuettes, and a relief in amber showing a Greek warrior in a style of about 500 B.C. (Fig. 65). The same site has yielded Greek bronzes of about this date.

The Greeks who arrived on the doorsteps of these barbarian or semi-barbarian neighbours had mixed receptions. They had little to do with the Illyrians, being more interested in the coastwise trade up the Adriatic. A very few Greek objects of the sixth century made their way up the valleys from the coast, and from Jerezine there is an unusual stone relief (Fig. 66) which looks as though it owed something, at several removes, to archaic Greek art.

Farther south, near Lake Ochrid in Macedonia, and at a point which may have been as readily accessible from the Greek cities on the Adriatic as from those on the Macedonian coast,

65. Incised amber plaque from Novi Pazar.

we come across rich finds of Greek *objets d'art* which rival and indeed closely match those from the great tomb at Vix in France which we discussed in the last chapter. At Trebenište Greek goods are already arriving in the seventh century, but in the second half of the sixth century there appear in native graves a series of superb Greek bronze vases, most of them clearly from the same school or workshop which produced the great crater at Vix. With them came a little Greek painted pottery and some Athenian and East Greek figurines, but the other tomb furniture betrays non-Greek funeral practice, although it may be that some of the objects, like gold masks, had been made by Greeks especially for customers in this region. Other native towns here, and in Thrace to the east, have yielded equally rich hoards of

Greek metalwork, but of later date. Duvanlij, north of Plovdiv in Bulgaria, is one of them. The earliest Greek finds here are of the first half of the fifth century and include Athenian pottery, East Greek figurines and a Chian wine jar. At Pesnopoj are more vases, a helmet, and a clay coffin with relief decoration of Greek

66. Stone stela from Jerezine.

type: all apparently sixth-century. To the west again there is a later grave at Demir Kapija, the first natural fortress up the River Vardar, which deserves a mention. It contained late fifth-century Athenian pottery, such as has been found in other graves there, but including two white-ground *lekythoi* of the type we have already had cause to comment on at Spina. Here again they may indicate the presence of an Athenian family.

The Thracians had proved the most hostile to the new Greek

colonies, for all their readiness to let their mines to Greeks and buy Greek goods in later years. The Greeks thought little enough of them except as fighters, and brought many of them back home as slaves. Thracian nurses seem to have been in some demand. We can recognize them on Athenian vases from the tattoo marks shown on their arms, their legs, and their necks.

67. Thracian women from Athenian white-ground and red-figure vases.

Fig. 67a and b show fifth-century pictures of a Thracian woman (attacking Orpheus) and a slave (attending Heracles).

THE BLACK SEA AND ITS APPROACHES

To the Greeks the Black Sea was at first the 'Inhospitable Sea'; then, when they had made it theirs, the 'Hospitable' Euxine. The earliest Greek foundations in the approaches to the Black Sea were not necessarily placed with an eye to further exploration of its shores, but they inevitably led to it. The approach itself is through the Propontis, which is like a broad vestibule with long narrow passages at each end – to the Aegean through the Hellespont (Dardanelles), and to the Black Sea past Byzantium (Constantinople) through the Bosphorus. Winds and currents made access to the Black Sea difficult, though by no means impossible for early ships, and passage through the narrow straits would be largely controlled by the cities founded along them.

Our evidence for Greek colonization here, and on the shores of the Black Sea itself, is unfortunately not of the quality of that available in Italy and Sicily, although most of the actual foundations were made at later dates than those in the west. The

literary record gives us names, but seldom any dates which can be greatly relied upon. The archaeological evidence is sadly incomplete: best perhaps for the cities in South Russia; but we still lack much of the sort of evidence for Greek expansion and influence which is readily forthcoming from the many excavated sites in Italy and Sicily. Our most important sources are the Russian excavations of late in the last century and early in this, and the excavations of the last fifteen years in Russia, Rumania, and to a lesser degree Turkey.

In the circumstances it seems the best course to summarize briefly what we know of the pattern of Greek colonization in this quarter, and reserve for a separte section an account of the better-explored Greek cities.

A growing number of scholars are today supporting the view that the Black Sea was being visited and its shores even being settled by Greeks in the eighth century B.C., and they are undeterred by the many excavations which have so far produced no evidence for it. The earliest material from the Propontis is said to be of the earlier seventh century; from the Black Sea cities there is nothing earlier than the latest seventh century. Literary evidence, not of the highest quality, puts the foundations of Sinope and Trapezus (Sinope's daughter-city) on the south shore of the Black Sea, and of Cyzicus in the Propontis, in the mid eighth century. In Herodotus' day there were stories hereabouts of a warlock, Aristeas, who, in the earlier seventh century, had visited the northern shores of the Black Sea; and there are indications too in ancient writers that something at least was known of the Black Sea by the end of the eighth century. The story of the voyage of the Argonauts, in particular, implies some knowledge of these parts, although the geographical detail of this region may well have been added to the story at quite a late date. This does not of course imply that Greeks were living there by 700 B.C., but there seems to be no particularly good reason for doubting that occasional voyages were being made into the Black Sea by East Greek sailors and merchants by that time, and it is not a historical point of the greatest moment. It is not until after 700 that we have any evidence for very active interest by East Greeks in any overseas trade or settlement in any other quarter.

An argument which has been used in favour of the early foundations of Sinope and Trapezus is that they were staging points in a 'North-east Passage' bringing oriental bronzes from the Urartu-Armenia region into the Greek world. In other words that this is another source of the 'orientalizing' influences in Greece, to be added to those we have discussed in Chapter 3. This is always possible, but the hypothesis is an unnecessary one. An overland route to Phrygia for these bronzes is now shown to have existed from the finds at Gordion. And the sort of orientalizing objects which it is assumed could have been passed by this route have their effect more in mainland Greece and Crete than in Miletus or other parts of Greek Asia Minor.

Sinope and Trapezus were said to have been founded by the Milesians, and it is the Milesians whom we shall find the first to exploit other parts of these remote shores. The motive for their move along the south coast of the Black Sea may have been in part a search for land, but they seem to have travelled far for it, and the extent of their colonization – if wholly occasioned by land-hunger – argues either a prodigious rise in the birthrate or a series of disastrous crop-failures. Even if these colonies did not necessarily serve to pass oriental bronzes to the Aegean, they would certainly have been well placed to encourage trade in metals with the rich mining areas of northern Asia Minor, Armenia, and the Caucasus.

In the Propontis the Milesians founded Parion just east of the inner end of the Hellespont. In this they were joined by other Ionians: Erythraeans, and Parians who perhaps at about this time had occupied Thasos. Cyzicus, on the south shore of the Propontis, was founded by Milesians alone as an agricultural community. In the Hellespont itself they had Abydos as well as several smaller towns. They had been allowed to settle at Abydos by the Lydian king Gyges; this must have happened before the middle of the seventh century, and it is likely that some of the other Milesian foundations in the Propontis belong about now. The story about Abydos is interesting. We should not, perhaps, look for Greek settlement on the margins of the Phrygian empire until that empire fell before the Cimmerians in the early seventh century, and was succeeded by the Lydians, who could at times be friendly to the Greeks, or at least to some of them. We have seen already how the Aeolian Greeks had established themselves on the mainland opposite Lesbos and to the north as far as Troy, which was resettled before 700 B.C. This coast was already theirs by the early seventh century, and they were later to press farther into the Hellespont, to the strong-point Sestos on the Thracian Chersonese. While the Milesians arrived, they had to move farther to the east, along routes which may or may not have been familiar to them already. One other important Ionian venture in the Hellespont which may be of this date was the

Phocaean settlement of Lampsacus, invited there, it was said, by the native king to share his land in return for help rendered by the Phocaean king. The same story has it that the natives became jealous, but the Greeks asserted their claim to the site by force of arms. The Samians came to Perinthus in about 600 and to other sites on the less hospitable northern shores of the Propontis.

This accounts for most of the important East Greek colonies on the Propontis, but they were not the only Greeks there. Megara, the town in central Greece just north of Corinth, which had already sent a colony to Sicily in the eighth century, also had an interest in this quarter. High dates are given for the Megarian colonies in the north-east, but it is generally agreed that their object was land rather than trade, and they were certainly slow to occupy any sites of strategic or commercial importance such as Byzantium. Their cities were at the remoter Bosphorus end of the Propontis, and this alone might suggest that they had been forestalled by the East Greeks on the nearer sites. They settled Astacus and Chalcedon on the Asian coast of the Propontis, Selymbria on the north coast, and eventually the commanding site of Byzantium (Constantinople) at the inner end of the Bosphorus. Even there, it seems, their first interest was in land, but they can hardly have overlooked its strategic value; 660 was a date given for its foundation, but nothing has been found there earlier than the end of the seventh century, and it certainly does not seem really necessary to believe in any Megarian colonization in this area as early as 700.

The general pattern of colonization along the Thracian and Asia Minor coasts would not lead us to expect that the Greek colonization of the Propontis began until the seventh century. The archaeological evidence is meagre in the extreme, and the earliest that can be offered is pottery of the first half of the seventh century at Dascylium, inland from Cyzicus, and Corinthian of little before 600 from Byzantium. It has been suggested that the story of Lydian Gyges letting the Milesians settle at Abydos really means that he put a Greek mercenary post there. Dascylium is named after Gyges' father, and it could be that the early pottery there betokens some similar Lydian venture rather than a wholly Greek colony. If so, it cannot be used as evidence for the date of foundations on the coast.

This need not necessarily deter us from believing in quite high dates for the earliest colonies on the Black Sea itself – Milesian Sinope and Trapezus. They must have been placed for trade as much as for land, and the same motive had prompted the relatively remote siting of the first colonies in Italy by the Euboeans. Ancient authors implied dates before the middle of the eighth century for the two Milesian cities. Sinope at least was supposed to have been re-founded after the Cimmerian invasion and occupation (see p. 108), so its first occupation by Greeks should on this reckoning be near 700. Nothing has been found there, as yet, earlier than about 600. There is hardly anything Greek any earlier from other Black Sea sites, so it may perhaps be wiser not to believe in actual Greek settlement on its shores any earlier than the Greek settlements on the Propontis. And it may well be that all the Black Sea cities are to be put later than the first of the Propontis cities.

The Milesians ringed the Black Sea with their colonies. To mention only the better known or better explored, they added Amisus to Sinope and Trapezus on the south coast. In the farthest east there was Phasis, which gave immediate access to the mineral and agricultural wealth of the Caucasus. On the west were Apollonia and Odessus, Tomi and Istros near the mouth of the Danube, Tyras at the mouth of the Dniestr, Olbia and an island city (Berezan at the mouth of the Dniepr–Bug. In the Crimea and approaches to the Sea of Azov are Panticapaeum and its daughter-cities. Near-by Phanagoria was founded by Teans in about 540, and we read that the Phocaeans were associated with the Milesians in some of their foundations. From the archaeological evidence, it would seem that the Chians were also well received in the cities founded by their allies the Milesians. At least, Chian pottery is found in many of them throughout the first half of the sixth century (and even a little later), especially at Olbia, Berezan, and Istros. What is more, at Olbia and Panticapaeum the only traces of early Ionic architecture are in a style which is most readily associated with the Chian school.

The Megarians were far less venturesome in the Black Sea. They did not stray far from their colonies by the Bosporus, and did not indeed attempt any colonization until some time on in the sixth century. To the north were Mesembria and Callatis, to the east Heraclea. And much later on, in the fifth century, they ventured across to the southern tip of the Crimea and founded Chersonesus, where the vine was grown with some success.

The overall character of the archaeological evidence from these Greek cities is fairly simple. Their siting and architectural history will be considered in a moment. The pottery from them should reflect the origins of their citizens and their most regular visitors. We do not know anything much of the pottery of either Miletus or Megara. There is plenty of East Greek pottery of what we conventionally call 'Rhodian' type, and this was probably carried and used by the Milesians. The quantity of Chian pottery in the Milesian cities has already been mentioned. It is worth noting too that many of the early wine jars found on the Black Sea sites are Chian. The predominant wares in the second half of the sixth century are still East Greek, and wherever there is evidence for Greeks at all, there Fikellura, Clazomenian (or related black-figure), and the plainer vases are found. There is a little Corinthian, inevitably, from the earliest days, and towards the end of the sixth century the Athenian vases become more common. They had begun to arrive in the second quarter of the century on many of the sites, just as soon as they became popular in East Greece itself. At the end of this chapter we shall have something to say about Athenian activities in the Hellespont and approaches to the Black Sea. Unexpected imports are one Eretrian vase at Olbia, of about 550 B.C., and three Boeotian vases alleged (perhaps rightly) to be from Olbia and Berezan.

The Megarian colonies are so late that we would hardly expect them to be receiving fine vases made elsewhere than at Athens. The Megarian cities are the least well-explored in their earlier levels, so we are denied the opportunity to test this.

In view of what has been said already about the possible date of the Greek foundations in the Black Sea area, it is interesting to observe that most of the earliest datable Greek finds are not from the colonies themselves, but sometimes from places far inland and not on Greek sites. Thus, there are East Greek vases of about 625 from a site near Panticapaeum; from Nemirov, 200 miles up the River Bug; and from Krivoroshie, between the Rivers Donets and Don, 250 miles from the sea. From the last is the top of a Chian vase in the shape of a ram's head (Plate 21b), and there is a slightly later one with a bull's head from yet farther off. Other early pieces are an early seventh-century jar of uncertain make said to be from Berezan (but the provenance is dubious) and a couple of Corinthian vases of about 640 or later from Olbia and 'South Russia'. These finds, at least those from sites which were never Greek, may well indicate pre-colonization exploration, although not necessarily trade or the presence of Greeks in the remoter places which their goods reached.

The material attractions of this region are easily listed. The good agricultural land on parts of the shores of the Propontis, and on the north and west shores of the Black Sea, guaranteed an adequate supply of corn for the new Greek cities, and in places provided a rich source for trade with the corn-starved areas of the Aegean. Here and there the Greeks were able to introduce the vine, and there were good supplies of fine timber for ships and building on the south shores of the Black Sea, as in Thrace. In its waters and rivers were plenty of fish, and there was a growing trade in dried or pickled tunny and other fish from the north and west shores. A notable feature of the excavations at Tiritaca was the discovery of twenty-four reservoirs for fish pickling, with the bones and scales of 'Kerch herring' on their floors. Of the River Dniepr (Borysthenes) Herodotus writes:

It provides the finest and most abundant pastures, by far the richest supply of the best sorts of fish, and the most excellent water for drinking – clear and bright, whereas that of other rivers in the vicinity is turbid; no better crops grow anywhere than along its banks, and where grain is not sown the grass is the most luxuriant in the world. An unlimited supply of salt is formed by natural processes at the mouth of the river, which also produces a very large spineless fish, good for pickling and known locally as *antakaios*, and a number of other most remarkable things.

The search for metals had probably inspired the foundations along the southern shores of the Black Sea and in the east, where the resources of the Caucasus and of Armenia might be tapped. The Chalybes were the traditional iron producers for the Greek world, and they were generally thought to live in northern Asia Minor, supplying their raw material to the Greeks through Amisos, on the coast. There was gold at Phasis, and remoter sources might also have been exploited.

Of relations with the natives on these shores we hear little. Troubles with the Thracians we have already mentioned, as also the relationship between the East Greeks and Phrygia and Lydia, whose empires spread far along the south coast of the Black Sea. In speaking of the archaeology of the Greek cities in the next section, there will be occasion to remark indications of contact with barbarian neighbours, who generally had to be displaced or 'persuaded' from a site before the Greeks settled. The most absorbing archaeological record of relations with the natives concerns the Greeks and the Scythians, but this deserves separate treatment later in this chapter. Other natives on the Black Sea coast, like those discussed by Herodotus, are related in varying degrees to the Thracians, Scythians, or Cimmerians. The Tauri in the Crimea were said by Herodotus to sacrifice 'all ship-wrecked sailors and such Greeks as they happen to capture upon their coasts'. The people west of the Black Sea shared in the European Hallstatt culture, but they are archaeologically undistinguished, and it is very rarely that their coarse plain pottery or bronzes have been recognized on the Greek sites.

THE GREEK CITIES

There are a few cities in the Propontis which may be briefly considered before we go on to the foundations on the Black Sea. The latter will be taken clockwise, around the coast. The Hellespont and Thracian Chersonese are discussed at the end of this chapter.

CYZICUS stood on a large island just off the south shore of the Propontis. It faced the mainland across a narrow strait, now bridged by a broad low spit of sand. Later building effectively seals, or has destroyed, any substantial evidence for the earliest city here, but pottery of the latest seventh century has been reported. There is evidence too for interesting archaic sculpture and architecture – a capital, and reliefs including a frieze with chariots. A recent find is part of a cylindrical basis with dancing women carved on it in relief. These works fall within the period when this coast owed allegiance to the Persian king. The city had access to gold mines on the mainland, which she exploited from the later sixth century for a notable issue of coins. The coins always show a tunny fish, which suggests another source of the city's wealth.

Inland from Cyzicus, some twenty miles away and on the far side of Lake Manyas, lies the site of DASCYLIUM. This became the seat of the Persian governor in later days, but excavations there have yielded pottery of the seventh century – some, it seems, of the first half of the century. It has been thought that this indicates an early date too for Greek foundations on the coast, but the town's Lydian name may imply that the first Greeks there had other business, perhaps as mercenaries installed by Lydia. From DORYLAEUM (modern Eski-Shehir) yet farther inland is an Ionian stela of the usual type, of about 520, but with relief decoration (Fig. 68). We cannot say whether it was for a Greek, Phrygian, or Persian.

On the north coast of the Propontis Samian PERINTHUS has yielded a little late archaic sculpture in an East Greek style and an inscribed gravestone of Samian type. Nearer the Bosphorus and on the south coast is CHALCEDON. In a tomb there of the second half of the sixth century most of the pottery was Corinthian, as we might expect in a Megarian town. There is also from near by a strange statue base of about 550 B.C., showing what might be a death-room scene and carrying an inscription in Ionic (not Megarian) lettering, and a small marble 'kore'. These stray finds of sculpture tell us little or nothing of the towns, since they are generally accidental finds, or from later buildings into which they had been set. Properly excavated evidence is still lacking.

It is little better with what was to become the greatest of the Propontis cities, BYZANTIUM. The ancient acropolis here lies at the east end of the city of Constantinople, behind Agia Sophia, overlooking the Golden Horn and the Bosphorus. It has been little explored, but trenches in the Great Court of the Seraglio Palace yielded some Corinthian pottery of the later years of the

68. Stone stela from Dorylaeum.

seventh century. Here again there might be good hope of more precise evidence from digging.

Within the Black Sea we turn first to those cities within the borders of modern Bulgaria.

Milesian APOLLONIA, by modern Sozopol, is the first of the important Greek cities on this coast. There is a peninsula with an offshore island (St Kiriak) just north of it, which may have been the centre of the earliest town. The earliest finds, however, were recovered from Sozopol bay. Most of these are East Greek vases, going back to about 600 B.C., with a little later Corinthian and Athenian. From the fifth century there are several interesting pieces of sculpture, the earliest a male figure of East Greek style of around 500. Later on the famous sculptor Calamis made for the city a colossal Apollo, which figures on its coins. There seems to have been no native settlement preceding the Greeks here. As well as its fisheries the city had ready access to good farmland and timber.

Megarian MESAMBRIA, at modern Nesebur, was a later foundation. It is a good peninsula site, of the sort so often chosen by Greek settlers, with an excellent anchorage to the south. It had first been occupied by native Thracians, and of the earliest Greeks there we hear only of sixth-century pottery. Its later archaeological history is better known.

ODESSUS, to the north again, is at the modern Varna. The site is on high ground overlooking the north side of a bay which is comparatively well sheltered for shipping. It was said to have been founded little before 560, and the earliest datable vase from the town is a Corinthian cup of these years. But so far the finds have been extremely slight.

The Danube formed a natural barrier between the north and the Balkans and also a natural channel for the passage of goods and peoples. It runs towards the Black Sea from the west along the present Bulgaria–Rumania border, but little over fifty miles from the coast it turns north for about a hundred miles, parallel to the coast, before turning again to enter the sea through a broad marshy delta. A rectangle of land is thus cut off, by the river to north and west, by the sea to the east, by a range of hills (now the Bulgarian frontier) to the south. This is the fertile Dobrudja, whose plains must have been as much an attraction to the Greeks who first came there as the riches carried by the Danube. Indeed they may well have been the greater attraction. The best positions from which to enjoy both lay not at the marshy delta but anywhere to the south, where there was ready access inland to the main streams of the river.

Probably the most convenient position is at TOMI, the modern port of Costanza, where there was a good headland protecting a south-facing harbour. The modern town effectively covers the ancient, but recent finds there include a number of Chian wine ars of the first half of the fifth century, so it may well be that Tomi is to be numbered with the other Milesian foundations of the sixth century along this coast.

The first Greek colony in this area lay at ISTROS (Histria, Fig. 69), half-way between Tomi and the Danube delta. Excavations have gone on since 1914, and the most recent work by

69. Sketch plan of Istros

Rumanian archaeologists shows that here we may expect perhaps the best picture we are likely to find of one of the early Black Sea colonies. Today the site lies at the edge of saline partly marshy ground, and seawards the approach is blocked by mud-banks deposited by the outflow of the Danube since antiquity. It is difficult to determine where the coastline ran in the seventh century B.C., but it seems likely that the site, a low hill, lay at the end of a peninsula, although it has also been thought that it was an island. The tip was the part walled off as the acropolis of the classical city, and there is sixth-century pottery here in the neighbourhood of a later temple. But the best sequence of early levels is on the northern edge of the peninsula, nearly half a

mile from its end, where it seems that there could have been
a good sheltered anchorage. A wall and a destruction level are
associated by the excavators with the Scythian raids of about 500.
There are only a very few scraps of native pottery in the earliest
levels, so the site may well not have been occupied before the
Greeks arrived. The earliest houses here were little more than
'wattle-and-daub' shacks, but there are also, from the acropolis,
pieces of an Ionic temple, no later than the early fifth century.
A cemetery lay to the north, now on the other side of a lagoon.
The tombs are covered by small tumuli, and contain mainly
Greek vases – the earliest are Attic of about 530 B.C. At the
centre of each tumulus is the pyre, but near by, sometimes outside the tumulus, horses, men, and women are also found buried,
unburnt. These were no Greek burials, but must be of native
(Thracian) notables who chose burial here, near the Greek city
which had brought them new prosperity. A Scythian mirror in
one of the tombs reminds us how near the Scythians were by
now. We are near in time to the Persian expedition against the
Scythians which carried Darius far beyond the Danube.

Istros has yielded a great deal of early pottery – the earliest
being East Greek of the latest seventh century, little after the
date for the foundation suggested by Eusebius. There is circum-
stantial evidence for early knowledge of the Danube in the vase-
fragment from Smyrna, of the mid seventh century, which bears
the name Istrocles – surely derived from the name of the river.
The sixth-century pottery is rich and varied. There are plenty of
the 'Rhodian' vases, both figured and plain, but other East Greek
wares are also well represented : Chian of the first half of the
century (one piece no later than about 600) and Chian wine jars
throughout it; much Fikellura and a very little Clazomenian,
mainly of the second half of the century. This reflects pretty
well the tastes of the East Greek world and the main pottery-
producing centres, without saying very much about the particular interests of any one state. Less expected is a clay relief *pithos*
(storage jar) of the later sixth century, probably from an East
Greek city or from one of the islands. Of other wares there are
Athenian vases of the second quarter of the sixth century, if not
earlier, as there are in East Greece, but there is very little

Corinthian indeed. Locally the Greeks made a plain *bucchero* pottery related to the known East Greek types.

There is evidence too for the early penetration of Greeks and Greek goods in this area. Less than fifteen miles west of Istros, a native town has been explored at Tariverde, and a number of Greek vases found, beside the local wares. Most are Athenian or East Greek, and the earliest are of the second quarter of the sixth century. Farther to the north west, at Barboşi, near where the Danube turns into its delta, late sixth-century Athenian vases have been reported. In the fifth century there is a stronger flow, and Athenian vases are found in several places along the Danube and its tributaries, as well as two fine bronze vases – one from a site near the Danube some 150 miles from the sea, another from the Carpathians about 400 miles from the sea.

TYRAS may be the site standing on a headland overlooking the southern waters of the estuary of the River Dniestr, and partly occupied by the Akerman fortress. Although early pottery has been reported here, none has been published. It was well placed to enjoy the cornlands of the Dniestr's broad valleys. Others take this for Ophioussa, and look for Tyras higher up the river, near where two inscriptions naming the town have been found; but the Akerman site was obviously an important one in classical and Hellenistic times, and has yielded many Tyras coins. It must have been the earliest of the settlements on or near the Dniestr, and so is probably Tyras, since the same name is used for the river.

OLBIA (Borysthenes) was the northernmost of the early colonies, and the richest. It lay on the right bank of the broad estuary of the River Bug as it flows into the broader estuary of the Dniepr. There was another early Greek town here which has no known ancient name, but is best discussed before Olbia, since some have thought it was the place which the Greeks first settled. It is on Berezan island which lies outside the estuary, nearer the open sea. It is not clear whether it was an island in antiquity, and it may be that this is another peninsula site, chosen more for its defensibility than any good anchorage. It now seems, though, that there had been a native settlement here before the Greeks arrived; one to which the Greeks, or at least

Greek wares, were admitted. The site has no architectural distinction, and most of the finds are from the cemetery, where an unusual crematorium-pit has been recognized. Apart from a vase of about 700, whose provenance is far from sure, the earliest pottery is of the late seventh century. From then on the town is well supplied with East Greek vases – 'Rhodian', Chian, Fikellura, Clazomenian, and other black-figure; plus a little Corinthian, Athenian after 570, and perhaps Boeotian vases.

70. (a) Chian jar from Berezan; (b) East Greek jug from Panticapaeum.

The presence of a Chian storage jar of a type with a wide mouth (Fig. 70a) which could hardly have been used for the carriage of wine or oil, rather suggests the presence of a Chian family here soon after 600. There are minor objects of faience, as on East Greek sites, and one of the more charming finds is a clay lamp of the late sixth century inscribed 'I am the lamp of –, and I shine for gods and men alike'. It was thought that the town did not survive long into the fifth century, and that its population had been absorbed by Olbia, but recent work has shown fifth-century and later settlement. Its main commercial value had probably been as a fishing station.

There are other towns on the Bug–Dniepr estuary, before we reach Olbia, which attracted Greek goods in the sixth and fifth centuries, and perhaps attracted Greek families too. Two are at Victorovka and Dneprovskoe (near Olbia); the tombs at Gute Maritzyn will be described at the end of the next section.

Olbia itself occupies a site shaped like an isosceles triangle, nearly a mile long and a half-mile across its base. The base at the north and the long west side are limited by ravines, the east side by the waters of the Bug, here four miles across. The archaic town lay around a hill at the southern point of the triangle, with the cemeteries to the north and west across the ravine. Later the whole triangle was occupied by the town, and fortified, with the acropolis located more centrally. Ships could be drawn up along the river bank towards the north of the site. Part of a good archaic house has been excavated in the area of the later acropolis, and it has been claimed that a proper 'grid' town plan was laid out by the end of the sixth century. There is evidence for earlier town planning of this sort in East Greece, at Smyrna. There is an elaborate architectural moulding of the later sixth century, which is close to contemporary fashions in Chios, and Herodotus speaks of a house which the Scythian prince Skyles had built for himself in the Greek city 'set about with marble sphinxes and griffins'. This and other stories reflect the town's good relations with the Scythians and its general prosperity. The earliest pottery closely matches that at Berezan already described, but is on the whole richer, and there is a greater variety of other objects: elaborate alabaster dishes, scraps of archaic sculpture, bronzes, and a painted clay coffin similar to the more elaborate types made in East Greece. There is more than a hint of the influence of Scythian taste on local products. This must have been one of the important centres for the production of the many Greco-Scythian works of art which we shall discuss in the next section. A good illustration of this is the find of a mould for casting an animal head of a type found on many of these Greco-Scythian objects. The earliest coins of Olbia may have been made early in the fifth century. They are of an unusual form: cast in bronze, not struck. Some are big discs with a gorgon's head and eagle with dolphin (Fig. 71); others are actually in the shape of dolphins.

CERCINITIS (crab-city) is not certainly located, but most Russian scholars identify it at a site (Eupatoria) about half way along the west coast of the Crimea in a rather exposed south-facing position. The old harbour may be represented by what is now a salt lake. In the early excavations nothing earlier than the end of the sixth century was found, and a report on more recent work says that the town was founded in the sixth century, without being more precise. Literary references suggest

71. Olbian bronze coin.

that Cercinitis should be sought farther north, in the Gulf of Perekop.

CHERSONESUS was founded by the Megarians from Heraclea at a point near the southern tip of the Crimea. This tip is, as it were, pulled round to the west, and the Greek city lay facing north. The site served long as a quarry for building stone for nearby Sevastopol. The earliest published finds, of the later fifth century, go back to the city's earliest days, but still beyond the limits we have set. However, earlier finds have been mentioned (sixth century), and it may be that there was a Milesian city here first.

THEODOSIA, towards the eastern end of the Crimea, had been founded by Milesians. It stood on the sheltered northern side of a steep headland. The earliest find – an Athenian vase painted about 570 – was from the old excavations, but work began again on the site in 1949.

At its east the Crimea stretches out a broad peninsula towards a headland (Taman) projecting from the coast north of the Caucasus. The straits between form a sort of second Bosporus – known as the Cimmerian Bosporus – an approach to the Sea of Azov, which the Greeks knew as Lake Maeotis. At its furthermost recess the Greek city of Tanais was later to stand, at the mouth of the Don, but we have seen already how Greek goods passed this way in the very earliest days of Black Sea colonization. The most important of the early towns lay on either side of the Cimmerian Bosporus, and in the fifth century were to form the nucleus of a Bosporan Kingdom. On the western, Crimean, shore are Panticapaeum (Kerch), Myrmekion, Tiritaca, and Nymphaeum; on the east are Phanagoria and Hermonassa. These are all certainly early foundations, although not all are mentioned as such by ancient authors. The Milesians were the most active in this area, but we hear of other Ionians, notably the Teans who founded Phanagoria after they had been driven from their homes by the Persians. Panticapaeum in particular has been a rich source of classical and later Greek antiquities, but no small part of the interest attaching to these Greek cities is the close proximity of some of the richest Scythian tombs, which were in part furnished with Greek jewellery, vases, and other objects.

The acropolis of PANTICAPAEUM became known as Mount Mithradates. It stands behind the modern town of Kerch, beside the sea. In antiquity it may have stood out more as a headland and enjoyed the use of a better harbour. The earliest Greek pottery may be of the last years of the seventh century, but recent reports speak of a pre-Greek town there with a Greek trading quarter in the seventh century. One of the arrivals of the early sixth century is an East Greek vase (Fig. 70b, p. 260) on which is painted a wine jar of the sort which was already being regularly supplied to the Greeks on the Black Sea. The early pottery is very much as that at Olbia and Berezan. There are scraps of what seems to have been an Ionic temple of about 500, with column bases carved in a manner best matched in the island of Chios. A gravestone carved with volutes and palmettes (Fig. 72) is in a provincial style rather far removed from the elegant stelae of East Greece. Part of an archaic bronze carries a dedication to 'Ephesian Artemis'.

MYRMEKION (ant-town) was to the north of Panticapaeum, looking across the bay, down the straits to the south. It has been the scene recently of joint Russian and Polish excavations. There is not much sixth-century pottery here, but what there is goes back nearly to the beginning of the century, and it seems likely

72. Stone stela from
Panticapaeum.

that this was a post established quite soon by the settlers at Panticapaeum. There is a report of a sixth-century fortification wall.

Some seven miles south of Panticapaeum is TIRITACA, which has also been shown by recent excavations to be an early foundation. There was an earlier 'Cimmerian' town here, but Greek houses of the second half of the sixth century are now reported. The pottery follows the by now familiar pattern. The earliest, in a strange orientalizing style which is not easily placed, may not be much later than 600 B.C. in date, but most of the vases are no earlier than 550 B.C. We have already noted its importance for the fish trade.

South again, some four miles, is NYMPHAEUM, which seems

to have been settled at about the same time as Tiritaca and presumably represents part of the same movement of expansion by the Milesians of Panticapaeum. Excavations since the last war have come upon an early sanctuary of Demeter by the harbour with Athenian vases of about 560 among the offerings, and temples of Aphrodite and the Cabeiri on the acropolis. A pre-Greek settlement is said to have been identified.

PHANAGORIA lay on the other side of the straits, at the recess of the deep bay. The site is low lying and undistinguished. From the literary evidence (see above) the foundation date should be about 540. The earliest pottery and figurines, East Greek in type, are very little later.

HERMONASSA is nearer the modern town of Taman. Here, and on other minor sites near by whose cemeteries have been partially explored, the earliest finds are pre-550.

The Greeks' hold on the eastern side of the straits seems to have been established roughly a generation after their first foundations on the Crimean shore, and it may never have been so firm. Not far to the east were some of the richest Scythian tombs. Near the famous group known as the Seven Brothers is a sixth-century native town described by the Russian archaeologists as most like a Greek citadel.

Of the remoter cities, TANAIS at the mouth of the Don and PHASIS at the extreme eastern shore of the Black Sea were founded after the period which we have set out to discuss. But we have seen that more than one Greek vase had passed up the Don to the hinterland in the earliest day of colonizing. Recent underwater exploration in the Taganrog Straits just west of Tanais has come upon East Greek pottery of the end of the seventh century, and this might represent a pre-colonial trading post, as early as any colony in the Black Sea and far more remote. Phasis (in Colchis) was to give immediate access to the Caucasus and its mineral wealth. The earliest Greek finds in the area may be local coins of the early fifth century showing the Milesian lion and a Minotaur. This was the logical step beyond the colonies which had already been founded along the southern shore of the Black Sea, to which we may now turn.

Of HERACLEA, the nearest to the Bosporus, and a Megarian foundation, we know almost nothing, although the city soon became rich, and sponsored other colonies at Callatis (between Odessus and Tomi) and in the Crimea (Chersonesus).

Sinope and Trapezus were the important Milesian foundations, and we have already had something to say about the early dates attributed to them.

SINOPE, modern Sinop, occupies a peninsula site which commands a superb sheltered harbour to the south-east. Exploration of the city has been made virtually impossible by later building, and only in recent years has part of the cemetery, on the mainland, been explored. The pottery from the graves is largely East Greek, but there is a little Corinthian too, which can be dated to little after 600 B.C. It seems likely that the earliest graves have yet to be found, but the scraps recovered from the town site are no earlier. Of equal interest is the quantity of Phrygian pottery which has been found, and which attests the close relations with the peoples of the interior (see also below, under Amisus). The city's main prosperity must have been derived from her trade. In part this would have been due to her possession of the only good harbour between the Bosporus and Trapezus. But she also had access to the mines and timber of the interior, and in later days was the major exporter of 'miltos', a mineral dye much valued by the Greeks.

TRAPEZUS (Trebizond) lay some 250 miles beyond Sinope, which was itself over 300 miles from the Bosporus. The city occupied a good acropolis site, but we know nothing of its early history from either excavation or casual finds. The city's importance for trade both with the Caucasus and with the area once occupied by the kingdom of Urartu, to the south-east, cannot be overestimated, though it may easily be dated too high.

AMISOS (Samsun) lies between Sinope and Trapezus, but much nearer the former. It is generally considered a later foundation, but in fact the little Greek pottery from the town is hardly any later than the earliest found so far at Sinope – after 600 B.C. It was perhaps better placed for trade inland, along the rivers, and we have already remarked that it was traditionally through Amisos that the 'steel-men', Chalybes, supplied the

Greeks. The finds here, and near by, reflect these relations with the interior. It will be remembered that the 'natives' here were the heirs to the old Phrygian empire, and this is the nearest point on the coast to the old Hittite and Phrygian city at Bogaz-koy. About ten miles inland from Amisos, at Ak Alan, East Greek pottery of little after 600 has been found beside local Phrygian painted vases. At the same site, and at Pazarli, farther inland, appear the painted clay revetments which owe so much to East Greek inspiration, and which we have already mentioned in Chapter 3 (Fig. 30, p. 109).

GREEKS AND SCYTHIANS

The Scythians of the South Russian steppes were originally nomad tribes who had come to settle in the plains and by the rivers. From the new Greek cities they were to acquire a taste for 'civilized' life and the trappings of urban civilization – wine and works of art. Not that the Scythians themselves were by any means uncivilized, as we shall see. But to the Greeks they must have seemed much as Red Indians do to the modern (or by now rather oldfashioned) schoolboy: a remote race of dusky warriors who wore long trousers and funny hats, were phenomenal bowmen and horsemen, and scalped their enemies. Their country was said to be one of darkness and intense cold, and the only Scythians most Greeks saw were either slaves or those enrolled in the Athenian police in the fifth century, although one Scythian (Anacharsis) was numbered by the Greeks with the Seven Sages. Their dress, which came to be standard uniform for archers, orientals, and Amazons in Greek art, may have been somewhat more familiar (Plate 21c; from a vase by Exekias).

It was generally held in antiquity that it was the arrival of the Scythians from the east that displaced the Cimmerians and set them on their many destructive raids into Asia Minor. We have already met the Cimmerians here, attacking Greek cities in the seventh century, and compassing the fall of the Phrygian empire.

The Scythians were thought to come from the east, and there is certainly much Persian in their culture and names. Of more immediate interest to us are their fortunes in the Near East, for what they learned there formed an important part of their heritage when they came to their South Russian homes, and this may affect our opinions about the influence of Greek art in Scythia. But first we should say something about what is known of the Scythians themselves, their tombs and their art, in the early period which is our concern in this book. Their customs and way of life are described in a full and picturesque manner by Herodotus, and we can learn something more of them from the contents of their graves. But most of these material remains date from the fifth century B.C. and later, and only a few of their tombs belong to the earlier period. These are, at all periods, their most impressive remains. There was generally a wooden tomb building, with an inner chamber to house the body. In the richer burials wives, servants, and horses were buried beside their master, who is fully dressed and armed. Over all a high earth tumulus was raised.

Scythian art too is best known from examples of the later period when Greek influence was already strong, sometimes paramount. Its native characteristics are fairly easily defined – an 'animal style' of decoration, with the bodies of the animals contorted into graceful curvilinear patterns. Extra limbs or heads of other creatures may grow from the bodies, to enrich the complexity of the compositions. We meet the style most often in plaques – often in openwork – of gold and bronze, which decorated furniture, equipment (especially harness), and dress. On larger objects, we can detect a desire to cover the whole available field, either by an almost endless development from the main central pattern or by the repetition of single motifs. There is a great deal here which looks back to the art of Persia, and Luristan in particular, and which looks forward to Celtic art, but there is much too which is not entirely foreign to Greek art. In East Greece, in particular at Ephesus, we find objects decorated in an 'animal style' which is very close to Scythian work. These are of the latest seventh and sixth centuries, but it would be wrong to think that the Scythians learned anything of this style from the Greeks. Rather, they were both drawing on older oriental traditions: the Greeks on that which developed in the town-civilizations of Mesopotamia; the Scythians on that which was evolved by the nomads of the European–Asian plains. The style is at its best on the sort of objects for which it was first adopted – like horses' harness or the traditional Scythian bow case.

In the eighth and seventh centuries, Scythian princes had invaded Asia Minor and the kingdom of Urartu, attacked the Medes and Babylonians, and even pressed far into Palestine. Of these years we find a few superb examples of the mixed eastern and animal style art, especially from Sakiz, the Scythian capital in the kingdom of the Mannai, beyond Urartu. In a very similar style are the earliest finds in the Scythian tombs of South Russia, which must belong to the last years of the seventh century, when the Scythians were already being pressed north and out of the lands they had won from the Medes and Assyrians. Thus the most sophisticated products of Scythian art in the period before any very close contact with the Greeks are profoundly affected by Near Eastern fashions. In two or three of the great tombs (notably Melgunov's, far north of Olbia, and others some 400 miles away near the Kelermes in the Kuban) there is fine relief gold work – on hilts, sheaths, etc. – which displays the developed animal style beside purely Assyrian motifs and figures (Fig. 73a). The artists were most skilful imitators of Assyrian

73. (a) From a gold sheath from Melgunov's barrow; (b) Gold plaque from Melgunov's barrow; (c and d) Gold plaques from the Kuban.

forms, yet they could enter fully into the spirit of the animal style. The best examples of this work were found as long ago as 1763 by General Melgunov, who took them to St Petersburg for the Empress Catherine II to admire.

It is at the end of the seventh century that the Greeks too reach the north shores of the Black Sea. With one of the earliest Greek vases to reach Russia, in the tomb at Krivoroshie (see p. 252), we find an example of the oriental goldwork which has just been mentioned. And in Melgunov's barrow, beside the Scytho–Assyrian objects, is a gold plaque with a monkey and birds in relief (Fig. 73b) which may be an early intimation of Greco-Scythian work. Greek art of this period is also 'orientalizing', but already much that was borrowed from the east has been changed and adapted beyond recognition. Still, it is not always easy to be sure whether some of the 'orientalizing' objects found in South Russia are Greek or genuinely oriental; for example, the fine ivory lions' heads from near Smêla (Fig. 74a). The fact that their eyes are inlaid with amber suggests that they were made either in South Russia or Greece; their style, that they were made by a Greek or an easterner.

In the sixth century we begin to find the clearest indications of the impact of Greek art on the Scythians. This is conveyed in part by imported objects, in part by the work of Greeks, Ionians, on objects or in styles calculated to attract the Scythians. Their work was probably done actually in the Greek cities of the Black Sea coast. We must, however, remember that this was no ordinary barbarian market that they were serving, but one already used to most accomplished works of decorative art in a quite different style, and one well acquainted with the best work of certain more formal Near Eastern schools.

In general we find the Scythians readily accepting Greek products of hitherto unfamiliar forms, for instance the Ionian bronze mirrors with volute handles, decorative bronze vases, and to a lesser degree painted pottery. The Scythian fashion of sewing metal plaques on to clothing was matched in East Greece, and we find East Greek motifs, some subtly acknowledging the native animal style, in the small gold plaques which have been found in many Scythian tombs (Fig. 73c and d, p. 269). Bracelets

74. (a) Ivory lion's head from Smêla; (b) Design from a
gilt silver rhyton from Kelermes.

with animal-head terminals had become familiar to the Greeks
from Near Eastern models, but some of their finest pieces seem
to have been made for the Scythian (and even the Persian)
market, and they set the standard for native work.

We have already mentioned the finds of Greek pottery of the
later seventh century far from the Black Sea shores where the
Greeks were founding their first colonies. They suggest the early
interest shown by the Scythians in their new neighbours, but it

is just possible that some of the Greek vases and settlers had arrived even before the Scythian princes from the south had established themselves near the great rivers of South Russia. Throughout the sixth century there are occasional finds of Greek pottery in Scythian towns far up the Dniepr, south of Kiev. The Scythians were not greatly impressed by Greek painted vases until the fifth, and particularly the fourth century, when the Athenian potters were producing lines especially designed for the Black Sea market. By far the greater part of our evidence for Greek goods penetrating Scythia, or the existence of Greco-Scythian art, belongs to the years after the end of the sixth century B.C. For the first hundred years or so, the new colonies prospered and enjoyed a lively trade with Greeks at home from the produce of their own agriculture and fishery, or from what they obtained from native farmers, but we cannot pretend that there is much evidence for very close intercourse between the peoples. It seems almost that they were brought closer together by their shared antagonism to the growing strength of the Persians, although the Scythians themselves should have found much in common with them, and for the latter part of the sixth century the Greek cities of Ionia, who had sent the colonies, lay within the bounds of the Persian empire.

A few Greek bronzes were already being sold in Scythia in the archaic period. From various important Scythian sites south of the Dniepr and some 200 miles north of Olbia, well on the way to Kiev, we find pieces of a large bronze crater very similar in appearance, if not origin, to those found in Illyria and at Vix, and a bronze mirror with, it seems, a Scythian handle. Late archaic are two more bronze mirrors with figure supports – both of women, one naked (Fig. 44b, p. 163), one clothed – from sites nearer the Greek cities at the mouth of the Dniepr.

As with the earlier, orientalizing objects, so with the Greco-Scythian, it is in relief goldwork that we find the most interesting products for the Scythian market. From the Kelermes tombs, where some of the best Assyrianizing pieces were found, there is a superb gilt silver mirror, with its back decorated in an almost wholly Greek manner (Plate 22). Completely Greek – Ionian, we might say, of the earlier sixth century – are the

Mistress of the Animals, lions, sphinxes, rams, goat, fox, eagle, griffin, and lion tearing a bull. The subjects are orientalizing, some of them; the treatment is Greek. But beside them we see a bear, a small crouching animal stylized in a Scythian manner, and an extraordinary scene of two hairy men grappling with a griffin. The last must be Arimasps – who, the Greeks thought, lived in the frozen north and stole the gold the griffins guarded: an appropriate scene for a Greek to choose, and one which again appeared often on the Athenian vases of the fourth century which were sold in some numbers in the Greek cities on the north coast of the Black Sea. Also from Kelermes, and by the same artist, was a gilt silver rhyton of Scythian shape decorated with a winged goddess holding two griffins (Fig. 74b), and various other figures, including a centaur and a hero fighting a lion. A gold diadem with a griffin's head projecting at the front imitates jewellery of the type being made in the Greek islands at this time.

Yet more remarkable, yet more remote, are the finds made near Vettersfelde in North Germany, little over fifty miles from Berlin. They are, it seems, from the burial of a single warrior, with his horse but no attendants. The equipment is Scythian. There are gold decorative pieces from the harness of the horse. One is in the form of a fish (Plate 24), the tips of its tail stylized into rams' heads and its body covered with small figures in relief – an eagle, lions with a stag and boar, fish, and a Triton merman. Another piece is in the form of five joined discs, four of them decorated with small animals in relief. There is gold work from a sheath and dagger, and one gold earring with other minor ornaments. The style of the figure and animal decoration on the larger pieces is wholly Ionian, and hardly any later than the end of the sixth century. But the form of the objects is quite un-Greek, and we are clearly dealing with one of the most distant and early burials of a Scythian chief who was equipped with the finest gold work from the Ionian cities of the Black Sea coast. That it is a burial, and not a hoard of gold captured from a Scythian, is suggested by the other less exotic Scythian finds of about this date in Central Europe, which bear witness to their damaging raids and expansion to the north-west.

Slightly later than the Vettersfelde finds is the gold stag from a Scythian tomb at Kul Oba, in the Crimea (Plate 23a). The animal is not wholly Scythian, but a Greek essay in the animal style, and its body is covered with small relief animals in a wholly Greek manner. We may contrast the more natural 'animal style' treatment of the same motif (Plate 23b). But with the Kul Oba stag and other gold work from Scythian tombs in

75. Sketch of a tomb at Gute Maritzyn.

Crimea and Kuban, we are beginning to meet the fully classical Greco–Scythian art of the fifth century which we cannot discuss in detail here.

To these earlier years of the fifth century belongs a remarkable tomb at Gute Maritzyn, on the Bug/Dniepr estuary between Olbia and Berezan. It, and others near it, well illustrate the way Greek and Scythian peoples and customs had already intermingled. The tombs are of Scythian type: wooden chambers in low tumuli. One was unusually well preserved, and its contents are worth detailing (Fig. 75). At either end of the body – of a man – stood a Chian Greek wine jar. Thirst was further served by a fine black Athenian cup, a Greek bronze dipper, and a strainer, the last carrying elaborate incised patterns. The man was a warrior. He had an iron sword, two spears with iron heads, three knives (two bronze, one iron); to one side of him lay his corselet with iron scales sewn on to it, to the other his stock of arrows. From the last, 377 bronze arrowheads were counted, all of the socketed type which the Scythians introduced to the Greeks. From other early graves came more Chian wine jars, Athenian black-figure pottery of about 500 B.C. and just after, and a mirror with the figure of a woman incised on the handle by a Greek artist. This was not a Greek town, but we would be hard put to it to say from the finds whether it is Greeks or Scythians who are buried there. A study of the skulls suggested that some from the cemetery were certainly Greek.

These apparently mixed communities, and the remarkable monuments of Greek work for the Scythians, are more eloquent testimony to the relations between the two peoples – the colonists and the natives – than the finds of objects imported from other parts of the Greek world. They show that the wealth of the Scythians and of the Black Sea trade attracted some of the finest Ionian artists to the northern colonies, where they adapted their natural style to the tastes and styles of the Scythians. We have noticed elsewhere – in Egypt, in the west, in Greece itself – the effect of the 'diaspora' of Ionian artists in the troubled years of the sixth century when their home cities were attacked or sub-jugated by the Lydians and Persians. The development of Greco-Scythian art was perhaps the strangest issue of the same movement.

ATHENIANS, PERSIANS, AND THE HELLESPONT

We have seen little enough of Athens taking any active interest in overseas foundations, although her pottery was carried so far by other Greeks and was appreciated so much by the barbarian neighbours of the Greek colonies. But in the sixth century Athens made a deliberate bid to secure a footing on, and indeed control of the Hellespont.

Sigeum, on the southern side of the entrance to the Hellespont, had been occupied by Aeolians from Lesbos. About 600, Athens seized the town and became involved in a protracted conflict with the Lesbians. Among these was the poet Alcaeus who sang, unashamed, of the time he threw away his shield and ran, to fight another day. The Corinthian tyrant, Periander, was called in as arbitrator, and he awarded the town to the Athenians. They seem to have lost it some time later, since the Athenian tyrant Pisistratus had to reoccupy it. In 510 his family took refuge there, but now it stood on the borders of the new Persian empire.

Earlier in Pisistratus' career Athens had also gained control of the northern shores of the Hellespont. Herodotus tells the picturesque story of how a deputation of Thracians (Dolonci) had come to Delphi for advice in their struggles with neighbours. They were told to invite as their leader the first man who offered them the shelter of his home after they left the sanctuary. They had to travel as far as Athens before they met the hospitable Miltiades. He was a rich man, perhaps a rival of Pisistratus, who was no doubt happy to see him go. The Dolonci lived in the Thracian Chersonese, the tongue of land on the north side of the Hellespont. Miltiades and the Athenian settlers he took with him occupied the whole area and built a wall across the narrowest point – just east of Gallipoli. We do not know on what terms his new settlements dealt with the Milesian and Lesbian colonies. The Lesbians probably suffered as they had in Sigeum. In the Thracian Chersonese Miltiades established a minor dynasty, which spent much of its energy fighting the Phocaean town Lampsacus, which faced it across the Hellespont. Miltiades himself was once captured, but freed when the Lydian king Croesus threatened the Lampsacenians. In about 516, the younger Miltiades was sent out from Athens, put down a revolt, married a Thracian princess, and occupied the islands of Lemnos (see p. 103) and Imbros in about 500.

There is some archaeological evidence for this period of Athenian interest in the Hellespont. On the Thracian Chersonese there is little enough to show for the earlier colonies founded by the East Greeks, and the only early find is a Corinthian vase of about 630 from Koila, a city nearly half way along the north coast which only much later became at all important.

The most interesting site for us is that of Elaeus, which must be an Athenian foundation of soon after 600. This stands on the broad promontory to the east of the small bay at the very mouth of the Hellespont. Excavations there were occasioned by the military operations in Gallipoli in the First World War, and the French continued to explore the area in later years. The new Turkish war memorial is now standing on the site, which is regularly visited, though seldom recognized, by Hellenic cruises. Most of the finds have come from graves to the east, although there is plenty of early pottery to be picked up on the town site. The few vases which can be attributed to the first half of the sixth century are Corinthian, and Athenian vases only become at all common from about 550 on. If Elaeus was lost – perhaps to the Lesbians – as Sigeum seems to have been for a time, this is understandable. We are coming to a time in which the identity of imported pottery, Corinthian or Athenian, is coming to mean little, but there is one group of vases from Elaeus which directly reflects the Athenian occupation. So far as we can judge, they were made around the middle of the sixth century or later, and were decorated quite simply with stripes and silhouette birds (Plate 21a). The type is Athenian, but this particular group is not found in Athens. Its distribution is significant – Elaeus and the Troad (including Troy), so it can plausibly be attributed to an Athenian pottery established in this area, most probably at Elaeus or Sigeum.

Coins can tell us a little too. Miltiades issued some labelled Cher(sonese), which combine an Athenian device with the Milesian lion – perhaps a reference to the Milesian cities in the Chersonese.

On the other side of the Hellespont the archaeological record is less informative. Troy was resettled by Aeolian Greeks before 700. From Sigeum there is a gravestone on which the epitaph was engraved once in Ionian letters, and again, somewhat expanded, in Athenian letters. The circumstances which led to the double inscription are not readily divined. The stone itself may well belong to a characteristically Athenian type of grave monument. Epigraphists date the inscriptions about the middle of the century. Pisistratus' son Hippias may have minted coins at Sigeum – of Athenian types but with his name upon them. Lampsacus was the other big city on this side of the Hellespont –

a Phocaean colony, hostile to the Athenians, and later a Persian base. Of the early town nothing is known, but there is in the writer's possession an East Greek cup of about the middle of the sixth century said to be from a grave there.

By the end of the sixth century the Persians were at the gates, and like the other leaders of the East Greek states, Miltiades acknowledged the suzerainty of the Great King. In about 513 the Persian Darius mounted an expedition against Scythia, and Miltiades, with other East Greek leaders, went with him. Herodotus says that Miltiades tried to persuade his fellow Greeks to destroy Darius' bridge over the Danube while his army was beyond it, but that they saw too clearly how precarious their own positions would be at home without Darius' protection. In 490 Miltiades met Darius' army again, on the battlefield of Marathon, but now he led his fellow Athenians against the Persian king.

The Persian occupation of the Greek cities of the Thracian coast is no part of our story. When Xerxes, Darius' son, led his army this way against Greece in 480 he bridged the Hellespont and watched the Greek grain ships going by to Aegina and the Peloponnese. His 'fighters drank the rivers dry' as they moved through Thrace into Greece, to Thermopylae, to defeat at Salamis and Plataea. Three centuries before, the Greeks had coveted the wealth and knowledge of the east. Now their own strength and skills stood as challenge to the greatest empire the east had seen.

Bibliography

ADRIATIC: Beaumont in *Journ. Hell. Stud.*, LVI, 1936. Roden-waldt, *Korkyra*, 1939–40. Alfieri, Arias, and Hirmer, *Spina*, 1958.

ILLYRIA, MACEDONIA, and THRACE: Casson, *Macedonia, Thrace and Illyria*, 1926. Filow, *Trebenishte*, 1927. The Thasos excavations are published in *Études Thasiennes* and reported annually in *Bull. Corr. Hell.* For Neapolis, *Arch. Eph.*, 1936, and *Praktika*, 1937, 1938.

BLACK SEA: Fundamental studies are: Minns, *Scythians and Greeks*, 1913; Rostovtseff, *Iranians and Greeks in South Russia*, 1922, and *Skythien und der Bosporus*, I, 1931. Rice, *The Scythians*,

1957, introduces recent discoveries. Schefold in *Eur. Sept. Ant.*, XII, 1938, for the art. For Olbia, Minns in *Journ. Hell. Stud.*, LXV, 1945. Recent work is published in *Materials and Researches*, and reported in other Russian periodicals (many are summarized in *Bibl. Class. Or.*). See also E. Belin de Ballu in *L'Histoire des colonies grecques*, 1960, and Boardman in *Arch. Reports for 1962–3*. Rumania: recent work reported annually in *Materiale și Cercetari Arh.*, the series *Histria*, I– ; a short survey in *Bull. Corr. Hell.*, LXXXII, 1958. Bulgaria: for Mesembria, ibid., LXXXIV, 1960, for Apollonia *Bull. Inst. Arch. Bulg.*, XVIII and XXIII, 1952 and 1960. Turkey: reports in Akurgal, *Sinope*, 1956, and *Anatolia*, I, 1956. Problems of entry to the Black Sea discussed by Graham in *Bull. Inst. Class. Stud. London*, V, 1958. On the siting of colonies on the west coast, Short in *Liverpool Annals*, XXIV, 1937.

INDEX

281